UNSEEN CITY

In *Unseen City: The Psychic Lives of the Urban Poor*, Ankhi Mukherjee offers a magisterial work of literary and cultural criticism which examines the relationship between global cities, poverty, and psychoanalysis. Spanning three continents, this hugely ambitious book reads fictional representations of poverty with each city's psychoanalytic and psychiatric culture, particularly as that culture is fostered by state policies toward the welfare needs of impoverished populations. It explores the causal relationship between precarity and mental health through clinical case studies, the product of extensive collaborations and knowledge-sharing with community psychotherapeutic initiatives in six global cities. These are layered with twentieth- and twenty-first-century works of world literature that explore issues of identity, illness, and death at the intersections of class, race, globalization, and migrancy. In *Unseen City*, Mukherjee argues that a humanistic and imaginative engagement with the psychic lives of the dispossessed is key to an adapted psychoanalysis for the poor, and that seeking equity of the unconscious is key to poverty alleviation.

ANKHI MUKHERJEE is Professor of English and World Literatures at the University of Oxford and a fellow of Wadham College. She is the author of two monographs and the editor of three essay collections. *What Is a Classic? Postcolonial Rewriting and Invention of the Canon* (2014) won the British Academy Prize for English Literature. She has been awarded fellowships and grants from the British Academy, AHRC, and Wellcome Trust.

CAMBRIDGE STUDIES IN TWENTY-FIRST-CENTURY
LITERATURE AND CULTURE
Editor:

Peter Boxall, *University of Sussex*

As the cultural environment of the twenty-first century comes into clearer focus, Cambridge Studies in Twenty-First-Century Literature and Culture presents a series of monographs that undertakes the most penetrating and rigorous analysis of contemporary culture and thought.

The series is driven by the perception that critical thinking today is in a state of transition. The global forces that produce cultural forms are entering into powerful new alignments, which demand new analytical vocabularies in the wake of later twentieth-century theory. The series will demonstrate that theory is not simply a failed revolutionary gesture that we need to move beyond, but rather brings us to the threshold of a new episteme, which will require new theoretical energy to navigate.

In this spirit, the series will host work that explores the most important emerging critical contours of the twenty-first century, marrying inventive and imaginative criticism with theoretical and philosophical rigor. The aim of the series will be to produce an enduring account of the twenty-first-century intellectual landscape that will not only stand as a record of the critical nature of our time, but also forge new critical languages and vocabularies with which to navigate an unfolding age. In offering a historically rich and philosophically nuanced account of contemporary literature and culture, the series will stand as an enduring body of work that helps us to understand the cultural moment in which we live.

In This Series

Joel Evans
Conceptualising the Global in the Wake of the Postmodern: Literature, Culture, Theory

Adeline Johns-Putra
Climate Change and the Contemporary Novel

Caroline Edwards
Utopia and the Contemporary British Novel

Paul Crosthwaite
The Market Logics of Contemporary Fiction

Jennifer Cooke
Contemporary Feminist Life-Writing

UNSEEN CITY

The Psychic Lives of the Urban Poor

ANKHI MUKHERJEE

University of Oxford

CAMBRIDGE
UNIVERSITY PRESS

CAMBRIDGE
UNIVERSITY PRESS

University Printing House, Cambridge CB2 8BS, United Kingdom

One Liberty Plaza, 20th Floor, New York, NY 10006, USA

477 Williamstown Road, Port Melbourne, VIC 3207, Australia

314–321, 3rd Floor, Plot 3, Splendor Forum, Jasola District Centre,
New Delhi – 110025, India

103 Penang Road, #05–06/07, Visioncrest Commercial, Singapore 238467

Cambridge University Press is part of the University of Cambridge.

It furthers the University's mission by disseminating knowledge in the pursuit of
education, learning, and research at the highest international levels of excellence.

www.cambridge.org
Information on this title: www.cambridge.org/9781316517581
DOI: 10.1017/9781009042680

First published 2022

Printed in the United Kingdom by TJ Books Limited, Padstow Cornwall

A catalogue record for this publication is available from the British Library.

ISBN 978-1-316-51758-1 Hardback

For Gayatri-di
&
Tiyash

Contents

Figures

Acknowledgments

I thank my editor, Ray Ryan, for readily placing his faith in the book when it was only half-formed. I am moved by the way he cares for his authors and feel fortunate to be counted in this number: his vision for *Unseen City* has kept me going. I am grateful to Peter Boxall for including this work in his series and his effusive encouragement along the way. I would like to thank the production team at Cambridge University Press for their highly efficient guidance through the publication process, in particular Natasha Burton, Edgar Mendez, and Leigh Mueller. The publisher's reviewers – Lyndsey Stonebridge, Tracy McNulty, and an anonymous reader – offered engaged and very affirmative reports of the draft manuscript, foreshadowing critical conversations the work will hopefully generate. It was most gratifying to see my hard-won insights and research findings scrutinized, challenged, and recoded by its expert readers in this way. The photograph by Teju Cole on the cover brings to mind a Derek Walcott poem about airplane windows reminding the "fortunate traveller" of the portholes of accursed ships with human cargo. Cole gifted it to me, for which I am still smiling in disbelief.

This book on traveling psychoanalysis came together on the move. I am grateful to colleagues who let me present sections of the book to different audiences: Sanjoy Bhattacharya (Centre for Global Health Histories, University of York); Sumit Chakrabarti (Presidency University); Zahid R. Chaudhary (Princeton University); Pheng Cheah (Hong Kong University); Hent de Vries (School of Criticism and Theory, Cornell University); John Frow (University of Sydney); Leela Gandhi (Brown University); Debjani Ganguly (Australian National University and University of Virginia); Rachael Gilmour (Queen Mary University of London); Maidul Islam (Centre for Studies in Social Sciences, Calcutta); Ranjana Khanna (Duke University); Chana Morgenstern (University of Cambridge); Avishek Parui (Indian Institute of Technology, Guwahati);

Rashmi Poddar (Jnanapravaha Mumbai); Ruvani Ranasinha (King's College London); Poulomi Saha (University of California, Berkeley).

I am extremely grateful to the Arts and Humanities Research Council (AHRC) for a Leadership Fellows grant (January 2017–June 2018) which enabled me to conduct research in the US and gave me the teaching relief I needed to start writing the book systematically. As a part of this scheme, I could host graduate workshops on the theme of "Humanitarian Fictions" at KCL and Warwick, and showcase innovative doctoral research. The AHRC-funded international conference "Global Hungers" featured key-notes by Gayatri Chakravorty Spivak, Leela Gandhi, Robert J. C. Young, and Honey Oberoi Vahali. The panels attracted scholars at various career stages from five continents. My research has also been supported by small travel grants from the Wellcome Trust (2014, 2015) and the John Fell Fund at Oxford (2015, 2017, 2020–2021), which proved essential for new and ongoing collaborations. Two visiting positions, a Fellowship at the Humanities Research Centre at the Australian National University in 2014, and the John Hinkley Visiting Professorship at Johns Hopkins University in 2019, opened vibrant new networks and dialogues. I thank Debjani Ganguly for the first. Christopher Nealon, Jeanne-Marie Jackson, and colleagues at the Department of English at JHU are thanked for the second, as are the students of my graduate course at Hopkins.

For informal introductions that have been crucial in an interdisciplinary and intercontinental project such as this, I thank Gautam Basu, Sanjoy Bhattacharya, Faisal Devji, Robyn Norton, Rewati Prabhu, and Neha Thirani Bagri; for the conversations that ensued, Vivek Benegal (NIMHANS), Matias Echanove and Rahul Srivastava (Urbz), Arup Ghoshal (Indian Psychoanalytical Society), Vibha Krishnamurthy (Ummeed), Kimberlyn Leary (Harvard Medical School), Vikram Patel (Harvard Medical School), Anita Patil-Deshmukh (PUKAR), and Andrew Scull (University of California, San Diego). The advice I received from Julian Stern (Tavistock Clinic), Tim Kent (Tavistock and Portman NHS Foundation), and Penelope Crick (London Clinic of Psychoanalysis) was instrumental in shaping the London chapter. Madeline Holland, a visiting student from Harvard whom I taught, very kindly introduced me to "grandma" Jimmie Holland, who defined Chapter 6.

I would like to thank colleagues in the English Faculty at Oxford who have contributed in singular ways to my research, writing, funding, and publication prospects: Ros Ballaster, Elleke Boehmer, Robert Douglas-Fairhurst, Merve Emre, Michelle Kelly, Laura Marcus, Helen Small, and Sally Shuttleworth. Ushashi Dasgupta, Adam Guy, and Graham Riach provided excellent teaching and pastoral care to Wadham undergraduates when I was on research or sabbatical leave in this period. Waverly March is thanked for making my audiovisual presentations objects of envy. I thank colleagues at Wadham College, in particular Warden Ken Macdonald, Hannah Bailey, Jane Griffiths, Tim Kirtley, and Lee Wootton for helping me to do my job well, and with continued enjoyment. My graduate students are thanked for the new explorations in thought and research they inaugurate: C. S. Bhagya and William Ghosh are thanked extra for their support as I wrote this book self-doubtingly. I remain grateful to the (Wadham) undergraduates for keeping my intellect supple, ideas perfectible, and the head and heart in synchrony in this area of academic life.

The powerhouse that is Ato Quayson heads the list of allies and collaborators I am most indebted to. I am sustained by his warmth, wit, his mentorship, the Akan proverbs he has loaded up for every occasion. I wish to thank for their unforgettable gestures of friendship Ranjana Khanna and Srinivas Aravamudan (Srinivas insisted I include "psychic life" in the title); Supriya Chaudhuri; Leela Gandhi; Debjani Ganguly. Joey Slaughter and Jennifer Wenzel helped immensely during the research stint in New York. Sree Banerjee Goswami is thanked for advising on cover graphics, as before. Lloyd Pratt and Karl Schoonover started out as amazing colleagues but have become a part of our nuclear family in Oxford. They are my rock. I admire Jeanne-Marie Jackson's fierce intellect and it is a bonus that Joseph K. Awotwi, Jeanne-Marie, and their baby are dear friends, Benji's photos providing bittersweet markers of the rush of time.

Purnima and Tarun Ramadorai, Rewati and Tushar Prabhu, Purnima and Raj Mookerjee, and Bipasha and Bhaswar Chatterjee are adored and thanked for showing that community and connectivity will survive against all odds if we try. Ma and Baba, Chitra and Chandrachur Mukherjee, make me feel rooted and sheltered even as these shade trees grow very frail with age. *Charaiveti*, they say: keep going, don't stop or pause. My sisters are thanked – Nayan for all the food pampering and Dithi for letting me use her photographic artworks on posters and websites. Saumya Banerjee, my love, my best friend, is gratefully acknowledged for the wild fun that is our life's uneven journey, and specifically for his handholding when I walk absentmindedly through the world in pursuit of words and abstractions. I learn a lot from his mathematical, economist's mind, especially when we argue!

I dedicate this work to our daughter, Tiyash Banerjee, an aspiring and idealistic human rights lawyer, and Gayatri Chakravorty Spivak, the strongest influence in my intellectual formation. To brilliant Tiyash because I want her to know this penpusher academic wanted to make a change for the better. To my muse Gayatri-di for the language of change – sometimes gnomic, sometimes plain as day – and the philosophy guiding modes of imaginative activism "outside in the teaching machine." It gives me a jolt of delight to audaciously link their names.

***

Sections of Chapter 1, "Eco-cosmopolitanism as Trauma Cure," appeared in two articles: "Affective Form," *Affect and Literature*, ed. Alex Houen (Cambridge University Press, 2020) and "Eco-cosmopolitanism as Trauma Cure," *The Cambridge Journal of Postcolonial Literary Inquiry*, 6.3 (2019).

An earlier version of Chapter 3, "Slums and the Postcolonial Uncanny," appeared in *Planned Violence: Post/Colonial Urban Infrastructure, Literature and Culture*, ed. Elleke Boehmer and D. Davies (Palgrave Macmillan, 2018), pp. 87–104.

Royalties from book sales will go to the charities I have written about.

Introduction: "The Poverty of Philosophy" – A Critique of Psychoanalytic Knowledge and Power

> Let me laugh aloud for a while. You see, you understand everything in terms of your schemas, your code, your imaginary, your fantasies ... which really are far too partial, in every sense of the word. For the most part, women's desires, words and *jouissance* elude them.
>
> (Irigaray, 102)

This is a passionate, often angry, essay by Luce Irigaray titled "The Poverty of Psychoanalysis," published in *Critique* in 1977. The addressee of the essay, which begins with "Gentlemen, psychoanalysts," is the male Lacanian. Adding "Ladies" would not change anything, Irigaray states, as long as we use a language [*langue*] masculinist in the grain, and where "the masculine noun always governs the agreement":

> The poverty of psychoanalysis? What next? The phallonarcissism you have duly invested in your function as analysts will not tolerate such a statement, though it is in fact a question. So you will protest, more or less consciously, just like those who want to preserve something of their desire in the repressed: in no way does psychoanalysis suffer from poverty [*la misère*], nor is it wretched [*une misère*]. (79)

Irigaray speculates of the elected audience of her essay that most of them will be unable to understand its title, meaning, history, or its full afterlife. The title, "The Poverty of Psychoanalysis," is referring, of course, to Karl Marx's *The Poverty of Philosophy*. Published in 1847 in Paris, *Misère de la philosophie* coincides with the early elaboration of Marx's historical and economic theory. Written in the reactive mode, it takes on the French Socialists of his time, in particular the *Philosophie de la misère* of Pierre-Joseph Proudhon. Marx attacks the economic doctrines of Proudhon on the grounds that he de-historicizes them, refusing to see them as the products of their time and socioeconomic milieu that they are: "these ideas, these categories, are as little eternal as the relations they express. They are *historical and transitory products*" (119). Capitalism, for instance, is a historically contingent mode of production, not the universal human condition Proudhon says it is.

> He borrows from the economists the necessity of eternal relations; he borrows from the Socialists the illusion of seeing in poverty only poverty. He is in agreement with both in wishing to refer it [and here Marx means economic relation] to the authority of science. Science, for him, is reduced to the insignificant proportion of a scientific formula. It is thus that M. Proudhon flatters himself to have made the criticism of both political economy and of communism: he is below both the one and the other. . . . He wished to be the synthesis, he is a composite error. (137)

Irigaray evokes the ghost of Marx to similarly critique a knowledge system that struts around as if it were self-begotten – "*whole*, absolute and without any historical foundations":[1]

> You refuse to admit that the unconscious – your concept of the unconscious – did not spring fully armed from Freud's head, that it was not produced *ex nihilo* at the end of the nineteenth century, emerging suddenly to reimpose its truth on the whole of history – world history, at that – past, present, and future. (80)

She objects in particular to the Lacanian code that the analyst's authorization comes from himself. This she categorizes as an "imperialism of the Unconscious," led by "the name of a father of psychoanalysis to whose unconscious any unconscious should be made to conform" (81). If we were to agree that the unconscious is both a result of a certain history and also something that is yet to come into being – Irigaray describes it as "*the reservoir of a yet-to-come*" (82) – psychoanalysis seems keen to fold the future back into the past, reducing "the yet-to-be-subjected to the already subjected" (82), the unspoken to something language has made explicit already, or already struck dumb. "Freud and the first psychoanalysts did not act quite like this," Irigaray states. For them, "every analysis was an opportunity to uncover some new facet of a practice and a theory" (83). According to Irigaray, the trouble with the Lacanian school is that it was brought up on philosophy – but not a philosophy predicated on searching questions. Its allegiance to castration, for example – and characteristic confusion about the interchangeability of the phallus and real genitals – makes its law "the law of the imposition of nothingness in the name of Nothingness" (87). In this "nihilistic religion," social reality is as nothing, Irigaray thunders.

When we think of psychoanalysis in the social contexts of race and class, we are likely to be staggered by the lack of intersection and "committed involvement" (51), a term I borrow from the Brazilian educationist Paulo Freire. Freud himself is notorious for writing, in *Civilization and its Discontents* (1930), that

> In an individual neurosis we take as our starting point the contrast that distinguishes the patient from his environment, which is assumed to be "normal." For a group all of whose members are affected by one and the same disorder no such background could exist; it would have to be found elsewhere. (144)

This, in turn, gave rise to the nomological claim that the primitive or the socially abjected did not have an unconscious: they were the unconscious. In his essay "The Unconscious," Freud ventures the wild opinion that "the content of the unconscious may be compared with an aboriginal population of the mind" (195). The primal or primitive, in Freud's work, refers both to an "early stage of development" and, as Celia Brickman points out, to "savages," who, "by virtue of their differences from European cultural norms and their darker skins, [were considered] to be less culturally advanced than their European cousins" (4–5). The primitive tends to be defined in terms of lack and deficit – that nihilistic religion Irigaray raged about, although Freud's ideas about the primitive are not as crude as the quick summary above suggests. In the "Uncanny" essay, for instance, he associates the violent inception of civilization with a forced "surmounting" (249) of animistic beliefs, and, in *Totem and Taboo*, the primitive is another name for the archaic (lending credence to Freud's invention of psychoanalysis as an archaeological science). In *Totem and Taboo*, one of Freud's key works on mourning, he talks about the "emotional ambivalence" around death demonstrated alike by "dreamers, children and savages" (62).[2] This ambivalence has two-fold implications: it stands for a love commingled with hostility toward the dead; it reflects also the remorse of murdering an adversary, in the context of war, for instance. As he elaborates in "Thoughts for the Times on War and Death," "savages" – and by this term he means "Australians, Bushmen, Tierra del Fuegans" – are "far from being remorseless murderers":

> when they return victorious from the war-path they may not set foot in their villages or touch their wives till they have atoned for the murders they committed in war by penances which are often long and tedious. . . . behind this superstition there lies concealed a vein of ethical sensitiveness which has been lost by us civilized men. (23)

While "emotional ambivalence" is usually associated by Freud with obsessional neurosis, here he is not simply positing in the primitive a prototype of the neurotic but bemoaning the unambivalent aggressiveness that the processes of civilization – ideas of sovereignty and liberal democracy in the West – have fostered. In chapter 6 of *Beyond the Pleasure Principle*, Freud uses "primaeval" and "primitive" interchangeably (53). In the same work, speaking of retrograde repetition, or the self-destructiveness of the repetition compulsion – the need to ruin what is whole in a bid (and in repeated bids) to become whole again – Freud gives examples from Plato's Symposium and the Brihadarânyaka Upanishad. The former is a possible repetition and derivation of the latter, dated 800 BC: in both Greek myth and ancient Hindu scripture, the unified, plenteous self feels lonely and wishes for a second. It is halved, with each part now desiring the other, "and eager to grow into one," writes Freud, repeating Plato (70). Again, "primitive" has the valence of primeval or ancient, and lessons lost to humankind.

As Daniel Boyarin astutely comments on the dual modality of reading Freud's racial (double) consciousness, if the ethnological comments posit him as a white subject enciphering black subjects, another critical vantage point would interpret "white" and "black" as stand-ins for Aryan and Jew: "In the first reading, Freud is the colonizer; in the second, the colonized" (219).[3] Freud's deconstructive take on the categories of "primitive" and "civilized" notwithstanding, sketchy intimations of the "psychic unity of mankind" at the inception of the field of psychoanalysis gave way to an engagement with non-Western cultures that was of "an appropriating kind," according to Sudhir Kakar:

> The paramount concern of psychoanalysis seems to have been in protecting and gathering evidence in support of its key concepts rather than in entertaining the possibility that these other cultures, with their different world-views, family structures and relationships, could contribute to its models and concepts. (*Culture and Psyche* 45)

These were territories to be annexed, Kakar states, "particularly for the Oedipus complex" (45). Freud's *Group Psychology and the Analysis of the Ego* (1921) is an interesting example for testing out Kakar's claim about the predominance of the Oedipus complex (and the concomitant denigration of mass psychology). This work reverses the trajectory of individuation (group to self) to read social neuroses transversally through individual neuroses. As individual psychology encapsulates the tumult of the individual's relations with others "as a model, as an object, as a helper, as an opponent" (*Group Psychology* 68), it is also, therefore, a social psychology. Narcissistic phenomena and social acts both fall "within the domain of individual psychology," Freud claims (96). *Group Psychology*, however, is not a clarion call to what Gustave Le Bon – whose 1895 work *The Crowd* informs Freud's argument – terms a "primitive communism" (cited in Brickman 104).[4] As the thesis unfolds, Freud characterizes the herd instinct observable in any group as "a regression of mental activity to an earlier stage such as we are not surprised to find among savages or children" (116). The Darwinian cadences of *Totem and Taboo* return in his pronouncement in *Group Psychology* that the group is, indeed, the primitive mental swarm of the "primal horde" (121): primitive peoples are particularly susceptible to this mentality. Reviewed in this light, individual psychology exists not in tandem with group psychology, but despite it. Each individual may have a share of "numerous group minds" (128) but they will have to transcend this collectivity to claim "a scrap of independence and originality," Freud states (128). If, in *Totem and Taboo*, individuality was made possible by the violent overthrow of the primal father, in *Group Psychology*, the process is presented more organically: life's intrepid and associative movement from self to group episodically returns, exhausted, to the somnambulant self.

> [B]y being born we have made the step from an absolutely self-sufficient narcissism to the perception of a changing external world and the beginnings of the discovery of objects. And with this is associated the fact that we cannot endure the new state of things for long, that we periodically revert from it, in our sleep, to our former condition of absence of stimulation and avoidance of objects. (129)

Celia Brickman is correct in assessing that Freud, despite not subscribing to Le Bon's antidemocratic intent in *The Crowd*, "retained [his] use of the category of the primitive as the critical term of opprobrium against which the desirable state of a modern, emancipated subjectivity could be measured" (105). Brickman's otherwise formidable analysis does not explicitly take into consideration that Freud was an Austrian Jew, whose ideas in works such as *Group Psychology* were influenced more by crowd theory rising out of World War I than by the psychodynamics of empire. As the historian Sander Gilman states, Freud "objected to the very concept of biological 'race' as early as the marginal notes he made in his university textbooks" (Gilman and Thomas 87) and his works on group behavior are haunted by the "insuperable repugnance" – a term he uses in *Group Psychology* (101) – bred by close physical proximity, not only in relation to cultural difference: "Every time two families become connected by a marriage, each of them thinks itself superior to or of better birth than the other" (100). The examples he gives here of squabbling groups include

English and Scot, the Spaniards and the Portuguese, the South German and the North German, the closely related "white races" and the "coloureds," the Aryans and the Semites (100).

Individuality, individualism, civility, and autonomy at one end, and a primitive communitarianism on the other: socialized entities on the winning side of the colonial divide, and narcissistic, puerile, fearful, and slavish hordes on the other. I will, in the chapters to follow, discuss in detail Frantz Fanon's critique of Octave Mannoni's theory of (primitive) enthrallment, and the global city's phobia of migrant swarms, but suffice to say here that the primitive in Freudian psychoanalysis is given a phylogenetic register, not an ontogenetic one. The primitive (and this includes indigenous communities) *is* the phylogenetic register for they have not graduated to "individual acquirements" from "noisy ephemeral groups" (*Group Psychology* 129). Brickman extrapolates two configurations of primitivity from Freud's writings:

> The familiar colonial tale of the primitive as a member of the evolutionarily prior, darker races, who lives in a hordelike community, desires his own oppression and lives in subjection to the leader of the community, is supplemented by a view of primitivity as determined by the unrestrained exercise of or compliance with authority. (114)

While the legatees of Oedipus shifted from "external to internal control" (Brickman 108) by transmuting beloved persons into "object-cathexes"[5] to be abandoned, thereby laying claim to egoic subjectivity, the primitive failed to author a similar history of maturing identifications. In fact, the primitive is outside history as we know it, hypercathected to external leaders, not idealized (internal) structures like the superego. Brickman reminds us that Freud had, in *Group Psychology*, compared the relationship of follower to group leader to that of the subject of hypnosis and the hypnotist. Freud had upheld these aim-inhibited, nonsexual relationships for creating enduring group ties. "On the other hand," Brickman says of Freud's interpretation, these relationships seem to "impoverish rather than strengthen psychic structure" (110). The primitive, therefore, is also poor.

Scrutinizing scientific papers published in the PEP-web in the seven decades between 1933 and 2003, Manasi Kumar suggests that psychoanalysis has had too much and too little to say about poverty. At first glance, there is an abundance of metaphoric appropriations: "ego's poverty" (Freud, 1918, 1919); "poverty of phantasy" (Ferenczi, 1923, cited in Berman, 2000); "poverty of interests" (Greenacre, 1941); "poverty of symptomatology" (Spitz and Wolf, 1946); "sensory poverty of dreams"

(Knapp, 1956); "affective poverty" (Esman, 1979); "the psychological poverty of present-day philosophy" (Eissler, 1963); "terror of poverty" (Khan, 1965); "voluntary poverty" (Anna Freud, 1967); "deprived child" (Winnicott, 1971); "poverty of instinctual experience" (Winnicott, 1975). In *Civilization and its Discontents*, we come upon Freud's powerful formulation of the "psychological poverty of groups" (74), which supposedly explains their capacity for enmity and what, in "The Taboo of Virginity," he had termed "the narcissism of minor differences" (199). These unreflective figurations not only distance the real thing but imply that to be poor is to have an impoverished inner life. As Kumar points out, "the description of the poor then is either too sterilised or so preachy that it sounds as though the poor do not have an unconscious or do not even have the capability to have one" (14).

Kumar does not mention Freud's technique papers in this extensive review, especially his "Further Recommendations on the Technique of Psycho-analysis," in which Freud frets on the structure, length, and cost of therapy and the impossibility of delivering a "short, convenient, outpatient treatment for obsessional neurosis" (128). Although he argues against gratuitous treatments – a therapy session is an investment of time equivalent to a seventh or eighth part of the psychoanalyst's monthly stint – Freud lets slip that he has offered free psychoanalysis. This was as an experiment, and removing the transactional and regulatory element vastly increased, instead of alleviating, the neurotic's resistances. Kumar also doesn't mention an extraordinary moment in the history of what Elizabeth Ann Danto called the "public involvement and accountability" (5) of psychoanalysis: the free clinic phenomenon. Two months before the Armistice, at the 5th International Congress of Psychoanalysis in Budapest, Sigmund Freud famously declared that: "The poor man should have just as much right to assistance for his mind as he now has to the life-saving help offered by surgery" (cited in Danto 1–2). This stance is elaborated in papers published soon after. In "Lines of Advance in Psycho-analytic Therapy" (1919), he states:

> the conscience of society will awake and remind it that the poor man should have just as much right to assistance for his mind as he now has to the life-saving help offered by surgery; and that the neuroses threaten public health no less than tuberculosis, and can be left as little as the latter to the impotent care of individual members of the community . . . institutions or out-patient clinics will be started, to which analytically-trained physicians will be appointed, so that men who would otherwise give way to drink, women who have nearly succumbed under their burden of privations, children for

whom there is no choice but between running wild or neurosis, may be
made capable, by analysis, of resistance and of efficient work. Such treatments will be free. (167)

In "Postscript to an Autobiographical Study" (1935) Freud adds: "[O]ut of
their own funds, local societies support ... outpatient clinics in which
experienced analysts as well as students give free treatment to patients of
limited means" (73). Whereas his theory aimed to be a de facto science,
Freud's clinical practice embraced the social-democratic ideology of post-
World War I Vienna. Between 1918 and 1938, the "indigent urban residents"
of Freud's Vienna, to quote Danto, were "students, artists, craftsmen,
laborers, office clerks, unemployed people, farmers, domestic servants and
public school teachers" (2). Freud's pronouncements on free clinics helped
to create a dozen cooperative mental health clinics, from Zagreb to London.
These were free clinics "literally and metaphorically," Danto states: "they
freed people of their destructive neuroses and, like the municipal schools and
universities of Europe, they were free of charge" (3). The movement,
however, was short-lived. In 1933, Freud's books were burned in Berlin;
the psychoanalytic institute closed and Max Eitingon fled to Palestine. Freud
is known to have quipped to Jones that he was fortunate: after all, in the
Middle Ages, they would have burned the author. It ended when, on
March 12, 1938, thousands of German troops armed with bayonets marched
the Nazi flag into Vienna. Looking back at Freud and the other psychoanalysts involved in this *debut-de-siècle* struggle, Helen Schur, wife of Freud's
personal physician Max Schur, states: "I think they saw that this would be
the liberation of the people. To really make them free of neuroses, to be
much more able to work, you know, like Freud said, to love well and to
work" (Danto 10).

A Social Psychoanalysis?

Despite the ongoing social work on the depredations of urban poverty in
areas such as neonatal health and infant nutrition, domestic violence,
housing, and human rights, the psychological toll of extreme disenfran-
chisement tends to be neglected by governments and NGOs alike. *Unseen
City: The Psychic Lives of the Urban Poor* is the culmination of a decade's
thinking and research on the causal link between damning sociocultural
perceptions of the mental capacity of poor populations and the lack of
state-funded mental healthcare provision for the same. Reading contemporary literature and theory, psychoanalytic theory and history, and

alongside empirical work with the free clinics on three continents, the book reveals the unseen city of its title. Exposing the entrenched contexts of mental illness through narrative, observational, and quantitative data, it urges the inclusion of the interpretive humanities in current debates on mental health.

Speaking of the relevance of psychoanalysis for the urban and raced poor, however, stands the risk of being top-down philanthropy if we do not take into account three key issues. First is the cost of psychoanalysis. The payment of a fee for treatment is traditionally seen to be crucial to the transference relation in psychoanalysis: both a transference relation – the displacement of feeling from one object, say the mother, to the analyst – and transference neurosis, an artificial neurosis built around the relationship with the analyst. Transference is, at once, an obstacle to the "talking cure" and the means of working through – that is, a way of cordoning off a tendency to repetition, to acting out, and running it through the transferential circuit. The analyst's task is to overcome the repetition controlling the transference and open the psychic avenues of remembering. Through the payment of a fee, the libidinal economy of the psychoanalytic dyad is set in play, the analyzand becoming bonded to the analyst, cathected but also invested in a kind of imaginative and financial speculation. The concept of "free clinics" is therefore not free of contradiction, for transference, as Michel Foucault notes in *The Order of Things*, is what differentiates psychoanalysis from the ethnological science it drew from.[6] While ethnology saw "primitive peoples" as being without history, psychoanalysis reads the history of the subject as being both held and withheld in the repetitions of the transference, which it interprets. This in turn poses questions to the practice of free psychoanalysis or psychoanalytically inflected psychotherapy in the West or East.

Second is the association between poverty and mental illness. Low- and middle-income countries (LMIC) carry the severest burden of poverty, and the highest number of depressed individuals are also to be found there. Do circumstances of poverty lead to "a higher prevalence of depression," or does depression "lead individuals to drift into, or remain in, poverty?" ask Crick Lund and Annibale Cois in a longitudinal analysis that tests the theories of social causation and social drift in an LMIC context for the first time (396).[7] According to the social causation hypothesis, adverse socioeconomic conditions related to financial stress (such as lack of education, food insecurity, increased exposure to violence) increase the risk of mental illness. The social drift theory proposes conversely that people with mental illness lapse into poverty because of disability, impaired productivity, increased health expenditure, and other adverse life events related to mental health. Examining data from the South African National Income Dynamics Study (NIDS), in a context where poverty is more extreme than in high-income countries and there is more income inequality, Lund and Cois conclude that depression is a predictor of poverty; depression is also a consequence of poverty. A breakthrough in global mental health research, this study shows that social causation and social drift may occur simultaneously. More policy priority, therefore, should be given to the diagnosis and treatment of depression, the authors recommend, just as there needs to be increased policy attention to the "social determinants of depression at a population level" (401).

A related question is whether a study of mental illness in poor populations contributes to a fuller understanding of urban poverty? It is my argument that such a study can fruitfully revise the rationalist humanism of economic concepts such as "poor but efficient" and "poor but neoclassical," which, Esther Duflo points out, assume that the decision-maker, however poverty-stricken, remains "unboundedly rational, forward-looking, and internally consistent" (367). Duflo, co-Director of the Abdul Latif Jameel Poverty Action Lab at MIT, won the Nobel (more precisely, the Sveriges Riksbank) Prize in Economic Sciences in 2019.[8] She argues that the *Homo economicus* at the core of neoclassical economics – the "calculating, unemotional maximiser," as Mullainathan and Thaler put it – would behave differently if they were poor than if they were rich (367). What is needed, she concludes, is a theory of how poverty impacts decision-making: such theory would give rise to innovative empirical research which was both "observational and experimental" (377). Bringing race to bear on poverty, the economist Glenn Loury postulates a discrimination theory that sees social inequality as inseparable from racial inequality in societies shaped by colonialism and chattel slavery. "The tacit association of 'blackness' in the public's imagination with 'unworthiness' distorts cognitive processes and promotes essentialist causal misattributions" (406). It is crucial to understand the maladies of raced bodies as the outgrowth of cumulative causation and examine the role of racial disparity in engineering speeds and forms of human development in Western societies, Loury argues. Poverty will not be eliminated by handouts and compensation, but through ongoing critical cognisance of "lives imperiled and devalued by a racial calculus and a political arithmetic that were entrenched centuries ago," as Saidiya Hartman has described it (*Lose Your Mother* 6).

Finally, how cross-culturally applicable is psychoanalysis? Can it cope with race and cultural difference, disparate paradigms of individual and collective trauma, and individuation *in extremis*? Psychoanalysis is culturally specific, as we know, traceable to not the beginning of time but the end of the nineteenth century. The sociologist Nikolas Rose argues that the "interiority" that is the stock in trade of psychological systems is best understood as "a discontinuous surface, a kind of infolding of exteriority" (*Inventing Our Selves* 37). The human material of modernity is an "inside" formed by discourses "outside": a being which is not an immutable entity but "a latitude or longitude at which different vectors of different speeds intersect," as Rose sums it up (37). In this parlance, psychoanalysis and the "psy-disciplines" (39) are a mode of subjectification, constructing relationships between the one and the many, external and internal, the universal standard and the aberrant example, the whole and the fragment. Can the theoretical reserves of a discourse complicit in colonial apartheid infrastructures be salvaged, mobilized, or strategically misread to articulate what Emily Apter, in a different context, terms a "dispossessive collectivism,"[9] a psychotherapeutic public defined by nonproprietary models of language and belonging?

"Psychoanalysis and its associated psychotherapies hold the key to transformative possibilities," concludes Celia Brickman's study on race in psychoanalysis, although they are also "potentially amenable to interpretations that lean too concretely on the racial theories that underpin some of Freud's theorizing" (198). *Unseen City* is a quest for a multimodal psychoanalysis – psychotherapy, counseling, group psychology, trauma-based cognitive behavioral therapy, horticultural therapy, among others – in an international frame. Translated and translatable, it aspires to a mode of improvisation we colloquially call *jugaad* in Hindi. Leela Gandhi claims this useful hack for postcolonial thinking, "a makeshift vehicle or style of frugal engineering that uses all the limited resources at hand" (178). The various elements of this assemblage "may not belong together and will likely disaggregate once the job is done, but their surprising combination is effective (it makes something work) and innovative (it builds something new)" (178).

To address the poverty of psychoanalysis, to aspire thereafter to the ampersand's amity between psychoanalysis *and* poverty, we need to make sense of the relationship between the individual and the collective in psychoanalytic reason. In *Civilization and its Discontents*, Freud imaged this collective along the broadening remits of families, races, people and nations, and, finally, what he termed "the unity of mankind" (122). I turn now to a literary text to examine how individual neurosis may be understood in the context of a group "all of whose members are affected by one and the same disorder" (quoting Freud again) and how individual regeneration may shed light on not just illness but the survivalism of grouped minds and a new universalism of the oppressed.

Psychic Life: Typification to Individuation

In his preface to Latife Tekin's *Berji Kristin: Tales from the Garbage Hills* (1984), John Berger compares the act of reading to losing his way in the labyrinths of the uneven city that is Istanbul: "And suddenly what I was watching, what I was brushing shoulders with, what I was turning my back on, what I would never see, what I was deaf to, was given a voice in her book" (6). The originality of Tekin's *Tales from the Garbage Hills*, Berger points out, is the power of its shanty voice, which makes the shantytowns, peripheral or nonexistent in the ken of the urban reader's vision, central to literature, "holding the stage and addressing the sky" (6). As Saliha Paker, the translator, points out in her introductory remarks, *Berji Kristin's* squatter settlements built on rubbish heaps, surreal though they seem, were an all-too-real phenomenon in the Istanbul of the 1960s. "[S]quatterland was an extension of the village" (12) for the millions flowing into big cities to make a living. Tekin's *Tales* give voice to the realities as well as dreams of these perishable settlements, Paker observes, in specific detail and lush figuration "without overlooking the humorous attitudes, ironic perception and emotional vitality of the community amid the filth and poverty of its living conditions" (13).

Berji Kristin uses the language of the deprived to describe "a complete neighbourhood ... fathered by mud and chemical waste, with roofs of plastic basins, doors from old rugs, oilcloth windows and walls of wet breezeblocks" (16). It deploys not a bird's-eye view or omniscient narration but the embedded, circumscribed, and occasionally traumatized reportage of the accidental witness-bearer of history. Characters are either stock – scavengers, wreckers, policemen, garbage owners, women, babies – or exaggerated caricatures around whose unusual and exemplary actions the tales are re-energized. In the second category belong Garbage Grocer, Nylon Mustafa, Liverman, simit-seller Mikail, Lado the gambler ("[you could] make a novel out of his life-story": 132), their identities and social relations deformed by commodity fetishism just as their names are. The second category of dissimilated[10] individuals also boasts of stand-ins for the author figure: Poet Teacher, who wrote "innumerable poems on the stifling odour, on the garbage glitter and the smoke that rose over Rubbish Road" (103), and Honking Alhaz, the community's own genealogist.

In her review of *Berji Kristin*, Güneli Gün observes that Tekin has given the "underprivileged masses a voice that can be heard by the world of literature" (886). To a compromised and bankrupted Turkish literature, Tekin brings "hijinks language, which bursts forth like the thousand-and-one flowers on hills of garbage": this is the language of the Turk's nomadic Central Asian past, replete with "tales, boasts, rumors, laments, riddles, ditties, gossip, exaggerations, jokes, adventures told around a campfire" (886). Resource-poor though they are, the subnational inhabitants of Flower Hill are not language-poor. To cite Gün again, Tekin makes them the rightful owners of lexical networks such as "eighth-century Dede Korkut tales and the folk tales surrounding the adventures of Keloğlan" (886): their life stories are tangled through testimony, gossip, superstition, ancestral and choral mediations. The title, *Berji Kristin*, combines innocent shepherd girl (Berji) with urban prostitute (Kristin), to signify relative identities in an embattled landscape of belonging. But how does the author reconcile the linguistic excess of the novel with its melancholic charge? How does she summon inner life from the heaps of ecstatic trash?

In *Knot of the Soul*, an "ethnography of madness" which sets up a dialogue between psychoanalysis and Islamic theology in the context of contemporary Morocco, the anthropologist Stefania Pandolfo addresses "the possibility of writing from the midst of trauma, taken at once as a historical event and as a window into the vicissitudes of the soul" (6). *Berji Kristin* poses a problem familiar to the literary handling of poverty, in which private and public worlds – "the historical event" and the "vicissitudes of the soul," to use Pandolfo's terms – seem indistinguishable, and illness, physical or mental, is an infectious epidemic. Freud himself had written, in the section from *Civilization and its Discontents* cited above, about his unease with the "diagnosis of communal neuroses" (144). The therapeutic application of psychoanalytic knowledge is powerless in the face of the "pathology of cultural communities," Freud stated (144), speculating that this is a venture for a psychoanalysis-to-come. As Dominic LaCapra observed in an article titled "History and Psychoanalysis," in the works of Freud "history in the ordinary sense often seems lost in the shuffle between ontogeny and phylogeny" (222). Even in the late moment of *Civilization and its Discontents*, Freud is more concerned with applying psychoanalysis to "the evolution of civilization at a macrological level," as LaCapra observes (222), than understanding individual case histories or the psychoanalytic method itself through wider historical processes, or processes of social reproduction crisscrossing the family unit yet operating beyond it. Works of literature such as *Berji Kristin* provide switch points between public and private or physical and psychic orders. In this way, individual malady is narrated against the shock, trauma, and collective suffering which is its composite slum milieu, but without subsuming the individual or the malady in the same. We learn, for instance, that Crazy Darsun, whose migration from Flower Hill to the Romany cardboard houses frames one of the tales, had suffered from a sunstroke as he polished shoes on Rubbish Road. This does not, however, adequately explain why he is subsequently peevish during the day and inconsolable at night, nor why, in an environment where sunstroke is an all-too-common occupational hazard, "*his* wandering wits never came back to their nest" (my italics, 122).

Yet another tale describes Sırma, who has a hysterical episode after one of the many cycles of rebuilding and demolition the Flower Hill populace endure. There, among the "broken and scattered belongings,"

> Sırma stood trembling before the ruins, embracing a complete, undamaged brick. As the other children gathered stones and bits of tin all over the hill, her trembling increased. Then she began to struggle and kick. She put down the brick and lay on it, tearing out handfuls of hair and throwing them to the wind. The women made a circle round her and tied her hands together. Holding her by her rough and matted hair, they shook her, scooped water on her face and stuffed a rag in her mouth to stop her teeth locking together. Exhausted with suffering, she fell quietly on the ground, her hands tied, and her eyes enormous. (20–21)

Tekin's use of the "undamaged brick" is masterful in its economy. The child is made hysterical by the necessity and futility of building structures which will be precipitately destroyed. Bulldozers follow the demolition men, rolling methodically backwards and forwards over the huts and Sırma is "seized with grief again," twitching in the air like the splintered wood or crumpled pieces of tin (20). She is brought to Güllü Baba, a prophetic savant, for succor. Güllü Baba is blind in both eyes and the slum dwellers come to believe that his tears of empathy have magical healing powers. "Seeing" Sırma's affliction, he "too was seized by grief" (21) and cried copious tears. Güllü Baba, who is "summoned to recite prayers which would heal her" (21), is presented as neither therapist nor Imam but an ad hoc and androgynous mixture of the secular and religious ministering to souls expected of each role.

The story of trauma is "a narrative of belated experience," as Cathy Caruth's field-forming work, *Unclaimed Experience*, states (7): it is an encounter with death which is lived twice, first as an experience that is not known, and iteratively as an experience that claims to be known, narrated, and eventually exhausted of meaning. With chronic stressors such as those suffered by the shantytown community, the psychopathological reaction may not operate at a temporal lag – but the symptomatology resembles trauma in that an embodied memory presents the event in the patient's mind without representing and processing it. Traumatic memory is not a verbal retelling of the past. Instead, it is a wordless mental automatism to cure which a "mnemotechnology," or a psychotherapy predicated on recollection and narration, would have to be formulated, as the French psychologist Pierre Janet had said (cited in Ruth Leys, Bessel van der Kolk, Judith Herman, and others). In his work, *The Body Keeps Score*, which I shall discuss in detail in Chapter 4, van der Kolk builds on Janet's theory of dissociation to add that this form of embodied memory simultaneously entails knowing and not knowing. Van der Kolk highlights the shamanic role of the analyst in addressing this intersubjective state and restoring the self-ownership and self-leadership of the patient in such cases. Unlike the French neurologist Jean-Martin Charcot – Freud's preceptor, Janet's colleague, and choreographer of the famous hysteria shows at La Salpêtrière – who was primarily interested in anatomizing the patients' physical symptoms, "Janet spent untold hours talking with them, trying to discover what was going on in their minds" (*The Body Keeps Score* 178).

Through the shamanistic Güllü Baba, Tekin is refuting taxonomy in relation to both the malady and the cure. We are forced to ask if there exists a mental or spiritual dimension to an experience of madness brought on by acute deprivation. Is Sırma special and different? And how might we understand Güllü Baba's talent? Is it to be interpreted as the gift of intent listening and imaginative insight – leading to a spiritual cure – or is it simply the instrumentality of reason treating unreason? In *Knot of the Soul*, Pandolfo evokes blindness as a form of preternatural vision into the fungible border of the temporal world and the world of the soul:

> For openness to the inner meaning of happenings requires the capacity to suspend judgment and welcome the penumbra of knowledge, which in the world of the visible attests to the Invisible – the "realm beyond human perception" which manifests itself as blindness. (17)

The anthropologist Veena Das also talks about healers who negotiate registers of luminous and dark knowledge in her monumental work

Affliction. Despite the vast difference in the knowledge systems each subscribes to, Das professes a "deep connection" with Hafiz Mian, a Muslim healer (*amil*) in New Delhi's Jahangirpuri, an affinity that derives from a robust skepticism regarding their experiences – "mine with anthropology, his with amiliyat" – the unlikely collaborators share (157). This skepticism or ambivalence about chosen epistemologies, Das says, "is not simply an opposition between theoretical formulations that are systematic and implicit ways of living, but a struggle over what gives reality to the stories we have heard and the experiences of suffering that have deeply moved us" (157).

The negotiation of "theoretical formulations that are systematic" and "implicit ways of living" also characterizes the psychologist Neil Altman's quest for the spiritual dimensions of psychoanalysis in *Psychoanalysis in an Age of Accelerating Cultural Change*. Instead of exoticizing or debunking faith-healing, he compares these belief systems to psychoanalysis and its simultaneous reinforcing and undermining of the dichotomy between subjectivity and objectivity, the rational and the irrational (42). Güllü Baba is pronounced a healer by the women of Rubbish Road who consider it miraculous that a blind man should weep for the unseen misery of those around him. The analyst confronts the invisible, the unapparent, and the undocumented – the realm beyond temporal vision – in search of a readable text. The aetiology of Sırma's affliction is known: what is not known is why it becomes pathogenic for her, and not any of the other children. Embracing the penumbra of knowledge and suspending judgment, it is only the blind healer, who weeps like a mother, whose telescopic apprehension can acknowledge the singularity of Sırma from the crowd around her. He sees her and talks to, not at, her: "don't cry, little dove, they'll free your hands; go and gather tin," he says (22). Sırma miraculously calms down and starts to collect tin as the peri-urban settlement embarks yet again on rebuilding homes in the landfill that are, or will soon be, "part rubble, part moulds, part shards" (22).

Moving from the class apartheid of Istanbul to the race apartheid of Turkish London, from magic realist fiction to the hallucinatory reality of great unequal cities, I want to dwell on a clinical case study that supplements Tekin's depiction of healing hysteria through talk and "therapeutic suggestion" (Makari 20). It is drawn from my collaboration with the Tavistock Trust in London, a not-for-profit public benefit corporation, which provides over half of all the NHS (National Health Service, the publicly funded national healthcare system in the UK) mental health provision. I focus, in particular, on a horticultural psychotherapy group run by two Turkish analysts.[11] The participants in this group, which meets in St. Mary's Garden, Hackney, once weekly over the four seasons of a year, are Turkish. They have experienced at least one major trauma in their lives: domestic abuse, political torture, complex multiple loss, severe poverty and deprivation. They are all migrants, most of them victims of trafficking, who have had to endure perilous journeys to arrive at the United Kingdom twenty or thirty years ago. They have no formal education, many of them illiterate in their own language. Most of them were menial laborers in Turkey, unable to work now because of the onset of psychosomatic presentations. Each has had to deal with the intrusive scrutiny of authorities to prove their eligibility for benefits from a healthcare system organized on socialist principles.

Ahmet Caglar, the integrative psychotherapist in charge of the group project, states in his report of this thriving initiative that almost all the participants have long-term physical debilitations, yet they "have almost no insight into possible links between their physical symptoms and early emotional traumas and losses."[12] To address this traumatic dissociation, the gardening therapy includes psychoeducation about the body in the form of mindfulness and grounding exercises. It sensitively addresses the "self-stigmatization"[13] the patients suffer from, relatable to the internalization of prejudice, hopelessness, and a debilitating lack of confidence. "One of the major tasks of the group work is to reverse this pattern and try to build resilience and capacity," Caglar states. This is achieved primarily through creating a safe environment in the horticultural group, training the members in principles of nonviolent communication and constructive criticism. Caglar mentions the Turkish word *sohbet* – a deep, intrapsychic "conversation" between therapist and group, and between fellow members – to explain the transformative connections this school of therapy aspires to. *Sohbet* is a form of social glue: Caglar cites a saying in Turkish that "you can miss or postpone a ritual prayer – which has to be performed at certain intervals in the day – but you can't postpone a *sohbet*." Psychodynamic, emotion-focused, and experiential therapeutic methods – which I discuss further in Chapter 2 – are used in this form of group therapy to triangulate person and conflict, understand patterns of repression, and help patients become aware of inhibitions, avoidances, and the devious workings of defenses and anxiety.

Caglar presents the case study of a 57-year-old man, a shopkeeper, with no record of mental illness, whose life takes a tragic turn following a road accident. His physical injury was not considered severe and he was discharged from hospital in a day. However, he deteriorates rapidly after this event, losing almost all of his meager language skills. Withdrawn, forgetful, unable to leave the house, the only words he can muster are "I do not know." At first the group coordinators are not sure he should join the Hackney gardening project, but they invite him anyway, and he agrees to come. As the weeks progress, he starts working actively in the gardening segment of the sessions and begins to share stories of his life. He has "small interactions" with those around him and shows interest in their lives, asking questions from time to time. In six months, he is the most loved group member, Caglar observes. Three months after the gardening cohort disbands, the therapists have a review meeting with the man, who arrives with his wife. They are "smiling and happy": he says that he is working with his son now, going out, carrying on with life. His relationships are more "fulfilling and relaxed," says the man, who, during his first assessment, could not string together answers, and "was not able to clear his nose when he cried." "What happened to this man during his time in the group may seem mysterious," Caglar muses. Like Güllü Baba's one-sided "conversation," the therapy in St. Mary's Garden is about a truth in parallax which restores functionality and capability in a world where historical truths kill – Sırma's hands are untied, literally and figuratively, and she begins to gather the tin with which to rebuild a home, albeit a future mound of bulldozed rubble. In Caglar's assessment, the care and compassion provided by the group in a safe and nonjudgmental environment "helped this man to connect to the healing potential which we all have" as he returns to the quotidian endurance of a care-filled life.

In her provocative study of subjection, *The Psychic Life of Power*, Judith Butler defines it as "the process of becoming subordinated by power as well as the process of becoming a subject" (2). She explains this further as she proposes a bringing together of the theory of power with a theory of the psyche (although not in a spirit of synthesizing Foucault and Freud): "power that at first appears as external, pressed upon the subject, pressing the subject into subordination, assumes a psychic form that constitutes the subject's self-identity" (3). The "tropological quandary" of this scene (4), Butler presses, is that by "subject" we refer to a figure that is not yet instantiated. Althusser termed the process "interpellation," Foucault "the discursive production of the subject" (cited in Butler 5). The former presupposes an authoritative voice which inaugurates the corresponding subjectivity in situ, while the latter captures the vagaries of "voice" beyond and in excess of the spoken word. There is more ambivalence in the Foucauldian interpretation, a "psychological valence," Butler observes: "the subject emerges in tandem with the unconscious" (7). If subordination is that which is forced on a subject[14] yet forms a subject, it implies also that the child, for instance, will emerge from the process with an attachment to those on whom they are dependent (and that their adult life will be inaugurated by the foreclosure of this attachment). Agency is thus predicated on subordination, or the very decimation of agency.

"If subordination is the condition of possibility for agency, how might agency be thought in opposition to the forces of subordination?" Butler speculates. Can the subject counteract and cancel power through (the catachresis of) power? Her answer to this conundrum is that although power is exogenous, it is assumed by the subject, "an assumption that constitutes the instrument of that subject's becoming" (11). Butler steers clear of the obscure lures of both fatalism (there is no outside of power) and optimism (agency can be extrapolated from power) here:

> If the subject is *neither* fully determined by power *nor* fully determining of power (but significantly and partially both), the subject exceeds the logic of noncontradiction. . . . . Exceeding is not escaping, and the subject exceeds precisely that to which it is bound. (17)

Impactful though this argument is in *The Psychic Life of Power*, Butler is talking about the norms and normalization of the psyche in relation to stable societies and healthy selves. What if the imposition of power had nothing to do with the (nascent) will or the equivalence of the subject? What if the vulnerability of the subject to this regulatory power was not a developmental phase to be (partially) overcome, like the child's willed overcoming of parental care? And what if the subject was rendered impossible through its need for affirmation from "categories, terms, and names" (20) not of its own making, and which pronounced it as a non-being, as nothing, as garbage? Finally, what might self-reflexivity, self-beratement, and melancholia – psychic processes through which desire is owned and managed, or transmuted into self-knowledge – entail in scenarios where the subject is not entitled to any sociality and remains unattached to the social? *Unseen City* is about these invisible legions, whom Butler does not write about when she considers the "socially dead" or "objects marked for death" (27). Her examples are AIDS victims, gay people, prostitutes, drug users. "If they are dying or already dead, let us vanquish them again" (27),[15] a phrase which has resonance for socially unassimilable garbage people of rubbish hills, such as the characters of a Latife Tekin novel, or those inhabiting Katherine Boo's documentary fiction, which I discuss in a subsequent chapter. It could also describe the impoverished Turkish patients of St. Mary's Garden, who have long suffered "medically unexplained symptoms"[16] in silence because they could not communicate their complex needs to their British general practitioners in the *lingua franca*. It is to this unseen city that we now turn.

Of Cities Unseen: Individuation to Unity

In a 1988 interview with John Clement Ball, Salman Rushdie insists that the "City Visible but Unseen" in the fifth – and longest – section of *Satanic Verses* is not an imaginary city.

> It is not an invisible city in the sense that Calvino's cities were invisible cities, fantasy cities; and this is a real city whose streets I know; you know, it would be possible to guide anybody down those streets and to show them the locations out of which, and the kind of life experience out of which, the experiences in the book come. But that city is certainly in English literature, and even in English society, ignored, not looked at – in fact is unseen. (*Conversations* 105)

A London ghetto is the laboratory of the lead characters' extreme mutations. Saladin Chamcha, the "translated,"[17] mimic man of an erstwhile colony, will be Indianized and humanized here, while the untranslated Gibreel Farishta – or the Archangel of his paranoid schizophrenic delusions – will lose, once and for all, his Indian and human self in messianic violence. Both of these larger-than-life characters anticipate the city walkers and analysts I will examine in the chapters to come. Saladin is forced to hide his Satanic billy-goat body – made grotesque, the magic realist novel will have us believe, by the racist discourse of the British state and society – in the boarding house of a migrant couple from Bangladesh. He is repulsed (and this foreshadows Julius's dodgy attitudes to race in Teju Cole's *Open City*, discussed in a later chapter) that Mr Muhammad Sufyan, proprietor of Shandaar Café, thinks Saladin is among his own people, his own kind. "'I'm not your kind,' he said distinctly into the night. 'You're not my people. I've spent half my life trying to get away from you'" (*Satanic Verses* 253). "Chamcha, the great projector of voices, the prestidigitator of personae, has turned into a goat and has crawled back to the ghetto, to his despised migrant compatriots," Homi Bhabha wittily describes the effrontery Saladin must feel (300). The irony of this saga is that if Saladin Chamcha, jaded urban sophisticate, is treated by the undiscerning British police as "riff-raff from villages in Sylhet or the bicycle repair shops of Gujranwala" (159), he returns the blast of blind prejudice to a subcontinental cousin less privileged but vastly more erudite than he: the Ovid- and Lucretius-reading, wisecracking, ex-schoolteacher Sufyan from Dhaka.

Cultural misrecognitions dog the steps of his apocalyptic double Gibreel too, as is the fate of the city walkers in the Aminatta Forna and Cole novels I shadow in Chapters 1 and 5. Here is Gibreel in the "City Visible but Unseen," stalking London as the self-appointed Angel of Recitation:

> He wandered its streets through that night, and the next day, and the next night, and on until the light and dark ceased to matter. He no longer seemed to need food or rest, but only to move constantly through that tortured metropolis whose fabric was now utterly transformed, the houses in the rich quarters being built of solidified fear, the government buildings partly of vainglory and partly of scorn, and the residences of the poor of confusion and material dreams. (320)

Gibreel is plotting a refabrication of the ungodly city in this tormented scene, but as his "angel's eyes" (320) penetrate superficial layers to reach the essence of meaning and being, he himself is seen by passers-by as a "poor bastard" (326) or a propositioning hobo (at which juncture he is punched in the nose). Despite the powerful "Archangel" psychosis, his is the phenomenology of a raced world. A kindly lady in a headscarf hands him a racist flyer, "demanding the 'repatriation' of the country's black citizenry" (326). She probably mistook him for a white angel, he thinks, though not white-white, "not quite pukka": "a Levantine angel, maybe, Cypriot or Greek, in need of her best talking-to-the-afflicted voice. 'If they came over and filled up wherever you come from, well! You wouldn't like *that*'" (326). In the interstices of Saladin Chamcha's and Gibreel Farishta's melodramatic transformations, playing out in the context of entrenched British race, class, and colonial politics, are the most unseen of the unseen citizenry. The formidable Hind, wife of Muhammad Sufyan, runs a B&B above the Shandaar Café, in the terraced house which is also home to her family of four. Here, sardine-packed in six rooms, live thirty guests. It is "temporary occupation," created in response to the public housing crisis, and the type that borough councils turned a blind eye to when it came to health and safety regulations (264). A nightly rate of £10 per person: for that money, Chamcha calculates, one could rent family-sized accommodation in the private sector, but there was "no central funding for such solutions" in the aftermaths of the (Thatcher) government's austerity cuts (264). Chamcha describes his silent but vigilant neighbors as "temporary human beings, with little hope of being declared permanent" (264). When the Shandaar Café is engulfed in fire later in the novel, "faceless persons stand at windows waving piteously for help, being unable (no mouths) to scream" (463).

The "unseen city" of my title is inspired by Rushdie's influential formulation of the city visible but unseen, either summarily dismissed or made abject in literary representations. My interdisciplinary work in this area is timely and urgent, revealing the entangled sociocultural contexts that have contributed to state-funded services not recognizing or meeting the mental health needs of poor and migrant populations. It is developed along two scholarly axes. The first is a critical interpretation of historical, literary, and cultural representations of urban poverty, with its constitutive nexus of vulnerable habitations, environmental crises, histories of displacement and migration, and racism. The second is related to tracing the history and afterlives of the "free clinic," the term coined by Freud in 1918, which I use to delineate clinics where psychoanalysis or psychoanalytically oriented services are provided to poor populations for free (or on a sliding scale). What interlinks these seemingly disparate fields is the psychogeography of the urban slum, shantytown, migrant ghetto, council estate, homeless shelter, and safehouses.[18] The invisibility *Unseen City* wishes to address and correct does not merely pertain to the urban cosmopolitan's field of vision: bestowing unimpaired sight to the hitherto oblivious city walker still leaves "faceless persons ... unable (no mouths) to scream" waving piteously at the windows of a house on fire. What it attempts, instead, is to disrupt the wordless, faceless image, the "image of the passive victim on display" (Chow 325), as the first step toward countering the absent, abstracting, or aggressive vision complicit in its victimization. As Rey Chow powerfully argues in "Where Have All the Natives Gone?" – and here she is talking specifically of the "native" as the silent object of anthropological vision –

> [T]he agency of the native cannot simply be imagined in terms of a resistance against the image – that is, *after* the image has been formed – nor in terms of a subjectivity that existed *before,* beneath, inside, or outside the image. It needs to be rethought as that which bears witness to its own demolition – in a form that is at once image and gaze, but a gaze that exceeds the moment of colonization. (342)

What Chow is advocating here is a mode of understanding the defiled racial, cultural other in which their existence predates the arrival of the colonizer and will obdurately survive it. Instead of functioning as an active episteme subjugating passive objects, the colonizer feels "looked at by the native's gaze" – a gaze that is, however, "neither a threat nor a retaliation" (342).

In *The Analyst in the Inner City*, the psychoanalyst Neil Altman's despatches from inner-city public clinics, he addresses the question of "analyzability," an exclusionary selection criterion in which "lower-class patients often end up on the unanalyzable side" (92). The psychoanalytic treatment of the poor or "culturally different" (68) is, indeed, challenging, Altman concedes. Such a patient may necessitate a more directive and prescriptive approach, which in turn triggers risks associated with suggestion. Material help may be sought by patients. Such patients are likely to be working class and "action-oriented" (68) and very unlikely to have the same communicational facility or educational background as the therapist: both of these socioeconomic markers enjoin a revision of the language-oriented treatment method. Altman takes each of the constitutive elements of the classic (ego psychological) model to suggest practicable revisions – capitulations to connectivity across class and race borders, as it were. If the classical model emphasizes insight as the mechanism of change, and this, in turn, makes verbal orientation imperative, what if the analyst located the mechanism of change "in the relationship, rather than in the insight of the patient" (68)? Verbalization is, after all, one of the many modes of relating. The distinction between verbal communication and action is further undermined, Altman argues, when we see verbal communication as forging a relationship, not simply facilitating an information exchange. Even silence, he suggests, could be re-evaluated as a "relational act," not non-action on the part of the supposedly recalcitrant patient (68). The ego deficit or deviance does not lie in the slum poor or the racial minority, but in the rule book whose norms are derived from the structurally advantaged to keep the structurally disadvantaged in their place.

According to Altman, it is not just the demonized poor, raced, patient who is at risk of messing up the interaction. In the inner-city clinic, "social class differences can provide the focus for projection and introjection by both patient and analyst," he cautions (92). He mentions the example of Ms B, a patient he saw in the Bronx, someone who came from a working-class family and had "considerable pathology," including alcoholism, and physical and sexual abuse (85). Ms B had once won a scholarship to an Ivy League university but had subsequently dropped out. In therapy, she identified powerful self-defeating tendencies based on her ambivalence about succeeding in life, which, she suspected, would alienate her from her backward family. One day, Ms B tells Altman that she had decided to quit her job "and do some ill-defined freelance work," going back on welfare in the interim (85). He diagnoses this as Ms B's characteristic self-sabotaging, only to realize, in the course of many weeks, that having a well-paying job had made Ms B feel isolated. In this case, she was performing neediness and subordination so as to make her analyst feel useful: as with her anxieties about losing her family, she had feared losing her therapist if she let him see her actual worth and resourcefulness. Altman wonders if her "relatively low social class position" contributed to his ready classification of her as helpless, and himself as the intrepid helper (92). "I have just illustrated a clinical situation in which what might be considered ego deficits in the patient turn out to be, in part, reflective of the patient's perception that the analyst is quite fragile and needs support," Altman soberly concludes (92).

Unseen City charts many such role reversals in what Altman calls a "three-person psychoanalytic perspective," which includes the role of social class in the psychoanalytic dyad (93). It brings together literary and cultural imaginings of the outcast poor of metropolitan centers with a survey of the prevalent protocols of psychoanalytic cure (and the implied notions of subject and subjectivity inherent to such protocols). As Kirkmayer and Swartz – psychiatrist and psychologist, respectively – state, "culture shapes all illness experience, and this influences the ways in which distress is communicated to others and presented in clinical settings" (46). *Unseen City* claims back for literature its potent role in the histories of humanism, human rights, justice, politics, and ethics – in particular, its instrumentality in uncovering and challenging cultural determinants. The function of literary and cultural analysis in a project that revolves around the ground reality of mental healthcare is manifold. Psychoanalytic case studies, particularly Freud's early work, are frequently read for their novelistic qualities, and the psychoanalytic cure, its linear progress baffled by digressions, distractions, and dead ends, has been a mainstay of narrative theory. Literature, like psychoanalysis, can allow an imaginative rethinking of affective life outside the deformations of colonial legacies and hierarchy, the determinations of neoliberal govern-ments and free market discourse, or the violent resurgence, in recent times, of de-globalized ethnic nationalisms. Writing against the injurious white-ness of the US literary canon in *Playing in the Dark*, Toni Morrison had adopted the language of reparations and repatriation when she said that literature can offer "a huge payout of sign, symbol, agency in the process of organizing, separating, and consolidating identity" (39).

Upholding this relationship of literature with its extradiegetic worlds is also a plea for an aesthetic education, with what Gayatri Chakravorty Spivak identifies as its "sensory equipment of the experiencing being" (*Aesthetic Education* 2). Speaking of withstanding the depredations of globalization – starting with the corporatized university, which lodges humanities departments – she asserts that only an aesthetic education can "continue to prepare us for this, thinking an uneven and only apparently accessible contemporaneity that can no longer be interpreted by such nice polarities as modernity/tradition, colonial/postcolonial" (2). Like humanism, which sought to secure human rights, justice, and power for the citizen-subject, the imaginative humanities aspires to human rights; social and gender equality; the queering and pluralizing of time; imagining the future of humankind in the age of climate breakdown; and the decolonization of knowledge. *Unseen City* enlists literary examples to illustrate the problem field of faulty psychoanalytical categories and provide ways of imagining these categories anew: this is not an ethnological salvage paradigm,[19] but a wakeful critique of what Johannes Fabian called the salvage paradigm's "denial of co-evalness" (31), which I have also identified in stadial or evolutionary accounts of the primitive in psychoanalytic literature.

Sigmund Freud's pioneering work of the 1920s and 1930s on the social conscience of psychoanalysis, leading to the foundation of "free clinics" in Vienna and other European cities, provides the historical framework for this undertaking. Following the lead of Elizabeth Ann Danto's *Freud's Free Clinics: Psychoanalysis and Social Justice, 1918–1938*, but revising the continental history of medicine for a postcolonial present, this work traces the afterlife of the free clinic phenomenon as seen in the emergence of a number of free or low-fee psychotherapy clinics in six global cities: Mumbai, London, New York, Kolkata, Bengaluru, Chennai. In arguing for technologies of subjectivity such as psychoanalysis to be made international, culturally translatable, and socially accessible, I will be building on works of collaborative scholarship such as *The Psychoanalysis of Race*, edited by Christopher Lane (1998), and *Unconscious Dominions: Psychoanalysis, Colonial Trauma, and Global Sovereignties*, edited by Warwick Anderson et al. (2011). Ashis Nandy's *The Intimate Enemy: The Loss and Recovery of Self under Colonialism* (1983) and Ranjana Khanna's *Dark Continents: Psychoanalysis and Colonialism* (2003) highlight both the pernicious ethnographical function of the colonial discipline of psychoanalysis and the ways in which it has been rehabilitated as a decolonizing reading practice. Neil Altman's *The Analyst in the Inner City* (2009) and *Psychoanalysis in an Age of Accelerating Cultural Change* (2015) have shown how psychoanalysis can subvert its medical commodification in capitalism to become a critical force in society. Celia Brickman's *Race in Psychoanalysis: Aboriginal Populations in the Mind* (2018) has helped me to make valuable connections between the colonial discourse analysis in

Nandy and Ranjana Khanna's scholarship and critical race studies. The vast and varied scholarship on international elaborations of Freudian thought – Mariano Ben Plotkin's *Freud in the Pampas: The Emergence and Development of a Psychoanalytic Culture in Argentina* (2001), Fethi Benslama's *Psychoanalysis and the Challenge of Islam* (2009), Rubén Gallo's *Freud's Mexico: Into the Wilds of Psychoanalysis* (2010), Stefania Pandolfo's *Knot of the Soul: Madness, Psychoanalysis, Islam* (2018), Christine Hartnack's essays on the Indian Psychoanalytic Society, and Omnia El Shakry's *The Arabic Freud: Psychoanalysis and Islam in Modern Egypt* (2017), to name a few – have reconfirmed my faith in the excursiveness of Freudian thought. There's life in the old dog yet!

The city is central to the psychic life historicized by *Unseen City*, which examines, in particular, the role of urban infrastructure in creating areas of radical underdevelopment. Case by case, I outline elaborations of biopower – the phenomena of zoning, segregation, profiling, and policing – and spatial interdictions such as noxious habitats; impoverished, migrant-only ghettoes with bad schools and poor social utilities; street and domestic violence; homelessness; substance abuse. The malaise I describe is linked to globalization's "spatial fix," as David Harvey terms it, or the outer transformation of civil society for the centralization of wealth and its periodic crises ("Globalization" 24). Harvey's argument is that "the hypermobility of finance and fictitious capital exists in a dialectical relation with . . . fixed capital investments of both the mobile and immobile sort" (28). One kind of spatial fix involves investing spatially, creating a new landscape for capital accumulation (building airports, for example); the other kind, Harvey claims, invests in production of space to resolve the crises of capital accumulation (here he gives the example of suburbanization, created to absorb excess labor and capital). To cultivate a "geographical standpoint," crucial for a materialist understanding of globalization's production of space and its "specific forms of creative destruction" (Harvey, "Globalization" 30), I will be drawing on relevant works of urban geography, architectural history, and anthropology. These include Harvey's *Social Justice and the City* (1973); Anthony Vidler's *The Architectural Uncanny: Essays in the Modern Unhomely* (1992); Bernard Tschumi, *Architecture and Disjunction* (1996); Mike Davis, *Planet of Slums* (2007); Suketu Mehta's *Maximum City: Mumbai Lost and Found* (2009); Swati Chattopadhyay's *Unlearning the City: Infrastructure in a New Optical Field* (2012); and Liza Weinstein's *Durable Slum: Dharavi and the Right to Stay Put in Globalizing Mumbai* (2014).

Methodologically, *Unseen City* breaks new ground in comparative theory, combining literary criticism with psychoanalytic theory, the history of medicine, public mental health, anthropology, and urban studies. Drawing on a complex body of epidemiological literature and quantitative data acquired through heterogeneous methods, instrumentation, study settings, and populations, it generates narrative and qualitative data to elucidate complex local realities and lived experiences. This ambitious interdisciplinarity of this book project has involved extensive, years-long collaborations and repeated cycles of knowledge-sharing. I have worked with prominent figures in psychiatry and psychoanalysis in each country: Vikram Patel (Harvard Medical School); Arup Ghoshal (Indian Psychoanalytical Society); Honey Oberoi Vahali (Ambedkar University); J. C. Holland (Memorial Sloan Kettering Cancer Center); Asher Aladjem (New York University / Bellevue Hospital); Julian Stern (The Tavistock and Portman NHS). Mine has also been a mode of "barefoot research" with local initiatives, working in the interface of urbanism, poverty, and mental illness. In India, I have worked closely with three non-profit organizations, interviewing seven in the run-up: Samadhana, a free (psychotherapy) clinic in Bangalore; Anjali, a human rights organization in Kolkata; and The Banyan, a mental health NGO in Chennai. In London, my collaborators were the London Clinic of Psychoanalysis, one of the "free clinics" inaugurated in Freud's lifetime; The Camden Psychotherapy Unit; Nafsiyat Intercultural Therapy Centre; and, finally, the Hackney unit, based in St. Leonard's Hospital, of the Tavistock and Portman Trust. In New York, I worked on the Program for Survivors of Torture (PSOT) at Bellevue, the oldest public hospital in the US; the William Alanson White Institute, one of the foremost training centers in the world for psychoanalysis and its applications; Sheltering Arms, a therapeutic nursery in Harlem; and TLC (Transitional Living Community), a psychotherapeutic shelter for homeless people with severe mental illness, also in Harlem.

I have organized the book under three rubrics – London, Mumbai, and New York – each with two chapters. The first chapter of each section examines literary works which bring into dialogue cultural discourses on poverty and mental health, while the second outlines reigning mental health paradigms in each world city, discussing the outreach of related services to impoverished populations. My literary examples are contemporary British, American, and Anglophone postcolonial works of fiction and narrative nonfiction that implicate race, class, migrancy, and gender in the endemic poverty of the geopolitical region in question, and my cultural examples include Hindi, Bengali, and English (American) cinema and television.

The twinned reading of *Berji Kristin*, a Turkish-language novel, and a case study from a Hackney psychotherapeutic experiment involving Turkish patients I offered earlier provides a snapshot of the contrapuntal and variational aesthetics of *Unseen City*. The three literary critical chapters (1, 3, 5) connect the language of cities "visible but unseen" to Freud's unfulfilled dream of free psychoanalysis in the clinical chapters (2, 4, 6). "Mumbai," "London," and "New York" become placeholders for not only Chennai, Bengaluru, and Kolkata, but also Srinagar, Freetown, Lagos, and Montreal. Unlikely affinities develop within the cases: Kashmir frames a chapter on London, while the racist pronouncements of a British Prime Minister shed light on a fictional character's unraveling in Canada. The cities overlap or clash further as I overhaul received readings of psychoanalytic and philosophical touchstones such as the uncanny; trauma; fugue; dissociation; touch as interruption; and time as spacetimemattering.

The Plan

The first chapter, "Eco-cosmopolitanism as Trauma Cure," focuses on Aminatta Forna's *Happiness* (2018), which, like its precursor, *The Memory of Love* (2010), critiques the global importation of psychiatric paradigms and the unilateral translation of culturally situated experiences into a universal diagnostic and classificatory language. Foreshadowing Chapter 5, with its city-walking analyst, we have a fictional psychologist and a fictional psychiatrist, recurring characters in Forna's oeuvre, who present the agonistic conversation between analyst and analyzand in changing geopolitical scenarios and times. Just as the ghost of Fanon haunts the protagonist of *Happiness*, the chapter is bookended by Fanon's theorizations of blackness at the intersection of ontogeny and sociogeny and his experiments with site-specific, grounded psychotherapy and ergotherapy at the Blida–Joinville Hospital in Algeria. I argue that Forna offers the eco-cosmopolitanism of urban living as trauma cure for her cast of *fugueurs* and transients, lost in perpetual motion between the war-torn landscapes they have fled and the phobic attitudes that greet them in London.

The second chapter, "The Analyst as Muse of History in Disaster Zones: Free Clinics, London," begins in the Government Psychiatric Diseases Hospital in Srinagar, as recorded in Sanjay Kak's 2007 *Jashn-e-Azadi*, a documentary banned from screening in India. Using the ad hoc treatment of trauma in this war zone as a frame narrative, and drawing on *Haider* (2014), Vishal Bhardwaj's restaging of *Hamlet* in the Kashmiri *intifada*, this chapter reads case studies from unseen cities nestling within London in the international frame of global and perpetual war. Here, I explore the following phenomena: new diagnostic categories articulating symptoms arising from the loss of a loved one to "disappearance"; filial refusals to mourn deaths denied by the state; intimate violence; disability and the loss of function associated with CTSD, or continuous traumatic stress disorder; the "universal" scripts of neuroanthropology and psychoanalysis pitted against cultural untranslatables. Drawing on the new materialist thinker Karen Barad's coinage, "spacetimemattering," I propose the term "psychomattering" to describe how the analyst in disaster zones tries to iteratively reconfigure time and space. This agential vocabulary is tested out in war zones as well as the embattled mindscapes of migrant London, a nonsynchronous, polylingual space throwing up a host of "medically unexplained symptoms." In this chapter, I dwell on the vagaries of intercultural therapy at Nafsiyat, a London NGO, and the horticultural psychotherapy at St. Mary's Garden, discussed briefly above. Case studies from both these sites echo insights on the racially exclusionary dimensions of classic psychotherapy we had heard articulated by the vexed or chastened practitioners in the Forna novels. As we will see in the final chapter, analysts in the inner city repurpose psychoanalytic concepts – transference, displacement, trauma, memory, and mourning – to aid brutalized historical selves achieve what Claudia Rankine calls the citizen-subject's "self self" (14).

The third chapter, "Slums and the Postcolonial Uncanny," examines the concept of the "uncanny" in relation to the worst slums and red-light areas of postcolonial Mumbai. The uncanny, in this definition, is a psychological avoidance mechanism that has its dark double in the way visibility is negotiated and manipulated by the colonial infrastructure dominant in global cities. Framing the argument primarily through works of narrative nonfiction on India – both published in 2012 and each with "beautiful" in the title – by Katherine Boo (*Beautiful Forevers*) and Sonia Faleiro (*Beautiful Thing*), and with references to Boo's Pulitzer prize-winning journalism on poverty, this chapter examines novel experiments in immersive reportage and kinaesthetic critique. The literary works are cross-referenced with cinema and documentary. If the upshot of the "Uncanny" essay is that space is a projection of the psychical apparatus, which confounds inside and outside, or self and other, the aesthetic interventions discussed here rescue subaltern space from being overwritten by this characteristically modern nostalgia.

The fourth chapter, "Psychoanalysis of the Oppressed, A Practice of Freedom: Free Clinics in Urban India," is an account of my extensive research on free clinics in urban India. It looks beyond the slum firmament, the staple of Western jeremiads on poverty, to find areas of underdevelopment in the fringes of exploding Indian metros, namely Bengaluru, Kolkata, and Chennai. Framed by my reading of Paulo Freire's libertarian pedagogy, it asks what revolutionary leadership, mobilized within and across class lines, might look like when it comes to the relay of psychoanalytic training from supervisor to lay therapist. The chapter provides a brief history of psychoanalysis in India, its travels and travails after the heady early days of the 1920s, to focus on psychotherapeutic initiatives which mobilize the figure of the lay counselor – the "vulnerable" expert (a term explained in this chapter) – a cornerstone of the historical free clinic movement. I describe and analyze the operations of Samadhana, a free clinic in Bangalore; the mental health cooperative model of Janamanas, an initiative of the NGO Anjali; and NALAM, a rural outreach program of the internationally renowned mental health NGO Banyan, which sends community "mobilizers" to the thousands left behind in poverty in the villages skirting Chennai.

Chapter 5, "Open, Closed, and Interrupted City," uses interruption as a chronotope, with its intrinsic interconnectedness of temporal and spatial relationships. I examine different pathologies of interruption here: that of unfinished, untold stories; truncated lives; the metaphysics of a non-tactilist touch; the clinical interruptions that structure immigrant psychoanalysis. As with Forna's fiction, the two Teju Cole novels have mental health professionals (psychiatrists-in-training) as their migrant protagonists. In *Every Day Is for the Thief* (2007), set in corrupt, neoliberal Nigeria, and *Open City* (2011), set in post-9/11, multiracial New York, the narrators' autopoiesis takes the form of forensically examining the unlived-out, erased, or buried lives of the city, including the bodies of slaves unmourned on both sides of the Atlantic. I read the dreamscapes and travelogues of these doppelgänger novels with reference to another *flâneur* narrative, Rawi Hage's *Cockroach* (2008): here, the insect-like protagonist, scuttling around for food and love, is the swarming unconscious of the icy city of Montreal, not its healer. Through the neurotic and psychotic episodes in this type of migrant fiction, we inhabit both the stratified spaces of a world city and the permissiveness of the mental underground: the restrictive immigration policy of the imperial metropolis is countered by its opposite, a self-annihilating fantasy of deterritorialization (without reterritorialization).

The final chapter, "Psychoanalysis of the Unhomed: Free Clinics, New York," repeats the themes and questions raised in the preceding ones as it looks at the delivery of psychoanalytically oriented psychotherapy in three "free clinic" settings: the PSOT at the Bellevue; a homeless shelter in Harlem for the severely mentally ill; and a therapeutic nursery, also in Harlem, for abused children. Can talk therapy address the quandary of raced subjects more spoken to than speaking? Can the prejudicial assumptions underlying the "non-analyzable" foreigner be replaced by a dynamic understanding of cultural difference? The "torture" clinic at NYU/ Bellevue is a microcosm of the city's radically dispossessed: AIDs victims and Tibetan refugees, survivors of West African genocide and rape victims from Bosnia, modern-day slaves from Mauritania and LGBT asylum seekers from the former Soviet Union. The chapter begins with a tribute to vigilante activists, guardians of the psychic life of urban poverty. It concludes with Altman's *Analyst in the Inner City* and his tireless championing of the cause of the "psychically disowned" (xix), those excluded from analysis due to the entrenched classicism, racism, ethnocentrism, and xenophobia of the discourse, and the logocentric ("talk, don't act") bias of psychoanalytic praxis.

In sum, it may seem contradictory to start the introductory chapter with Irigaray's "The Poverty of Psychoanalysis," given the project's elaborate and obsessive investment in psychoanalysis. This is not in error. The free clinic phenomenon, which followed Sigmund Freud's speech act in 1918, is the starting point of my speculations on this topic, and I question the philosophy of psychoanalysis for more democratic and pluralist treatment protocols which were once promised but did not come to fruition. Marx had attacked Proudhon the speculative philosopher in the latter's *Philosophy of Poverty*, critiquing the "absolute method" of an Old Hegelianism which read the functions of political economy according to eternal logical categories. Citing Hegel (from "Logic," vol. III), Marx states: "Method is absolute force, unique, supreme, infinite, which no object can resist; it is the tendency of reason to find itself, to recognise itself, in everything" (118). To forcibly stop the contestation of meanings constitutive of philosophy would be to impoverish philosophy, he implies. In a lecture delivered in Kolkata in 2019, Gayatri Chakravorty Spivak, in fidelity to the title of the French original (*Misère de la philosophie*), has translated the "poverty of philosophy" as the Bengali phrase "chintar durdasha" – which I translate back to English as the "travails of ratiocination."²⁰ To be held hostage by a reason which does not allow imagination to ameliorate and emancipate it is, according to Spivak, tantamount to foreclosing the very vocabulary of the ethical. Spivak has argued elsewhere that "Reason is the best grounding error upon which we can locate ourselves in order to make the most productive mistakes" (*Through the Roadblocks* 44). In the 2019 lecture, she counteracts the poverty of philosophy with what she calls "aparashokti" – "kalponar sahajye aparer antarey probeshadhikar labher proyash." To translate, "aparashokti" is the power of self-othering, which endeavors to imaginatively approximate (without gobbling up) the psyche of the other. *Unseen City* urges that psychoanalysis overhaul its own identifications to see imaginatively the psychic life of the poor, without which it remains complicit in the denial of "legitimate community"²¹ to the socially disenfranchised. This restructuring involves not only a revision of what Freud called the "foreign policy"²² of global psychoanalysis, but a contingent repurposing of its temporal logic, technique, aims and outcomes, and its archival and death drives, as we shall explore in the following chapters.

PART I

London

CHAPTER I

Eco-cosmopolitanism as Trauma Cure

The fourth chapter of Frantz Fanon's classic work *Black Skin, White Masks*, titled "The So-Called Dependency Complex of the Colonized," is a powerful critique of Mannoni's *Prospero and Caliban: The Psychology of Colonization* (1956). Born in France of Corsican parents, Dominique-Octave Mannoni had come to know the African colonial condition primarily through his ethnological work in Madagascar, where he spent twenty years. The argument of *Prospero and Caliban* is that colonial "situations" are the product of "misunderstanding, of mutual incomprehension" (31). The situation, Mannoni observes in the introduction, is created the very moment a white man appears in the midst of a tribe, and he elaborates on its distinctive and varied features: dominance of a majority by a minority, economic exploitation, the seemingly benign paternalism of the civilizing mission, and racism. The colonizer's "grave lack of sociability combined with a pathological urge to dominate" gives him a "Prospero Complex" while the colonized Malagasy, forced out of their own history, genealogy, and tradition, and victimized by a failed European interpellation, develop a corresponding "Dependence Complex" (102, 41). Neither inferiority nor superiority, "dependence," Mannoni claims, is Caliban's reliance on colonizers fostered by a sense of abandonment.

"We propose to show that Monsieur Mannoni, although he has devoted 225 pages to the study of the colonial situation, has not grasped the true coordinates," states Fanon at the outset (65). Intellectually honest and insightful on colonial psychopathology though he may be, and the research sincere, Mannoni's "objectivity" becomes increasingly suspect when he claims that the germ of the inferiority complex in the Malagasy was latent in them:

> Here we see the mechanism at work in psychiatry, which explains there are latent forms of psychosis that become evident following a traumatic experience. And in surgery, varicose veins in a patient are caused not by having to

stand for ten hours, but rather by the constitutional weakness of the vein walls; the work mode merely deteriorates the condition further, and the employer's responsibility is assessed to be very limited. (66)

Fanon delineates the colonial industrial complex whose moral justification is derived from an opportunistic confusion of the psyche and soma of the oppressed, the denigrated body standing not for the causative brutalization of colonization but for the racist ideology animating the same. Monsieur Mannoni "has not endeavored to see from the inside the despair of the black man confronted with the white man," writes Fanon (66). From the inside, objectivity is not possible, states Fanon, nor is it possible to differentiate between colonial and other forms of racism. Fanon excoriates Mannoni's argument that the depredations of colonial rule are traceable to petty officials, small traders, and colonials, not the mind of Europe. He states defiantly that "European civilization and its agents of the highest caliber are responsible for colonial racism ... every citizen of a nation is responsible for the acts perpetrated in the name of the nation" (70, 72).

Turning to the so-called "dependency complex," and the supposed lack of an inferiority complex among the colonized, Fanon is equally scathing. In South Africa, there are 2 million whites to 13 million blacks, yet it has never occurred to a single black person to consider themselves superior to a member of the White community. They, in fact, feel inferior, an "inferiorization" which is a "correlative to the European's feeling of superiority" (73). Mannoni's pernicious misunderstanding is that he gives the native no choice between dependence and inferiority. In fact, caught up as he is in the contest of meanings between schools of ethnographers, Mannoni fails to consider that "Malagasy" itself is a concept metaphor which exists only in relation to the European. Moreover, Mannoni's interpretation that it is the demand for equality which makes the "dependent" Malagasy positionally "inferior," because the demand is unappeasable and no measure of equality can ever suffice, is based on deeply flawed assumptions.

> A Malagasy is a Malagasy; or rather, he is *not* a Malagasy, but he lives his "Malagasyhood." If he is a Malagasy it is because of the white man; and if, at a certain point in his history, he has been made to ask the question whether he is a man, it is because his reality as a man has been challenged ... I start suffering from not being a white man insofar as the white man discriminates against me; turns me into a colonized subject; robs me of any value or originality; tells me I am a parasite in the world. . . . So I will try quite simply to make myself white; in other words, I will force the white man to acknowledge my humanity. But, Monsieur Mannoni will tell us, you can't, because deep down inside you there is a dependency complex. (78)

I quote Fanon at length here because it encapsulates three recurrent themes in literary representations of the nervous condition of the colonized: the discursive construction of paradigms of identity, health, and pathology; the physical and psychic violence that determines the identity, health, and pathology of what Fanon calls the "colonized subject"; and, finally, the impasse in which the racist neuroanthropology puts the colonized subject, unable to move backwards or forwards. If Mannoni had, in his analyses of the seven Malagasy dreams that Fanon critiques,[1] highlighted the dominant theme of terror – in particular, the existential terror of the immobilized as well as the fugitive victim of violence – Fanon provides a practical, historically relevant interpretation instead: the black bull, in the Malagasy dream, is not the phallus but the feared Senegalese in the criminal investigation department. "Freud's discoveries are of no use to us whatsoever," Fanon cautions.

> We must put the dream *in its time*, and this time is the period during which 80,000 natives were killed, i.e., one inhabitant out of fifty; and *in its place*, and the place is an island with a population of 4 million among whom no real relationship can be established, where clashes break out on all sides, where lies and demagoguery are the sole masters.[2] (84)

In *Crazy Like Us: The Globalization of the Western Mind*, Ethan Watters accuses the pervasiveness of diagnostic categories emanating from American psychiatry of "flattening the landscape of the human psyche itself" (1). Aminatta Forna's 2010 novel *The Memory of Love*, similarly, is scathing in its critique that Western theories of trauma and trauma cure are not self-reflexive enough about their foreign provenance and cultural particularity in relation to the specific and local histories, geographies, traditions, and conceptions of self to which they are indiscriminately applied. Forna, born in Glasgow to a Scottish mother and Sierra Leonean father, is Sierra Leonean and British, and has expressed surprise at her reception in academic circles as an African writer: "We hyphenated writers complain about the privilege accorded to the white male writer, he who dominates the Western canon and is the only one called simply 'writer'" ("Don't Judge"). *The Memory of Love*, which Kiran Desai described as "a profoundly affecting work," is a novelization of the brutalizing effects of the Civil War (1991–2002) in Sierra Leone. Set in Freetown in 2001, the aftermaths of the genocide are narrated by three voices: Adrian Lockheart, a British psychologist trying to come to terms with a therapeutic scene where "ninety-nine percent of the population was suffering from post-traumatic stress disorder" (319); Elias Cole, a former history professor at the city's university and Lockheart's only private patient; and Kai Mansaray, a Sierra Leonean orthopaedic surgeon who befriends Adrian.

Lockheart is a trauma specialist who has flown in to help the nation "heal" from the Civil War. His connection to Sierra Leone or Africa is accidental: at a professional crossroads, mindful that the momentum of his career may have dissipated, he had seen an advertisement by an international agency "for a government-sponsored psychologist to work overseas" (66). Adrian's application had failed, and he would not have embarked on the six-week project in Freetown in 2001 had the successful applicant not taken ill. While it is eventually revealed that Adrian's connection to Sierra Leone is not as tenuous as it had seemed – his mother had "nearly" been born there – the fact that he "knew a little more about it than most, at the very least he knew its correct location" (67), is more an indictment of his savior complex than a justification of it. Lockheart is the nervous focalizer of some of the novel's key themes: the incommensurability of the "universal" diagnostic and classificatory language of psychiatry with the quotidian and exceptional catastrophes visited on the local population in a brutalized postcolonial nation; the incommensurability of taxonomies of normalcy and pathology with the on-the-ground reality of Sierra Leone in the aftermath of a decade-long armed civil war; the uncanny correspondence between gender injustice in peacetime and the sexual violence that is used in the Sierra Leonean genocide as a military tool against civilians.

When Forna won the Windham Campbell Prize in 2014, the citation said "Aminatta Forna writes through and beyond personal experience to speak to the wider world in subtly constructed narratives that reveal the ongoing aftershocks of living through violence and war."[3] If *The Memory of Love* references the carnage of the 1990s in Sierra Leone, her third novel, *The Hired Man* (2013), tells of the aftermaths of ethnic cleansing following the break-up of the former Yugoslavia. Forna's first novel, *Ancestor Stones* (2006), archives subaltern voices and spaces in a decolonizing nation: while it is not ostensibly about the states of exception the civil conflict in Sierra Leone or Croatia present, it too is ravaged by personal loss and bloated with melancholia. "Somebody must stand guard over the past," says Duro Kolak, custodian of a Croatian town named "Gost," with all its echoes of guest, host, and ghost (*Hired Man* 43). Sometimes, the best way to remember is a willed forgetting. Faced with the resounding silence of his patients in *The Memory of Love*, Adrian Lockheart has to learn not to file it away under the rubric of "psychological avoidance" in the style of the PTSD diagnosis. The upshot of the novel is that he must learn to read faltering, ambiguous, and euphemistic speech, as well as silence, as strategies of symbolic containment in a melancholy nation space.

Forna's *Hired Man* reminds the reader of J. M. Coetzee's style, as bleak as *Ancestor Stones* is sumptuous. The more unspeakable the reality, the more forensic and meticulous the prose gets. Forna is a method writer: she learned to shoot as part of her research for *Hired Man*, and, for *The Memory of Love*, she spent time at a hospital in Sierra Leone watching amputations. The book reviews tend not to pick up on the preternatural sensitivity to the nonhuman world, which she is shooting in more ways than one. Deer, elephants, ants, chicken, fish, conger eel, stones. Jean Turane, one of the key characters of Forna's fourth novel, *Happiness* (2018), is a wildlife biologist fighting to keep London foxes safe from the rapacity of urbanization and its eugenicist biological imagination with relation to the nonhuman animal. As Nilanjana Roy observes in the *Financial Times* review of *Happiness*, for Forna, "the wilderness is never far away" ("*Happiness*"): parakeets, a falcon chasing down a pigeon, skeletal remains of horses archived in the riverside mud. The quest for truth, "the desire to examine every inch of her surroundings in a way that went beyond childish curiosity" (207), is pitiless, as any reader of the rats-in-winter scene in *The Hired Man* will testify. In *Ancestor Stones*, Forna calls it "the African way of seeing" (6), although it would be equally applicable to Croatia or Sierra Leone.

The "African" way is a way of seeing patterns and logic in signs "invisible yet visible, apparent to those who belong" (*Ancestor Stones* 6). Forna's poetics of third spaces – neither sleep nor wakefulness, neither past nor the present, neither head nor heart, neither real nor unreal – finds trenchant expression in the aesthetics of the liminal state of "Rothoron" through which some of her female protagonists in *Ancestor Stones* survive their short and brutish lives, or the "fugue" states and dissociative episodes she describes in *The Memory of Love*. This psychic navigation system informs the way Forna traverses geopolitical difference. When British interviewers describe her as having "two such different cultures," she asks them how they know if they've never been to Sierra Leone:

> I point out that in Scotland my family belongs to a clan, which, when we are talking about Sierra Leone, is renamed a tribe. In Sierra Leone people tell stories of mischievous spirits who play havoc in the world of humans, using the same word the English colonials used: "devils." In Scotland my grandmother told me stories of "faeries" who stole horses and babies, and

essentially behaved in the same way as the devils in Sierra Leone. ("Don't Judge")

This "different way of seeing," which recalibrates a phenotype-dependent identity politics, informs Forna's choice of Croatia for *The Hired Man*. Sierra Leone and Croatia are quite similar, she observes, in size, population, natural beauty, peasant cultures, and as tourist destinations. What drew her to Croatia in the first place is that it has, like Sierra Leone, suffered decades of dictatorship, civil war, human rights violations, and economic deprivation. "Just because things look a certain way on the surface, doesn't mean that's the way they really are" ("Don't Judge").

Fugue: or, Crossing

In her influential genealogical study *Trauma* (2000), Ruth Leys takes issue with experts who see psychic trauma, especially in the institutionalized form of PTSD (post-traumatic stress disorder), as "a timeless diagnosis, the culmination of a lineage that is seen to run from the past to the present in an interrupted yet ultimately continuous way."[4] Although the shock of an acute sensory overload is a known cause of psychological disturbances that manifest over time, Leys points out that it was the British physician John Erichsen who, faced with victims of railway accidents, invented trauma syndrome in the 1860s. The term "traumatic neurosis" was coined by the neurologist Paul Oppenheim and acquired its psychological dimensions in the work of J. M. Charcot, Pierre Janet, Alfred Binet, Morton Prince, Josef Breuer, Sigmund Freud, and others. The waning interest in trauma, which Leys attributes to Freud's problematic debunking of the seduction theory – from 1897, he prioritized erotic infantile fantasy over actual incidences of sexual seduction or assault – and Babinski's dismantling of Charcot's hysteria discourse, changed with eruption of the Great War. The tide of collective trauma resulting from modern trench warfare, captured in makeshift descriptors such as "war neurosis" or "shell shock," ushered a return to Freud's ideas of dissociation and the Breuer–Freud cathartic method. Despite the work of psychoanalysts such as Sándor Ferenczi and Abram Kardiner in the interwar period, or the pioneering therapies advocated by William Sargant, Roy Grinker, and John Spiegel in the aftermath of World War II, Leys notes that it was only after the Vietnam War that "the American Psychiatric Association's *Diagnostic and Statistical Manual of Mental Disorders* [*DSM*] (1980) accorded the traumatic syndrome, or PTSD, official recognition for the first time" (5). An outcome of the mobilization of support by collaborations between Vietnam Veteran pressure groups and anti-war psychiatrists, PTSD would soon come to signify not merely the psychic response to an exceptional event outside the range of human experience, as the American Psychiatric Association initially suggested, but also to violent though not unusual occurrences such as rape, incest, and child abuse.

I discuss the provenance of (and false universals associated with) PTSD in greater detail in the next chapter. Arguably a blunt instrument, the Post-traumatic Stress Disorder Reaction Index (PTSD-RI) – alongside instruments such as the Depression Self-Rating Scale and the UCLA Grief Inventory – is nonetheless widely used to screen for mental health issues in post-conflict populations. The diagnostic criteria elaborated by DSM-5, summarized briefly, are as follows: exposure to death, injury, or (sexual) violence; intrusion of symptoms associated with the traumatic event; persistent avoidance of stimuli associated with the traumatic event; negative alterations in cognition and mood; marked alteration in arousal and reactivity, including aggressive and self-destructive behavior; duration of disturbance for over a month; impairment in social and professional functions; disturbed behavior not attributable to medication, drink, drugs, or a medical condition. "Despite the majority of contemporary wars being located in non-Western countries, Western ideas of trauma currently dominate," observe David Winter et al. in their substantive study of the aftermaths of the Civil War in Sierra Leone (9). The scholarship they draw on – Masten, Bonanno, Westphal, Mancini – suggests that, unlike the psycho-pathological responses shored by initial trauma research, "there is now overwhelming evidence that most people respond to trauma with minimal disruption to their overall function, and, instead, demonstrate resilience" (6). The outcome pattern following a Potentially Traumatic Event (PTE), as suggested by Bonanno (2004) and Bonanno, Westphal, and Mancini (2011) are: resilience (35–65%); recovery (15–25%); PTSD (5–30%); delayed distress (0–15%). While the lay public continues to believe that the absence of prolonged distress and dysfunction (in populations who have suffered a PTE) is abnormal, recent scholarship proves that "resilience is the prevailing response to a PTE," state the authors of *Trauma, Survival and Resilience in War Zones* (Winter et al. 7).[5]

Similarly, an article on a fourteen-year longitudinal study of war-affected youth in Sierra Leone, which also examines the impact of short-term group CBT (cognitive behavioral therapy), asserts that "exposure to violence in conflict settings is not necessarily determinative of long-term health outcomes" (Simmons Zuilkowski et al. 66). The effects of war exposure on mental health were indirect, moderated by the stresses of daily life, and tended to manifest in the form of interpersonal conflict: aphonia, aggressiveness, high-risk behavior, struggling to access education services. This research highlights the association of social capital with lower levels of depression and social impairment in post-conflict youth and advocates the cultivation of supportive relationships, alongside the cognitive restructuring achieved by group psychosocial interventions such as CBT, for reintegrating war-affected youth into community and society.

The Memory of Love is scathing in its critique that Western conceptions of trauma and the methods proposed for curing the same do not sufficiently declare self-interest or their entanglements in specific histories, geographies, or what David Scott terms "the conscripts of modernity." The "conscripts" of Scott's book title are modernity's ostensible strictures, often a colonial inheritance, but he argues that these could be repurposed as critical conceptual resources to remake the postcolonial present.[6] It is possible to test this argument in relation to the diagnostic toolkit of psychiatry, undoubtedly a conscript of colonial neuroanthropology. Moreover, as *The Memory of Love* – as well as Forna's latest novel *Happiness* – suggests, it is possible to prevent the coercive epistemology of psychiatry from superseding postcolonial futures. In fact, interventions such as Forna's show how psychiatry and the Euro- or America-centric "psy-ontology" (Rose 190) of the trauma cure, instead of hollowing out interiority, could provide an expedient affective form for agential modes of post-traumatic recovery in the postcolony.

"If you were an ambitious researcher in psychology or psychiatry in the 1990s, PTSD was where the action was; by 2004, more than 20,000 articles, books and reports had been indexed in the National Center for Post-Traumatic Stress Disorder's database," observes Watters (72). The Ghanaian psychiatrist Attila Asare, whose character finds its full flowering in *Happiness*, makes his first entrance in *The Memory of Love*. He tells Adrian about a visiting medical research team who had pronounced, after a mere six weeks of study, that 99 percent of the Sierra Leonean population was suffering from post-traumatic stress disorder. "You call it a disorder, my friend. We call it *life*," he says memorably (319). Lockheart is troubled by the dwindling numbers of patients to see him at the Freetown Hospital: the idea that he was "neither wanted nor needed . . . had simply never occurred to him" (320). Frustrated and made restless by his lack of patients, Adrian fixates on the diagnosis of a local woman called Agnes, an "enigma" whose "dissociative" episodes of unconscious wandering whet Adrian's curiosity (112, 359). Having first encountered Agnes in a state of confusion in a marketplace, Adrian later recognizes the woman on a visit to a psychiatric ward at the local mental hospital. The resulting trajectory, reminiscent of the end-oriented speed of a sensation novel – its atmosphere of mystery building up to the exposure scene – showcases Forna's most damning indictment of the psychiatric paradigm. As Kai says of humanitarian conquistadors like Adrian:

> It was errantry that brought them here, flooding in through the gaping wound left by the war . . . [t]hey came to get their newspaper stories, to save black babies, to spread the word, to make money, to fuck black bodies . . . Modern-day knights, each after his or her trophy, their very own Holy Grail. (218–219)

This allegation holds for colonial administrators like Adrian's grandfather, District Commissioner Silk, as well as the influx of journalists, foreign investors, counselors, and NGO workers to Sierra Leone in the twenty-first century.

Adrian ascribes to Agnes the illness identity of a complex amnesia listed in the DSMs as "fugue": "Characterised by sudden, unexpected travel away from home . . . often coupled with subsequent amnesia," the disorder, which first appeared in 1887, as the novel cites, is a "rarely diagnosed dissociative condition" whereby sufferers appear "to inhabit a state of obscured consciousness from which they eventually emerged with no memory of the weeks, months or even years they had spent away" (325). The 1994 DSM identified "fugue" as a dissociative disorder. The psychiatrist Herbert Spiegel, Chair of the Dissociative Disorders Committee for the DSM-IV, claimed that dissociation was caused by trauma, though this was not substantiated by the "Comprehensive Review" of psychogenic amnesia and fugue conducted before the publication of DSM-IV. As Adrian synchronizes Agnes's behavior to Eurocentric taxonomies, he feels the "anxious euphoria of a person who happens upon what they think might be a lost treasure in a field" (128). Keen to build on the lukewarm reception of a past paper, Adrian's humanitarian enterprise is a corollary to vulture capitalism. If he could demonstrate the presence of fugue in this wasted population, it would be a considerable achievement; if he could "also demonstrate a clear link to post-traumatic stress disorder? Well, that could make his name" (168).

In *Mad Travelers: Reflections on the Reality of Transient Mental Illnesses* (2002), Ian Hacking makes the thought-provoking claim that "fugue" was a *fin-de-siècle* phenomenon, and that its "ecological niche" (Hacking pointedly uses the term "ecological" instead of the Foucauldian "discursive") was France and a few other European countries (13):

Fugues, that is to say strange and unexpected trips, often in states of obscured consciousness, have been known forever, but only in 1887, with the publication of a thesis for the degree of doctor of medicine, did mad travel become a specific, diagnosable type of insanity. (8)

According to Hacking, it is a mental illness that could only have existed in a specific space-time configuration and in the context of specific vested interests. The following vectors led to the emergence of this "transient" disease: the greed and competitiveness driving medical taxonomy in the scientific community; the polarity of romantic travel and criminal vagrancy; an emerging culture of surveillance in France and Europe, which regulated moving bodies; and, finally, the medical relief that was in place for the *fugueurs*. It could be argued that the dominant affect of *The Memory of Love* is a fugue state, with its haunting landscape and haunted characters. The novel is crowded with transients and travelers – Adrian, Attila, Kai, Agnes, Ileana – although it is only the African locals whose border crossings are pathologized. Adrian "feels like a sleepwalker" (45), the train timetables ordering his London existence giving way to the abrupt timekeeping of a country without twilight or the intermediary seasons of spring and autumn. Attila, the chief psychiatrist at the mental hospital, is also a lurker in margins. Here, for instance, mocking the absurd national PTSD diagnosis rate, he moves uncertainly between native informant and colonial subject: "When I ask you what you expect to achieve for these men, you say you want to return them to normality. So then I must ask you, whose normality? Yours? Mine? . . . This is *their* reality" (319).

In *The Memory of Love* as well as *Happiness*, Forna seems also to be questioning the cultural assumption, tacitly supported by the medical establishment, that the immobilization of PTSD is tantamount to victimhood. In a *Columbia Law Review* article, Saira Mohamed critiques the victim-oriented approach of academic trauma theory and international criminal justice today, albeit in a different vein: highlighting the reality of "perpetrator trauma," she argues that monsters suffer from PTSD too (1157). Mohamed cites the well-known argument between trauma theorists Ruth Leys and Cathy Caruth, where the former challenged the latter's reading of Tancred and Clorinda from Tasso's *Jerusalem Delivered*. Ruth Leys takes issue with Caruth's depiction of Tancred as the subject of trauma – hasn't he (unwittingly) killed Clorinda, the woman he loves? Disaggregating PTSD from the narrative of victimhood, Forna describes the way in which psychoanalysis and psychotherapy can use a repatterning of traumatized states to change not only the prototypes of narration and historiography which bear witness to the same, but the very material-discursive logic of the cure. Attila, whose own perpetually fugitive state cultivates a healthy disdain of boundary protocols, wants to stop at roadblocks and ask the violent perpetrators about their dreams. "Nobody funded those kinds of conversations" that would psychoanalyze war outside the self-serving frame of liberal guilt (*Happiness* 67). It is true that a perpetual war is raging in the space-time crimped globe, and no one can sleep these days, Attila observes. However, he forcefully protests against the ubiquity of the vocabularies of trauma and valorizes endurance, resilience, and flexibility instead. He has never known an African to ask, "why me?" he tells Kathleen Branagan: "the script of life for most of us is, dare I say, a great deal more fluid" (202).

Adrian's temporary loss of control, "surrounded by languages you don't understand" (27), or the selflessness he tries to cultivate, is defeated by overriding self-interest: "There were too many like Adrian, here living out their unfinished dreams" (220). In Sierra Leone, the mainstays of globalized psychiatry cause misrecognition and missed cultural encounters. There is, for example, the Swedish doctor's diagnosis of a "possible suicide attempt" when he sees wrist injuries in a patient (339). The local surgeon Kai has never treated an attempted suicide, nor has he heard of it once in his career. "Perhaps the Swedish doctor imagines himself trying to end it all if he lived here," he thinks, convinced himself that the emotive response to postwar trauma in Sierra Leone was more likely to be obdurate survival: "Survival was simply too hard-won to be given up lightly" (341). In *Happiness*, Attila's ideals and prognoses are far from compromised by the Western perspectives on trauma cure he constantly negotiates but he feels co-opted nevertheless by ruthless military governments, "tasked with the job of trying to keep the young men sane while what they were being asked to do was an insanity itself" (210).

Forna's narrative in *The Memory of Love* is structured around elisions, secrets, and mysteries, but these have an added function beyond formally signifying the lacunae of traumatic memory. The gaps stand for cultural untranslatables, and also phenomena in plain sight that the mental health tourist refuses to see. "Do they help, the local methods?" Adrian asks Ileana about local healers. "It's just care in the community under another name," replies she, something Adrian hadn't contemplated, just as he was taken by surprise to learn that some of the antipsychotic drugs of modern medicine were discovered by faith healers in Sierra Leone "hundreds of years ago" (87, 277). Adrian initially attributes the reluctance of Sierra Leoneans "to talk about anything that had happened to them" to the collapse of witnessing built into trauma (321). When not irritated by the opacity or banality of uttered speech, he feels ill at ease with the silences that punctuate verbal exchanges: "the notion that a conversation is a continuous act is bred into his bones and silences like nudity should be covered up lest they offend" (48). "[I]t's as though the entire nation is sworn to some terrible secret" (322). Ileana reminds him that the elected muteness could well be a function of a failed interpellation: "After all, it was us Europeans who invented the talking cure. And most of the maladies it's designed to treat" (169). It is when he begins to treat these silences not as dissociative absences, but as full and present signifiers, that Adrian achieves a breakthrough: he learns to read the use of ambiguous and euphemistic speech as well as muteness as strategies of containment in a nation space destabilized by outbreaks of extreme violence. Faced with complex riddles, such as the story of Agnes, and with little grasp of local visual, verbal, or etymological nuance, Adrian drifts to intersubjective spaces where alternative loci of enunciation may be uncovered (187).[7]

The locals, both Adama's companion and the nurse Salia, claim that Agnes is "crossed": "If a spirit possesses you, you become another person, it is a bad thing. . . . But sometimes a person may be able to cross back and forth between this world and the spirit world" (129). To be "crossed" is to inhabit the in-between world, and to be in neither world fully. With the aid of Salia's cultural translation, Adrian learns that "when a spirit enters a person sometimes it makes them act a certain way, what people call crazy" (115). Differentiating between "crossing" and "possession," Salia explains the former as a co-inhabiting of the material and spirit worlds. Not the negative determination of fugue, then, or the stigma of dislocation, migration, and refugee camps associated with the figure of the asylum seeker, but an intersectional mode of belonging: trans- and inter-, it is, Adrian realizes, a viable way of being in a disjointed world. Kai Mansaray, the Sierra Leonean surgeon, does not dismiss the fugue diagnosis offhand but, as Fanon had done with the Malagasy dream, he reads the symptom in the context of the patient's contingent history. Agnes, he discovers, was leaving home compulsively to flee the unbearable condition of cohabiting with the murderer of her husband, whom her daughter had unknowingly married.

If Forna flouts a hegemonic (Western) understanding of consciousness in *The Memory of Love*, she is also wary of nativism and forced cultural dualisms. The narrative of Kai, the "worldly" (49), cosmopolitan Sierra Leonean, draws on interlocking memory systems. Kai *can* be analyzed because he is Western-educated, always already a product of colonial soul-making. Repressed memories flood his mind at unguarded moments: "a sudden intrusion of conscious thought upon his world of sleep" (286). In the final chapter, we see the surgeon, driving across the bridge where he was abused, and which he has avoided in the previous chapters. His successful recovery is attributable to the newly reciprocal engagement between the two men, Adrian and Kai, which results in a transformation of (traumatic) memory. With Adrian's help, Kai moves from what the trauma theorist Judith Herman calls "passively experienced symptoms" to the traumatic reaction, a symbolic repetition of the primal event, which leads to "an active understanding" ("The Politics of Trauma," 141). As the philosopher Catherine Malabou states, "being affected means to be modified – that is altered, changed." Turning to Jacques Derrida's notion of "heteroaffection," Malabou asks "Is the affected subject, then, someone else, the presence of another subject within itself? Or is it just nobody, the absence of a substantial first person?" (Johnston and Malabou 8). Adrian gets the answers he had once doggedly sought after he has stopped grasping for them: the aetiology of Agnes's fugue comes unbidden, in a letter from Kai, enfolding the coast of Norfolk in the coast of West Africa. In *The Memory of Love*, affect is heteroaffection, the affect of the other, intersectional affect. Here, we see the self-disjunction Brian Massumi talks about, whereby a vocabulary of affect, while putting "matter unmediatedly back into cultural materialism," can also provide a situated understanding of "the real incorporeality of the concrete" (*Parables for the Virtual* 4, 5). "One day perhaps he will return," Adrian thinks, unable to let go of the past or the future (440).

The wandering figures sometimes cross over novels, like stories which, as Forna said in *Ancestor Stones*, "started in one place and ended in another . . . [worn] smooth and polished like pebbles from countless retellings" (10). This has more to do with the connected world of late capitalism and late liberalism, global war, terrestrial catastrophism and the refugee crisis than with the border crossings of comprador classes specifically. Adrian Lockheart himself is a revenant from Forna's first novel, where he made a fleeting appearance as a rookie counselor, with the barest whiff of a colonial hang-up ("His grandfather's fondness for our country made Adrian want to see it for himself," Mariama observes: 303). She assumes that he had come to this West African country with the hope of treating child soldiers, and if he was disappointed to get Mariama (christened Mary) instead, he didn't show it. Mariama is suspected of having a breakdown, hence the counseling sessions arranged by her employer, but the conversations are far from therapeutic: Lockheart is naïve and earnest and she is condescending, teasing, even rude in response. In a novel spilling over with the stories of four interconnected lives – and the relays of these stories – the therapy session is a curious chapter where the narrator sets up her only audience to fail. What Mariama says to Adrian Lockheart is an admixture of autological fantasy and hallucination, genealogical myth, and historical fragments snatched in the throes of a violent civil war: "This was the story I told Adrian Lockheart. By the end he was leaning forward, his eyes glistening, the picture of professional caring" (309). It is not that he doesn't care. Narrative therapy fails in this scenario because Mariama sees him as nothing more than an altruistic foreigner, and he sums her up as a PTSD case, albeit a harmless one. Forna's latest, *Happiness* (2018), sees the return of the Ghanaian psychiatrist Attila. If repetition is at the core of trauma, Sierra Leone returns too in this novel, in the war-weary Sierra Leoneans posted in Iraq, "used to war conditions, hardship, and jolly happy to be earning $750 a month" (194), or in the dislocated lives of Ibrahim and Adama, adrift in London.

Collision: Black, White, Light Bright

"Everything Adrian had known must be true but had never been able to discover, never been able to prove" (441), writes Forna, describing his reaction on receiving Kai's eight-page letter describing the story of Agnes. *The Memory of Love* as well as *Happiness* have, at their core, the quest for a serviceable narrative form for postcolonial trauma: in the precursor novel, this is made available to Adrian only after he has attuned himself to a discourse whose terms of exegesis are deferral, displacement, and silence. The novel hints that Adrian's failure to fit the symptomatology of "fugue" neatly to Agnes's malaise – as Kai observes, she is not searching for something, like the classic fugueur, but is fleeing something instead – constitutes a productive failure, resulting in a more empathetic mode for the secular ministering of souls that is therapy. Fighting the stereotyping diagnoses, as he and Kai had done with PTSD verdicts in Freetown, and the political marginalization concomitant on the affixing of labels to disenfranchised minorities, the Attila of *Happiness* challenges the nascent orthodoxies and prevalent misconceptions around trauma, especially when they readily attach to raced bodies historically subjugated by symbolic overdeterminations. The designation of victimhood to the trauma sufferer forecloses the empowering potential of trauma, the hopefulness, if not the happiness, Attila thinks. Trauma, he argues, is not merely damage: suffering may well lead to change, and it is more often than not transformed into resilience. Psychiatry is "more art than science," his mentor Toure, a philosopher-psychiatrist, had argued (231). In "the era of the asylum, of electroshock therapy, the prefrontal leucotomy, insulin-coma therapy . . . psychiatric methods to control the political dissidents of the USSR" (231), the Senegalese Toure had turned instead to the works of Frantz Fanon, whom he had known personally. His old mentor now spent his retirement in his Gorée Island home, reading up on a range of subjects. Toure had once told Attila about the role of forest fires in habitat vitality and renewal, about an ecological process called "succession" whereby the burned trees in a fire-adapted ecosystem will come back stronger after the fire. He had taught Attila "that their field of study was not one of either/or, rather it was one of and/but. . . . the path to reason was not always a straight line" (232). Forna's complex explorations of the vicissitudes of trauma theory in cross-cultural applications similarly show how intellectually curious and adventurous psychological interventions, like her instigating and nonlinear narratives, can provide expedient affective form for unheard testimonies from the war zone, whether it was Bosnia, Sierra Leone, or migrant London.

The main narrative of *Happiness* begins with a collision on Waterloo Bridge. "A man so tall he appeared to be wading through the crowd was crossing the bridge in the opposite direction to the fox" (10). It is Attila Asare, the psychiatrist specializing in the treatment of post-traumatic stress disorder in noncombatant populations, as is revealed (a pleasant surprise for the reader of Forna's *The Memory of Love*). Attila is in London to deliver the keynote at a very large (800 delegates and counting) conference on PTSD. His self-situation as a native informant and international trauma specialist is not without its contradictions and limitations and Forna subtly points out that his world-weariness is a badge of privilege:

> [H]e described his work in Sri Lanka, Northern Ireland, Bosnia, Afghanistan, the Turkish/Syrian border and all the other places he had travelled in the last decade, where he stepped off planes to be driven through streets of shelled buildings, devoid of people and colour, it might be thirty degrees centigrade or minus fifteen, the air clouded with dust or with snow, the landscape flat or mountainous, from his perspective conflict looked very much the same in one place as in another. (24)

The woman who runs into him, all in black, with hair of a "rather remarkable pale silver" (11), and in hot pursuit of a fox, is Jean Turane, a wildlife biologist fighting to keep London foxes safe from the rapacity of urbanization and its eugenicist biological imagination. She falls foul of twitterati for suggesting that a rare incident of a child being bitten by a fox is insufficient grounds for the extirpation of the species. Trauma is a recurrent theme in Forna's fiction, as, I will argue, is her eco-cosmopolitanism (Ursula Heise's term), an ecologically urgent imperative that we see ourselves and our social groups as "imagined communities." Referring to Benedict Anderson's concept of the nation as an imagined community, Heise proposes a planetary model, a cosmopolis of species "of both human and non-human kinds" (61). This collision of two people moving across wide geographic distances is not simply symptomatic of the global flow of goods, commodities, and ideas, but demonstrates transnational connections and planetary identifications which may transcend what Franco Moretti calls the "subdivided reality of the modern world" (5). The dissimilar but overlapping paths of two foreigners to the metropolis bring to light the affiliative networks that may arise where filiation has failed. Finally, in a novel which is framed with the dispassionate and professional killing, in Greenhampton, MA, in April 1814, of the last wolf in the United States, signaling that the birth of postindustrial modernity is tainted by the death of nature, the absent referent of a fleeting fox, jolting together the worlds of Attila and Jean, provides a corrective association with the natural world instead.

Later in the novel, Attila is brought in as expert witness to validate a PTSD diagnosis, which would absolve defendant Adama Sheriff of the crime of arson (thereby preventing her punitive deportation). The West African Adama, a non-naturalized resident in the UK, is the wife of a man who was once kidnapped in Iraq, and is supposedly suffering from the belated shock of the prior event and the more recent one of her spouse's death. She sets fire to a pile of sewing (Adama is a seamstress), and Attila quickly realizes that it is not a response to the racism of her neighbors, but an explosive expression of the grief and rage the widow feels at being isolated and shunned by happy families. Instead of the incapacitated victim of PTSD, staving off "intrusive recollections," Attila finds a woman who is "sad and angry" (258). Refuting the diagnosis of trauma and complicated grief arrived at by Dr. Greyforth, the specialist appointed by Adama's solicitor, his rejoinder is a hollow echo of the words he had uttered to Adrian Lockheart: "You call them symptoms, I call them emotions" (259). Adama needed neither diagnosis nor treatment, Attila insists. The medico-legal establishment wouldn't have come after her had her despair been implosive, not explosive. As Michel Foucault argues in the *Abnormal* lectures, the most insidious form of power is not negative, repressive, or superstructural: it is positive, productive, and inventive, legitimizing its exercise by the creation of polemical and political concepts which multiply its effects, and through regimes of normalization.

> How to construe normality was not a new argument, but it remained the fact that preventing practitioners in places like this from defaulting to the values of the West was to wage an unending campaign. Attila suspected that Greyforth was the kind of person who when he said "people" meant "white people." (Forna, *Happiness* 258–259)

As he prepares to address members of his profession in the conference in London, Attila speculates whether the traumatized can be imagined in theoretical debates, as well as clinical practice, as active, not passive, resilient and capable, not the "compliant mad": "suffering and damage are not the same," he insists to an incredulous group of colleagues (251, 228). If Attila's is an African way of seeing, it is not made explicit. In fact, Forna avoids the reverse essentialism of such a stance by suggesting that trauma, to quote Didier Fassin and Richard Rechtman, is "a commonplace of the contemporary world, a shared truth" (2). Not a universal, but a shared, truth, which can connect dissimilar social systems to begin addressing shocking inequities. The work Attila consults last-minute for his lecture is Robert Graves's World War I memoir, *Goodbye to All That*. Dr. Toure had introduced him to the book. Reading again about the tyranny of the medical establishment behind the Great War, which saw Siegfried Sassoon's pacifism as insanity, and to placate whose wrath Graves had argued that his friend (Sassoon) was shell-shocked, Attila writes out new key words: "Hope. Humour. Survival. Adaptability. Expectations. Impermanence (acceptance of)" (Forna, *Happiness* 291).

In *Happiness*, survivalism and psychic recuperation are associated with embracing the eco-cosmopolitanism of urban living. Earlier in the novel, Attila Asare had collided with Jean Turane. This is not coincidental, they both agree, but a statistical possibility given their unrelated yet intersecting trajectories. Jean is in London to conduct a study on urban foxes on behalf of Southwark Council, with funding from a European Commission urban development grant. In a world of vertiginous migrant motion, she ponders the congeries of wild creatures in the city, their nonsynchronous arrivals and the genius of variant adaptations.

> How had the Argentinian parakeets come to live in this northern European city? And found a way to survive, to make it through the winters, just as the coyotes had when they'd moved from the western plains up north and east, from dry plains to snow-covered mountains,

from creosote bush to hemlock forests, from one hundred plus degrees
Fahrenheit to five? (48)

Jean's stream of consciousness is occasioned by a run through the
Nunhead Cemetery in South-East London, a dead and disused graveyard
greened by bright moss, lichen, and ivy, and resurrected by the rude life
of vernal flowers and parakeets overhead: "So much life, fed by the bones
of the dead" (50). While she loved this stuff in Hollywood blockbusters,
"the world being given back to nature" (131), she is ambivalent about an
uninhabitable earth: cities built at sea level would flood with nobody to
clear the drains, work the pumps, and monitor the flood barriers; fires
would rage without fire engines to call; cement and asphalt would break
up; invasive tree species would run amuck like weeds. "But maybe that
wouldn't happen" (132), and maybe the interrelated web of organic life
can animate public imagination before it is too late. "They told him
things, not because he was a professional full of a professional's intrigues
or dispassion, but because he wanted to know" (221), Attila says of his
successful therapeutic technique. An ecological analogue of this is the
communication Jean Turane instantiates with a coyote in New England.
"*She stood as still as she was able and held his gaze,*" before the Eastern
Coyote relents to her felling him and putting on an electronic collar, like
a talisman (184).

The heterogeneous team of road-sweepers, traffic wardens, street
performers, and security guards (immigrants to the city, all) which is
mobilized to find Tano, Attila's great-nephew and a boy who has gone
missing after his mother and he had immigration problems, is the very
body of urban vigilantes Jean has created to spot and track migrant foxes.
Jean has named the foxes of her study: Jeremiah and Babe, Finn and
Black Aggie, and her favorite, Light Bright. In the environmental
imaginary of the global city, the eviction of parakeets from a graveyard
sycamore, the culling of pests and feral animals, and the hounding of
illegal immigrants are manifestations of the same phobia of alien invasion that structures ownership and entitlement. Happiness, here, is
Jean's patient knowledge that the tropical birds taking off from the
branches of the dead tree at the end of the parking lot will return
from their peregrinations come dusk, and her lover, "his tall figure
moving through a landscape of rock and dust" (308) in Raqqa,
Fallujah, and Mosul, will come back to her momentarily.

Happiness

Attila Asare's theories are based on the work of Boris Cyrulnik, Forna declares in the acknowledgments of *Happiness* (311). Cyrulnik, a renowned neurophysicist and psychoanalyst who teaches at the Université du Sud, Toulon-Var, France, is a Holocaust survivor who popularized the idea of psychological resilience in his self-help books, most notably *Resilience: How Your Inner Strength Can Set You Free from the Past* (2009). According to Cyrulnik, history is not destiny: "Traumas always strike differently because they occur at different times and affect different psychic constructs" (11). Resilience, he insists, is natural and automatic, a mechanism by which we use our "ecological, emotional, and verbal environments to 'knit' our-selves" (13). Cyrulnik evokes the rhetorical device of the oxymoron to describe the antinomic definition of a subjecthood which is wounded yet resistant, "that suffers but is happy enough to go on hoping despite everything" (19, 20). The tension of the opposing terms binds and holds up the psychic edifice. It is not cruel or reckless to tell the victim it is possible to "get over it," Cyrulnik argues, nor does it trivialize the crime.

> Anyone who publishes a paper on resilience gets a virtuously indignant response: "How dare you say war is nothing?" someone told the Lebanese speaker who had just explained that lots of children were able to "get through the war" without too many scars, provided that the adults who were responsible for looking after them did not make their problems worse by talking about their own worries. (29)

Trying to understand resilience does not imply a failure of empathy for the individual's suffering. Similarly, trying to understand a criminal is not an attempt to justify the crime, but is intended to be a preventive measure. Resilience is not a solid substance but a pliable mesh, one that we "are forced to knit ourselves, using the people and things we meet in our emotional and social environments" for cladding (51).

Attila's is the "filthy work of clearing up after other people's wars, listening to the survivors' accounts of what had been done to their sisters, mothers, brothers, fathers, themselves," he thinks, waiting for a mediation in Bosnia with the UN peacekeeping team (*Happiness* 69). Attila's ideas about resilience are crystallized for him by an erstwhile child soldier, Komba, among others. He had crossed paths with Komba in the midst of yet another flare-up of the war at a checkpoint in Sierra Leone. The rebel fighter had allowed to pass the car in which Attila was smuggling out to the capital a UN official ("the Kenyan") in the guise of a psychotic patient. When they accidentally meet in London, Komba discloses this act of mercy on his part, telling Attila also that he, the misguided boy Komba, had joined the rebels only because he had wanted to be like his grandfather, a signalman on the railway. The perpetrator of war, who is revealed to be an accidental perpetrator – "Komba was not a fighter, he was a signalman's grandson" (290) – is at peace with the life he has made for himself in these foreign parts, down to his uniform, which reminds him of his grandfather. "I am hopeful," he says (289).

Critical interpretations of Forna's work tend to prioritize an "empire writes back" model of revisionism in the novels, whereby the authoritative epistemologies of trauma theory are challenged before they are supplanted by non-Western scripts of trauma management and what Stef Craps calls "local coping mechanisms" (64).[8] In my argument, not only does the fiction – *Happiness*, in particular – go beyond such a reactive mode, it valorizes the metapsychological, the foundation of psychoanalytic and psychodynamic theories, as that which can lead to realms of freedom. Psychoanalysis, whose "dynamic understanding of human consciousness" can transcend the "sterile nosological preoccupation" of psychiatry (Keller 318), provides a holistic vocabulary for understanding individual trauma, as well as the traumatizing disease of colonial racism or civil war which affects the group. Moreover, Forna seems to say that neuropsychiatry and psychoanalysis are not just imports in the concurrent spaces of the neo- and post-colony, but that they can return from the (sobering) colonial encounter with disalienist, dialectical methods, as Adrian Lockheart does. What Attila brings to psychiatric London is an African way of seeing, albeit self-consciously derived from the interimplicated colony where "African" and "European" used to be unequal yet mutually constitutive discourses. This is not glorified nativism or reverse ethnography but a commerce of ideas across history and geography, without which, Forna seems to be saying, the global institution of psychoanalysis can be neither international nor multilateral.

"Attila understood more codes than most people," Forna writes in *Happiness*, a generous characterization denied her other (white, British) therapists in the novels (83). He understands British, Ghanaian, Sierra Leonean, Iraqi, and Bosnian cultural codes, among others. Attila is a man of big appetite but with no visible appetency – in a world sharply divided between the dogmatic slumber of the unaware and the sleeplessness of the traumatized, the affected, and the "woke,"[9] his is the gift of being able to choose "when and whether to sleep" (13). His talent as therapist lies in the fact that he can start and take charge of a conversation even with the most estranged and isolated of his interlocutors. He repurposes psychiatry to raise from the dead the "compliant mad" of modern Bedlam, the drugged patients who "shuffled and drooled, keened and slept and when they spoke they spoke in whispers" (251). Robert Graves, whose memory he invokes while jotting notes for that keynote to the 800-strong psychiatry convention, had found society so unbearable that he had chosen to return, unbidden, to the war. Jean returns Attila, war-weary yet preferring war to "insufferable civilisation" (244), to the unacknowledged resilience of small creatures fighting human predation every day. Jean and Attila's London is a temporal economy where the hippos, which once "wallowed" in Trafalgar Square, are buried but not forgotten and where "nature's immeasurable adaptability" can lead the way in countering Anthropocene damage with cycles of geological repair (132, 101). The outlook is hopeful, if not happy. *Happiness* had begun with the catastrophic killing, in April 1834, in Greenhampton, MA, of a pair of wolves without pups, which wiped out the species. We are left, in the end, with a vision of the *fugueurs* – Attila, Jean, Komba, Osman, Tano, and Ama – patiently assembled at Rosie's memorial, an imagined, affiliative community, albeit short-lived and inherently dispersive. "We are wanderers but we have a sense of direction," they seem to say, echoing Cyrulnik. Light Bright, however, has (been) disappeared from the city.

The Arab Doctor

I started this chapter with a reading of Frantz Fanon's epochal work *Black Skin, White Masks,* one of whose most influential insights is that "the Black's alienation is not an individual question. Beside phylogeny and ontogeny stands sociogeny" (11). *Black Skin, White Masks* turns the mechanisms of fixed racial signification against themselves in order to begin to constitute new subjectivities, new positions of identification and enunciation. The celebrated cultural theorist and sociologist Stuart Hall saw in the works of Fanon – psychiatrist, intellectual, and anti-imperialist writer – a "re-epidermalisation, an auto-graphy," a new politics of the black signifier (27). Speaking at a conference on film, performance, and visual arts work by contemporary black artists at the ICA (the Institute of Contemporary Arts), Hall dwells on the "spectral effect," the ghost of Fanon, the colonial man who wrote for his people:

> Rather than trying to recapture the true Fanon, we must try to engage the after-life of Frantz Fanon ... in ways that do not simply restore the past in

a cycle of the eternal return, but which will bring the enigma of Fanon, as
Benjamin said of history, "flashing up before us at a moment of danger." (14)

This enigma of Fanon haunts the fictional Attila Asare and Kai Mansaray
and speaks forcefully to the interventions in community mental healthcare
I have chronicled in three of the chapters of *Unseen City*. Like Fanon, many
of my real-life examples have a hospital-based clinical practice, and, like
him, they question the limits "of reducing the mental to the neurological,"
to quote Jean Khalfa (*Alienation and Freedom* 175). *Black Skin, White Masks*
was written at a traumatic colonial intersection. World War II had brought
Fanon to France and combat in the black units of the Free French Army,
and he wrote *Peau noire, masques blancs* (translated into English in 1967)
while preparing for the exams that would enable him to join the august
ranks of France's psychiatric health system. The book came together in
Lyon between 1951 and 1952, a period marked by, as his biographer Alice
Cherki puts it, "a triple junction" (24) of encounters and experiences:
psychiatry; the influence of schools of thought such as phenomenology,
existentialism, and psychoanalysis; and, finally, the Francophone black
subject's encounter with a racist white French society. The doubt and
trepidations of the introduction – "Why write the book? No one has asked
me for it" (Fanon 9) – juxtapose with the author's quiet determination that
the book will be a "mirror with a progressive infrastructure, in which it will
be possible to discern the Negro on the road to disalienation" (184).

Fanon situates the man of color in a world where he is seen and heard
by others and *is* for others. The look of the Other, rather than giving
oneself back to oneself, fixes one in an epidermal scheme. Trapped in
their respective "whiteness" and "blackness," white settler and black
native create one another, though without any reciprocity. Fanon,
whose mother was of Alsatian descent, grew up in Martinique thinking
of himself as white and French; his painful reconstitution as a black
West Indian occurred only when he arrived at the French capital. In
France, Fanon had come to realize that volunteerism on behalf of
abstract principles of "freedom," "France," "anti-fascism," counted for
nothing in the eyes of the majority of French citizens, for whom he
remained a black man, inferior, inassimilable, nothing but an interloper.
Black Skin, White Masks uses psychoanalysis to understand the visual,
aural, and olfactory economies of racialization in the colony (French
Antilles) as well as the imperial metropolis (Paris). The analyst becomes
a sort of radio receiver, Ian Baucom suggests, recording the voice
consciousness of the impoverished black subaltern.[10]

Fanon never went back to Martinique, and his decision to leave France for Algeria in 1953 was sudden. While Fanon identified with Algerians on the basis of their colonization by France, and it was evident that he had an obvious preference for working in the colonies rather than in the metropolis, David Macey suggests that he did not move to Algeria in 1953 out of any sense of political commitment. "I'm going to Algeria," Fanon states in an undated letter to his brother Joby: "You understand: the French have enough psychiatrists to take care of their madmen. I'd rather go to a country where they need me" (Macey 204). Blida – Algeria's capital of madness, as it was called – was a typical colonial town with the "interstellar distance of colonialism" separating the European and Arab quarters, as a liberal pied-noir put it (cited in Macey 211). The Blida–Joinville hospital was similarly divided along ethnic lines, and Fanon had 165 European women and 220 male Muslim patients under his care. The culture at the hospital was racist and punitive, marked by mutual incomprehension and mistrust between the colonizers and the colonized. Fanon would write in his letter of resignation to the Resident Minister that "the Arab, permanently an alien in his own country, lives in a state of absolute depersonalisation" (cited in Foreword, *Black Skin, White Masks*, ix). Fanon's work between 1953, when he joined Blida–Joinville, and 1956, when he resigned from service to the French colonial state to join the cause of Algerian liberation, not only is a watershed in his psychiatric writings (1951–1960) but provides the foundation for a postcolonial psychoanalysis to come, its insights based on ontogeny, phylogeny, *and* sociogeny.

Frantz Fanon was perhaps the most thoroughly assimilated of Francophone colonial activists, and the person who imbibed contemporary French philosophy, literature, and culture more voraciously than any of his African or Caribbean contemporaries. He "used the resources of Western thought against itself," as Robert Young states, translating its "epistemological location" (276). Henry Louis Gates suggests that we neither elevate Fanon as a "Global Theorist" nor simply "cast him into battle, but to recognize him as a battlefield in himself" (471). Martinican, Algerian, French, and black, Frantz Fanon identified with the French, the Algerian, and the Antillean in his wide-ranging political and ethical sensibilities, saddled all the while with what he called a "dark and unarguable" blackness (*Black Skin, White Masks*, 117). Fanon's was a political psychoanalysis in Algeria (if it was psychoanalysis at all). Blida–Joinville was a second-line, 700-bed, colonial psychiatric hospital ideologically oriented along the lines of the Algiers School of Psychiatry and psychoanthropology, which saw the Arab (and the sub-Saharan black African) as creatures of primitive mentation. Years later, in the *Wretched of the Earth*, Fanon condemned the ethnopsychiatry of the University of Lyon-trained Antoine Porot, founder of the Algiers School, for claiming that the native Muslim Algerians were "born slackers, born liars, born robbers, and born criminals," their brains dominated, like the "inferior vertebrates," by the diencephalons, which implied that the cortical functions were feeble, if they existed at all (213). Fanon, who is credited to have invented the concept of racialization, was one of the first of the colonial psychoanalysts to examine the false universalism of psychoanalysis and its collusion with the civilizing mission of the French empire.

In the Algerian hospital, and later the Algerian Revolution, Fanon was doubly an outsider for being a black man and a French colonial. He wrote also about how the French police occasionally mistook him for an Arab. David Macey, Fanon's biographer, describes the failed psychoanalytic techniques at Blida. The noisy thoroughfares of the psychiatric wards offered little privacy, and Fanon failed to establish transference. There is no doubt, however, that, while working tirelessly at the hospital – the nurses recall running into him any time of day or night – Fanon was revisiting his childhood and youth and claiming the moment in which he became African: the Senegalese infantry man "crouches in the labyrinth of his epidermis," he said in "Africains Antillais," completed in 1954 (Cherki 77). As Alice Cherki states, until 1945, "the African was a Negro and the Antillean a European" (77). The imposture of the Arab Doctor and the Blida experiment on social morphologies of the Arab occasion Fanon's psychoanalytic testimonials on the painful transition from colonial erasure and anti-colonial resistance to postcolonial ideality, from "the great white mistake to the great black mirage" ("Africains Antillais," cited in Cherki 77).

Fanon's clinical and critical work in Algeria bridges psychopathology and his political sociology. His 1955 article "North African Syndrome," for example, testifies to this. "North African syndrome" is itself the terminology of racial biologism, invented to describe the malingering Arab, the work-shy social parasite who seeks out the warmth and inactivity of the hospital environment. The damning diagnosis, Fanon observes, rises from negative presuppositions, and he stresses that the absence of lesions to which the painful symptom can be traced back does not necessarily mean the absence of pain. Fanon's recommendation is not to ignore the profiling of organic lesions but to engage with the social situation of the expatriate North Africans, their lives reducible to fruitless searches for work and perfunctory sex with prostitutes. French colonization had forced a redistribution of resources. What was once collectively owned property was now divided asymmetrically between a few major land holdings, owned privately by Europeans, and small parcels of the worst land, on which the mass of small proprietors worked. Fanon's term for the plight of the poor was "proletarianization": as Jock McCulloch observes, the bulk of the Muslim patients at Blida were the victims of a systematic de-tribalization in which communal ties were destroyed (129). "Without a family, without love, without human relations, without communion with the group, the first encounter with himself will occur in a neurotic mode, a pathological mode," Fanon observed in *Toward the African Revolution* (23). The Arab Algerian resisted psychotherapy, a resistance that Fanon came to see as a justifiable response to a colonial imposition. In his essay on medicine in *A Dying Colonialism*, Fanon argues that even colonial medicine, which "in all objectivity and all humanity" should be seen as beneficial, was perceived by the colonized as just another part of colonial oppression – so much so that "When the colonised escapes the doctor and the integrity of his body is preserved, he considers himself the victor by a handsome margin" (128). In this light, the constitutional stubbornness of the Arab that Fanon's precursors at Blida, Antoine Porot and Jean Sutter, had identified, and which they precipitately diagnosed as a mental puerilism, can be interpreted as civic resistance instead. The indigenous North African does not confess, Fanon observes, because they do not want to legitimize and authenticate an oppressive system through that confession. The accused Muslim's refusal to confess his act is not pathological mendaciousness, as the colonial masters accuse: "his often profound submission to the powers-that-be (in this instance the power of the judiciary) . . . cannot be confounded with an acceptance of this power."[11]

As Diana Fuss has noted, psychoanalysis's investment in the notion of identification provided Fanon with the critical tools "to treat not only the psychological disorders produced in individuals by the violence of colo-nial domination but also the neurotic structure of colonialism itself" (*Identification Papers* 141). In "Ethnopsychiatric Considerations," Fanon calls the psychiatry of North Africans "an arresting condensation of racism with scientific pretensions" (Khalfa and Young 405). Similarly, in "Social Therapy in a Ward for Muslim Men: Methodological Difficulties," co-authored with his intern Jacques Azoulay and published in 1954, psychiatry is exposed outright as a colonial science. As in "North African Syndrome," Fanon offers a scathing critique of the colonial policy which reproduces whiteness, and wherein the proposed cure for mental disorders involves not a restitution of personality but systematic deracination and depersonalization:

> The psychiatrist, reflexively, adopts the policy of assimilation. The natives do not need to be understood in their cultural originality. It is the "natives" who must make the effort and who have every interest in being like the type of men suggested to them. Assimilation here does not presuppose a reciprocity of perspectives. It is up to one entire culture to disappear in favour of another. (Khalfa and Young 362)

In "Social Therapy," Azoulay and Fanon examine the failure of their attempts to create a vibrant collective life in the Muslim ward (when these very attempts had yielded noticeable improvement among the European patients). While the European side participated in the publication of a weekly journal and film evenings – and the "climate had become therapeutic" (Khalfa and Young 362) – the Muslims were locked in a vicious cycle of agitation and punishment. The failure of therapy at Blida could be attributed to the inability of metropolitan psychiatry to see the North African subject as anything but French mimic men, and also to the paucity of research on Muslim Algeria, Fanon and Azoulay propose. They take a hard look at their own Westernized approach, influenced by the Algiers School, which had not fully grasped the "North African social fact" (363).

A group of Algerian women, who had attended the celebrations held in the European wards, help the breakthrough – their joyous ululations in response to a visit by local musicians inspire Fanon to develop musical therapy with an Algerian artist. "Socio-therapy would only be possible to the extent that social morphology and forms of sociability were taken into consideration," Azoulay and Fanon write (364). The psychotherapeutic practice of listening would subsequently be sutured with the construction of a Moorish café, the celebration of traditional festivals and Muslim holidays, and visits by traditional story-tellers for his Arab patients. The men who could not be persuaded to weave raffia baskets were thrilled to be given spades and mattocks for digging and hoeing.

Fanon's encounters with Algerian women contributed richly to his nascent ideas of *socialthérapie*, in particular the episodes involving the Thematic Apperception Tests, or TATs, that Fanon had been trained to administer. As he writes in a 1956 essay, "TAT in Muslim Women," co-authored with Charles Geronimi, the patient is shown a set of cards with indistinct human figures engaged in indeterminate activities: the patient's interpretation allows the therapist to identify conflict and defense mechanisms in their psyche. The young women – Arabs and Kabyles – who had been hospitalized for maladies including minor hypochondria, anxiety, emotional disorders, and (juvenile) mania, seemed unable to nominate gender, let alone create a narrative. "I don't know if it's a boy or a girl. I think it's a girl. I don't know what she's doing. I don't know what to say" (Khalfa and Young 429). Almost all the sessions ended with patients feeling tired or distressed by the exercise. Fanon does not lapse into ethnopsychiatry to explain the patients' inability to think abstractly or symbolically. By asking them to describe and "to live a scene elaborated by westerners and for westerners, we immerse them in a different, foreign, heterogenous and non-appropriable world," he states (431). The patients offered dry enumerations at best, devoid of narrative structure or psycho-affective content. They refused to "make anything up" (431), some attributing it to their fidelity to the Quranic injunction not to lie. When presented with a white card – a blank text – however, the patients, unimpeded by "foreign cultural fetters," spun "rich and varied stories" (432).

The "Social Therapy" essay documents the perils of cultural translation in an analytic scene where the doctor cannot make his diagnostic through language. Fanon had neither Arabic nor the Berber languages spoken in Algeria and needed interpreters to listen to his patients. In the absence of professional translators, nurses, orderlies, and, occasionally, other patients were pressed into service.

> While the face is expressive and the gestures profuse, it is necessary to wait until the patient has stopped talking in order to grasp the meaning. At which point, the interpreter sums up in two words what the patient has related in detail for ten minutes: "He says that someone took his land, or that his wife cheated on him." Often, the interpreter "interprets" in his own way the patient's thinking according to some stereotyped formula, depriving it of all its richness: "He says that he hears *djnoun*" – indeed, one no longer knows if the delusion is real or inferred.[12] (368)

Unable to speak Arabic, Fanon and Azoulay fail to synchronize verbal and gestural articulations. They see the animation on the patient's face but have to be content with the terse summation of the interpreter, who is giving them what he thinks they want, the plot summary, and not its desirous elaborations and digressions, wherein lies the individual story. The very apparatus of talk therapy is rigged in Algeria, Fanon and Azoulay imply, as in the projection experiment with Maghrebi women: "meetings soon came to an abrupt end because one no longer knew what to talk about" (368).

Fanon would eventually distance himself from the project of social therapy but his meditations on Muslim patients in Blida–Joinville testify to the psychiatric institution's legacies of racial domination and the obdurate sovereignty of the colonized mad, manifesting in silence, elective mutism, nonconformity, nonviolent resistance. They shed light on the fictionalized Adama's angry eschewal of a PTSD diagnosis, and to the "*fugueur*" Agnes's unconscious improvisation of short flights to ameliorate an inescapable and unbearable life situation. Acknowledging the reality of the men of the Muslim ward, most of whom were illiterate sharecroppers or day laborers, Fanon (and Azoulay) realize that they were unlikely to want to sing in a choir, stage a play, enjoy *Little Women* or *Rio Grande*, or participate in journaling faithfully the social life of the hospital. Nor did they want to weave baskets or mats, associated in their culture with women's work. The resocialization of these men would have to be imagined otherwise. It turned out that all Fanon had to do was give them a shovel or pickaxe to get them to till the earth:

> These peasants are close to the land; they are one with it. And if you succeed in getting them hooked on a particular patch of land, in getting them interested in the yield gained from farming, then work will genuinely be a factory of re-equilibration. (371)

Fanon's term for this was "ergotherapy." In the next chapter, I will examine modes of intercultural therapy relatable to the social therapy Fanon conceptualizes and experiments with at Blida: it ends with "ergotherapy," with Turkish migrants in a garden in Hackney.

CHAPTER 2

The Analyst as Muse of History in Disaster Zones: Free Clinics, London

About an hour into *Jashn-e-Azadi*, Indian filmmaker Sanjay Kak's 2007 documentary on the Kashmir *intifada*, we find ourselves in the Government Psychiatric Diseases Hospital in Srinagar. It is a very busy ward. As Seema Kazi notes: "In 1980, Kashmir had the lowest suicide rate in India; presently it is among the highest in the world" (119). Since the insurgency started in 1989, the outpatient ward of the psychiatric hospital has seen patient numbers soar from 3,000 to 18,000.[1] We are in the chamber of Dr. Mushtaq A. Margoob, Assistant Professor of Psychiatry, and hear snippets of the conversation between the doctor, patients, and their relatives (a not uncommon sight in the delivery of mental health services in the subcontinent, where patients are brought in by relatives or neighbors).

> You are on fire, [experience] suffocation?
> Restless and a bit scared?

Cut to an everyday street scene in Srinagar, the army washing blood from the streets. As if in a fugue, the camera wanders into the shrine of Makhdoom Sahib with its hollow reverberations of the dirge-like chant of "When will we be rid of our sorrows?" A Zarif Ahmed Zarif *ghazal* is the soundtrack of the documentary's restive excavations:

> My gaze has been silenced
> What frenzy is this?
> Sukrat [Socrates] did me no favour in dying
> I shouldn't be saying this but . . .
> He didn't drink my share of poison.
> What frenzy is this?

Back in the hospital, Dr. Margoob is asking a middle-aged woman in a white headscarf, "What faces do you see?" She says "he" asks her to "go somewhere." He says, "Don't stay here." "Are they humans or something else?" the doctor asks of the sightings. "The last time [I saw you] you were fine for several years," Margoob remarks, indicating that the psychotic breakdown has happened before. "When did her brother die?" Margoob asks the relative who has brought in his patient. "1994, I think," he says. He wasn't a militant, just a civilian. He was getting on with his day when he was shot dead. The voiceover explains that in this conflict, "there are no bystanders, no civilians." The militancy that started in the Kashmir valley in 1989 and reached a peak in the 1990s started winding down in the early 2000s. In 2007, when Kak's documentary was completed, there were less than 1,000 armed militants, yet 700,000 soldiers continued to wage the war against an "unseen enemy," in Kak's words. That's 700 for every armed militant or *mujaheed*, 1 soldier for every 15 Kashmiri civilians. At hotspots such as Kashmir, Chandra Talpade Mohanty observes, "neoliberal and militarised state and imperial practices are often sustained by development, peacekeeping, and humanitarian projects, thus illuminating the new contours of securitised states that function as imperial democracies" (77).[2]

The segment on the Government Psychiatric Diseases Hospital is preceded by a scene in Bandipora, North Kashmir, shot in the winter of 2004. The Jammu and Kashmir Civil Society is conducting a survey of those killed during militancy and we see flashbacks of the untimely deaths which have triggered public and militant displays of mourning. A mother keens over the dead:

> What did you do at the moment, my martyr?
> Did you cry out, my martyr?
> Were you in pain, my martyr?
> My life for you, my martyr.

The much-repeated word "martyr," mimicking the repeated intrusion of traumatic memories, is *shaheed*. In Arabic, *shaheed* means martyr as well as witness. *Shahaadat* is the act of martyring oneself and the act of bearing witness. To bear witness is to be a martyr, Kak says. From Dr. Margoob's analytical perspective (and I am quoting from Rumana Makhdoomi's *White Man in Dark* now), "Patients see someone get killed in their presence, some friend, some relative, and they get stuck in that moment" (121). The gaze is silenced, as the Zarif Ahmed Zarif *ghazal* goes. In the Sanjay Kak documentary, Margoob explains the temporality of "clear-cut classical PTSD": the "first event," as he calls it, is severe, gruesome, its implications belatedly grasped at the sight of a televised killing or a graphic news report. TV is a stress multiplier. When the secessionist violence first broke out, there were no satellite channels commuting disturbing images to homes. However, the digital revolution of the twenty-first century, which has made possible "experience of wartime as an everyday horizon of living," as Debjani Ganguly describes it (136), has had a doubly detrimental effect on populations who physically inhabit these hypermediated deathworlds. As a study conducted by Margoob and others at the Government Psychiatric Diseases Hospital in 2006 demonstrates, the Department of Psychiatry diagnosed 469 PTSD patients, and 53.73 percent of these were women. Children were also seen to be suffering from PTSD. Referring to the period between 1991 and 2006, Margoob and co-authors argue that "due to prevailing violent conditions in Kashmir, there has been a phenomenal increase in psychiatric morbidity, including stress related disorders" (S58).[3]

In *Remnants of Auschwitz*, Giorgio Agamben puts forth two definitions of witnessing: the "*testis*" or third party, the external observer who offers a neutral perspective; and the "*superstes*" the person who has directly experienced the event (17). *Jashn-e-Azadi* shores some of these third-party testimonials too. A teenage girl bears witness to a civilian death. A young man had put his hands up, as asked, but was nevertheless shot in the leg, chest, and head. "His eye fell out." From 1.30 to 7.00 p.m., the body lay uncared for in the street. The soldiers threatened to shoot anyone who ventured to offer a drink of water or cover the body. This is Kashmir, "a netherworld of disappearances, military torture, and extra-judicial killings," as the *New York Times* review of Vishal Bhardwaj's movie *Haider* described it.[4] Mirza Waheed's 2011 novel, *The Collaborator*, set in the 1990s in Nowgam, near the Pakistan border, describes a sleepless population, mourning the lost boys who have left for Pakistan to join the insurgency or have been hunted down in the Indian army's reprisals as they crossed back. Everyone had turned to tranquillizer (*araam*) pills: "our quirky medicine man had put the whole village on Alprax and Calmpose" (248).

In this chapter, I explore the transformative interventions of two therapeutic services in London that reach out to resource-poor non-Anglophone migrant populations. I have chosen to frame this with cultural examples and representations of Kashmiri grief because of the stark parallels these offer to the formulations of trauma and improvisations of cure in the London sites. "Kashmir" is an unspeakable name in India today. It has been in security lockdown since August 4, 2019, when the Indian government revoked Article 370, which defined Jammu and Kashmir's unique relationship to India for the seventy years of Indian independence.[5] Integrating the Muslim-majority state of Kashmir has been an election manifesto of the Hindu nationalist Bharatiya Janata Party and Prime

Minister Narendra Modi: the revocation of this special status, a unilateral breach of the Instrument of Accession by means of which the former Princely State of Jammu and Kashmir acceded to India in 1947, cancels the autonomy hitherto exercised by the state in formulating rules around property ownership, permanent residency, and fundamental rights. Kashmiris have been barricaded in their homes since, with no phone or internet connectivity. Security forces patrol the streets and even moderate and reconciliatory political leaders have been put under house arrest. In a trenchant critique of this move, which also provides a potted history of the case of Kashmir, Booker prize-winning author and activist Arundhati Roy urged readers to punctuate the vulgar celebrations in majoritarian Indian with the "loudest sound": "the deathly silence from Kashmir's patrolled, barricaded streets and its approximately seven million caged, humiliated people, stitched down by razor wire, spied on by drones, living under a complete communications blackout."[6] The mental health fallout of this rendering of Kashmir into a "giant prison camp," to quote Roy, remains unseen and largely unimaginable. My examples refer to an earlier time, the cycles of violence in the valley after the "rigged" state legislative elections of 1987, following which Kashmir was infiltrated with foreign fighters – including Jihadists trained to combat Soviets in Afghanistan during the US Cold War – and ruled by militants from both sides of the border.

Bhardwaj's *Haider*, a 2014 adaptation of Shakespeare's *Hamlet*, show-cases a unique Kashmir valley phenomenon, the enforced "disappearances" of dissidents, which make for a curious unraveling of the present – without the ability to mark the past as past, there is no imagining of the future.[7] The year is 1995 and Hilaal Meer, MD, has been marched off by the security forces for offering shelter and medical treatment to Ikhlaq Latif, a "terrorist," not any irrefutable act of insurgency. All of Kashmir is a prison, Haider muses upon his return to Srinagar from university at Aligarh, where he has been writing a thesis on the revolutionary poets of British India. His uncle, the unscrupulous Khurram, says "Kashmir mein upar khuda hain, neeche fauj" (In Kashmir, God is above and the army below), the Indian military emboldened by the notorious Armed Forces Special Powers Act (AFSPA) of 1990. The psychological toll of this state of emergency manifests in predictable and unpredictable ways across the population, albeit most dramatically in the tragic unraveling of Haider/Hamlet and Arshia/Ophelia. We come across a man who is unable to step across the threshold of his own home without a frisking, so accustomed is he to being body-searched by border patrols.[8] We inhabit the twilight zone of the women rendered "half-widows," on vigil for "disappeared" husbands who will never return, alive or dead. The boredom of the quotidian is a luxury in 1990s Kashmir: its earth is unclean, the river Jhelum colored blood-red with killings, and its homes rent by whisperings of filial betrayal, *badla,* and *inteqam* (revenge and reprisal).

Khurram Meer has built a career and a counter-insurgency force by using captured militants to kill militants. His brother, Hilaal, on whom he turns informant, is collateral damage for his political ambition (this is perhaps not unrelated to the lust he has long harbored for sister-in-law Ghazala). Arshia's military officer father, in cahoots with Khurram, betrays his daughter's love and trust just as callously. "I wanted to make *Hamlet* in Kashmir. In my film, in a way, Kashmir becomes Hamlet," Bhardwaj said in a 2014 interview.[9] Haider, his head shorn, talking into the loose strand of a rope he has tied around his neck in the presence of a gathering crowd on the town square, is momentarily the "antic disposition" (*Hamlet* 1.5.172) of Indian-occupied Kashmir.[10] "The UN Council Resolution 47 of 1948; article 2 of the Geneva Convention; article 370 of the Indian Constitution": Haider recites these talismanic laws, underscoring their failure to prevent extrajudicial encounters, torture, and killings of civilians. Do we exist or do we not? Did we exist or did we not? he asks.[11] Jacques Derrida has related the difference between law and justice to the difference between the "deconstructability of law (*droit*), of legality, legitimacy or legitimation" and the "indeconstructability of justice" ("Force of Law" 15).[12] Justice is indeterminable and has an *avenir,* a dimension "to come." However, while it is true that justice is unrepresentable, infinite, and irreducible (because it is owed to the other), justice also doesn't wait: "It is that which must not wait" (26). "Incalculable justice," Derrida emphasizes, "*requires us* to calculate" with the incalculable (28). Haider's madness is the unreason of trying to find infinite justice in the superstructures of law: it is an impossible endeavor that painfully points out the divide between the singular and the universal (Haider and Kashmir, or Kashmir and India), between petty juridico-political calculations and incalculable justice.

There is no ghostly figure of the father triggering the emplotment of *Haider* because the Kashmiri King Hamlet – Prince Hamlet's father – is one of the 8,000 to 10,000 enforced disappearances brought about by the crackdown on armed insurgency in the region. It is as if without the production of a corpse in the field of vision there can be no sanction for the invisible and ghostly afterlife. Without the Oedipal overcoming of the body, there is no name-of-the-father for the bereaved son, no law-of-the-father, no rites of initiation into language or society, and Haider descends into psychotic violence. There is, however, a spirit medium in the form of the self-named "Roohdar" who makes audible the disappeared father's vengeful voice. Writing of the haunting of James Joyce's *Ulysses*, Maud Ellmann sees in ghosts a perplexity of the visible:

> Ghosts are almost always hungry, and they are usually angry too, for "ghost," as the *Oxford English Dictionary* informs us, derives from the Teutonic word for "fury." A "ghost" in optics is a bright spot, like a livid mole, produced by the reflection of a lens. It is, in other words, the mark of a mediation, and people who see ghosts, like Hamlet or Macbeth, know better than to overlook the bright spots embedded in the visible. (86)

Haider, the hapless Hamlet re-imagined in Kashmir, does not see his father's ghost. Roohdar narrates to him the timeline of his father's imprisonment and killing, revealing also the roles his mother Ghazala and uncle Khurram played in Hilaal Meer's fatal apprehension by the military. Profoundly shocked as he is by Roohdar's narrative, Haider does not know whom to believe when it comes to his (ghost) identity: is Roohdar an idealistic freedom fighter radicalized by the very (Indian) state-sponsored terror which took Dr. Meer's life, or is he, as Haider's uncle Khurram claims, a Pakistani spy turned double agent, preying on the vulnerabilities of the local Muslim population to create the militancy which has derailed democratic process in Kashmir? In my reading, Roohdar, the so-called holder and keeper of the soul, is the analyst par excellence, resurrecting spirits, and making available the memory of a traumatic event Hamlet has viscerally experienced despite not witnessing or experiencing it in person. But he is not the only analyst vying for Haider's soul.

Hamlet, as we well know, is as haunted by the missing father as he is by the fleshly, demonical mother. If Roohdar revives the ghosts that the mourning self will have to confront in order to overcome the same, Ghazala/Gertrude in *Haider* appropriates the violence of this overcoming so that the son is spared its consequences and finally free to walk away from the scene of carnage. Ghazala, like Roohdar, is a ghost identity to herself: a half-widow is at best a half-bride, she says. The last scene shows her contemplating her fractured reflection in the parts of a broken mirror: wife, lover, mother, Kashmiri, Indian. In Vishal Bhardwaj's retelling of *Hamlet*, Haider's existential questioning – do we exist or do we not? ("hum hain ki hain nahin") – implies also that in occupied Kashmir, to inhabit dualities or multiplicities, to exhibit divided loyalties or cultural ambivalence, is to be a persona non grata. Roohdar is ghoulish because he is at once Shia and Sunni, the river Jhelam and the Chinar tree, Muslim and (Hindu) Pundit, alive and undead. "Main tha, main hoon, aur main hi rahunga," he states philosophically: I was, I am, and I alone will continue to be. The self-divided Roohdar and Ghazala, in singular ways, act as analyst and healer to Haider's delirium. Each helps him to confront the contradictions of life hystericizing Kashmir. Here, everyone suffers from "a psychological disorder called the 'new disease,'" Roohdar tells Arshia with comic seriousness: there is no distinction between pathology and normalcy in the rotten state Haider has returned to.

"To go or not to go?" Rosencranz and Guildenstern, recast in *Haider* as the cartoonish Salmans – friends of Haider (and diehard fans of their famous namesake, the Bollywood superstar Salman Khan) turned spies – wonder as they watch Haider walk away with the mysterious figure that is Roohdar. To be Kashmiri, Bhardwaj is asserting, is to be ill with procrastination, paralyzed like Hamlet by the impossible interdiction of setting right the out-of-joint time. The stimulus to action comes from Roohdar and Ghazala. If the first facilitates the transmigration of the father's ghostly wrath which will help Haider consciously self-situate in Kashmir's history and politics, Ghazala, monstrous wife but a selfless, primal mother, offers up an alternative material corpus (to the father's ghoulish one) for Haider to escape from the vicious cycle of violence such history and politics entail. Echoing Grandpa Meer's words, Ghazala enjoins Haider to seek freedom beyond the self-begetting violence of revenge. The mother's flesh, its carnality the object of Haider's violent disgust and rage, becomes the very material of the explosive ending of *Haider*. Ghazala dons the suicide vest, avenging Hilaal's murder on Haider's behalf by blasting through Khurram and his forces, an act which ensures that her son's life, unlike his Danish precursor's, is spared.

Vishal Bhardwaj's *Haider* uses Hamlet as a patient whose trauma is related not to a dread of the unknown but the cold certainty of the known. His immobilization reflects not merely the irresolvable conflict of his warlike and peaceable selves – or a crisis of masculinity, for that matter – but the powerlessness of the Kashmiri mind in the vice-like grip of the autocratic Indian state. Reading *Hamlet* with modern and premodern theories of the mind – such as those propagated by Gilbert Ryle, Putnum, Augustine, Pomponazzi, and Jeremy Taylor – Paul Cefalu points out that Renaissance philosophy and theology gave rise to cognitive science that resembles modern non- or anti-dualist accounts of behaviorism and functionalism. Cefalu claims this non-Cartesian intellectual tradition as a vital interpretative tool for the play:

> When Hamlet famously asks, "to be or not to be, that is the question, / Whether 'tis nobler . . ." (H 3. 57–58), the query is not specifically concerned with Hamlet's reversion to an inner state or essential interiority. Nor does it suggest that Hamlet's mind is a mirror to the world, subject to self-inspection. Hamlet's question is about his existence as an object among other objects in the world. (405–406)

In *Haider*'s characterization of its eponymous hero, similarly, we are not confronted with the psychological curiosity that is the human mind at odds with the social reality its alienated body inhabits. "To question one's existence does not necessarily entail apprehending or exploring one's mysterious interiority, or even seeing oneself as an isolable subject, alienated from the objective realm," Cefalu argues (406). Haider, the Kashmiri Hamlet, does not or cannot separate the world from his mind: he cannot carry out the revenge-mandate because he remains conflicted till the end about the veracity of the ghost as well as the external verifications that cast doubt on its existence. Echoing Hamlet's "To what base uses we may return, Horatio!" (*Hamlet* 5.1.203), Haider, skull in hand, contemplates the imaginable transmogrification of Sikandar (Alexander) to earthenware, just as Hamlet had pondered the Macedonian king's afterlife as a beer-barrel stop. There is no such thing as a disembodied soul, and no matter how exaggerated the grandeur (or grotesquerie) of the life – Alexander, Akbar, Hitler, or Gandhi – it turns and returns to clay. In the scene with Yorick's skull, Hamlet suggests that "radically transformed monistic substance can be put to a variety of perfunctory and menial uses, most of which are defections from the function the substance as human constitution had originally performed" (Cefalu 426). For the analyst in the disaster zone that is Kashmir, as well, thoughts and minds will have to be restored in relation to their contingent existence in the midst of physical happenings in the external world.

Margoob deals with another case, that of a 9-year-old girl, studying in class 3. Relatives had noticed something odd when they found her sitting, benumbed, on the bench where her father's dead body had been placed. She had seen her sisters and mother crying but was mute herself. Fifteen days later, she started suffering fainting spells and hallucinations. The dead body of her father, splashed with blood, started surfacing in her dreams. She refused to look at pictures of the father or go to the graveyard – refused, in other words, to mark and commemorate the finality of his death.

Margoob talks to the neighbor who is visiting the doctor on the young girl's behalf for her quarterly report. Margoob enjoins him to not discontinue treatment: "I will give you bus fare" as he hands him pills. There is improvement, the neighbor says: she is going to school and is more active at home. However, she continues to dream of her father.

Psychomattering

Nikolas Rose, who argues that the human being is a discursively spatialized and subjectified entity, finds the contemporary regime of the self profoundly disquieting, even in identity talk where the sovereign self is negatively defined, as in the psychoanalytic decentering of the ego or the Marxist critique of bourgeois individualism. The ideas about the self in the human sciences – psychology and its affiliates – have, Rose argues, constituted the very knowledges behind "governable subjects" (*Governing the Soul* vi). However, although he no longer finds Marxism or psychoanalysis "good to think with," he gives qualified assent to Marxism and psychoanalysis for their "refusal to celebrate the sovereignty of the autonomous and self-identified subject of self-realization and their suspicion of the 'humanist' values that come along with this sovereignty" (xxiv).

The case studies in the final section of this chapter will show how psychiatry and the Euro- or America-centric "psy-ontology"[13] of the trauma cure, instead of hollowing out interiority in the guise of positing interiority, can indeed provide an affective form for post-traumatic recovery – cures which happen in a variety of agential improvisations, such as mutuality and intercultural dialogue, environmentalism, a commitment to the group as a social entity. Questioning the diagnostic category of trauma to read non-Western and non-military traumata may also prove to be an expedient way of revising psychoanalytic reason, its disciplinary organization and governance, and its privileging of psychiatric disorder over nervous sequelae with confused aetiologies. As Ruth Leys has pointed out, the history of medical apprehensions of trauma from the 1860s, when John Erichsen discovered the railway spine, is actually non-genealogical and nonlinear, frenzied with twists and turns, and a free-for-all as far as terminology is concerned.

> [A] scrutiny of pre-1980 psychiatric literature on the survivors of concentration camps and victims of military combat, civilian disasters, and other traumas reveals a wide diversity of opinion about the nature of trauma, a diversity that has been obscured by the post-Vietnam effort to integrate the field. (*Trauma* 6)

Arguing that PTSD is not a "timeless entity with an intrinsic unity" (6), Leys quotes the work of anthropologist Allan Young, who sees it as a historical construct of not only the practices and technologies with which it is diagnosed and treated, but also the "various interests, institutions, and moral arguments that mobilised these efforts and resources" (6). Acknowledging these reservations about trauma studies as a non-cohesive and controversial field, I would like to extrapolate and develop three key aspects in the medical literature on trauma and dissociation which are relevant for the psychic harms seen in migrant London. These three interconnected issues are as follows: non-military traumata; non-dualist and neurobiological understandings of trauma; the disavowed relationship between traumatic embodiment and trauma ecologies.

First, non-military traumatic disorders. The study of trauma, pertaining to scholarly as well as psychiatric analyses, has primarily been associated with the Holocaust or military combat: the attention to domestic violence or collective suffering and civilian trauma afflicting victims of necropolitical state power is relatively recent. "Not until the women's liberation movement of the 1970s was it recognized that the most common post-traumatic disorders are those not of men in war but of women in civilian life," observes Judith Herman (28).[14] Herman, whose pioneering scholarship was inspired by her work with the Women's Mental Health Collective in Somerville, Massachusetts, contests the American Psychiatric Association definition of PTSD as outside the range of usual human experience. Whether it is rape, battery, sexual or domestic violence, or military trauma associated with perpetual global war, none of these can be described as outside the range of ordinary experience for the civilian populations concerned. A reaction is traumatic, Herman observes, when neither resistance nor escape is possible, and the human system of self-defense becomes overwhelmed and disorganized. The DSM-III and DSM-III-R (the revised third edition, published in 1987) emphasis on the traumatic event as greater than "usual human experience" was eventually broadened in the DSM-IV-TR (2000), which added a couple more definitions, including one which focused on the effect rather than the cause of trauma:

> (1) the person experienced, witnessed, or was confronted with an event or events that involved actual or threatened death or serious injury, or a threat to the physical integrity of self or others; (2) the person's response involved intense fear, helplessness, or horror. (467)

Next, the non-dualist interpretation of trauma. As I have detailed in the previous chapter, the symptoms of trauma, as enumerated in the diagnostic criteria for PTSD in DSM-III, include recurrent recollections of the event; repeated and distressful dreams; experiencing or acting out of the event in response to environmental or ideational triggers. Placing traumatic experience at the heart of PTSD diagnosis raises two tricky questions, as Callard and Papoulias point out:

> To what extent could these re-enactments of traumatic events – "acting or feeling as if the traumatic event were recurring" – be termed memories and anchored back to a specific event? Second, to what extent was trauma an "experience" that the subject underwent and then "re-experienced"? (*Memory* 254)

The traumatic experience and the welter of nonrepresentational memories it generates are not identical, and the French psychologist Pierre Janet's 1889 *L'automatisme psychologique*, which coined the term "dissociation," was one of the first works to articulate the theory of trauma-related amnesia. According to Janet, trauma, which could not be integrated into the normal memory system, produced dissociated, non-declarative "traumatic memories" instead. Dissociationism in Janet, Matthew Erdelyi observes, is a "deficit phenomenon": "Insufficiency of binding energy, caused by hereditary factors, life stresses, or traumas, or an interaction among them, results in a splitting off of personality clusters from the *ego*, the core personality" (9). Unlike Freud, who regarded dissociation as an active and voluntary defense phenomenon, Janet saw the traumatic event resulting in a splitting of consciousness and described how the dissociating patient became attached to "an insurmountable obstacle":

> unable to integrate their traumatic memories, they seem to lose their capacity to assimilate new experiences as well. It is . . . as if their personality has definitely stopped at a certain point, and cannot enlarge any more by the addition or assimilation of new elements.[15]

Because of the dissociation, trauma is not assimilated in normal, comprehensible memory, and creates a different archive instead of these fragments of unmastered history. Janet made a distinction between "narrative" and "traumatic" memory, the first repeating the past *as past* and the latter unconsciously repeating the past. In an oft-quoted passage, Janet clarifies that memory is not simply recollection:

> Memory, like belief, like all psychological phenomena, is an action; essentially, it is the action of telling a story. Almost always we are concerned here with a linguistic operation. . . . The teller must not only know how to [narrate the event], but must also know how to associate the happening

with the other events of his life, how to put it in its place in that life-history which each one of us is perpetually building up and which for each of us is an essential element of his personality. (cited in Leys, "Traumatic Cures" 654)

Involuntary repetition is a form of affliction. In order to be cured, in order for the trauma to be erased, the patient needs to assume a critical distance from the ur-event by narrating the story to themselves and others. Not remaining in the modality of amnesia through debilitating repetitions but recovering and narrating traumatic memory are necessary for its eventual "liquidation," a process which, as Leys points out, "sounds suspiciously like 'exorcism' or forgetting" (660).

Following Janet's "mnemotechnology,"[16] the psychiatrist Bessel van der Kolk claims that the overload of affect in trauma produces an embodied memory which presents the past without representing it: a psychopathological expression of trauma is produced without comprehending and processing its meaning. This memory is experienced, at least initially, van der Kolk states, "as fragments of the sensory components of the event: as visual images, olfactory, auditory, or kinaesthetic sensations, or intense waves of feelings that patients usually claim to be representations of elements of the original traumatic event" (van der Kolk et al. 287). "Dissociation means simultaneously knowing and not knowing," van der Kolk muses in his later work, *The Body Keeps Score* (120). Commenting on a case study on maternal disengagement, he observes how, in these situations, the child blocks out the parent's hostility or neglect and pretends to be indifferent, but the neurobiology of trauma makes the body remain "in a state of high alert, prepared to ward off blows, deprivation, or abandonment" (121).

The final point to be transported from the vicissitudes of trauma studies is that the embodiment of trauma has an added significance for studying its manifestations in man-made disaster zones: it necessitates that psychic suffering be interpreted in the context of collective and chronic trauma ecologies. Not recognizing the traumatized societies that generate traumatized individuals could mean that the trauma repeats itself – as public, personal, or interpersonal violence – outside of cognition and representational memory.[17] In *The Body Keeps Score*, van der Kolk remarks on the psychiatric establishment's "obtuse refusal to make connection between psychic suffering and social conditions":

When I give presentations on trauma and trauma treatment, participants sometimes ask me to leave out the politics and confine myself to talking about neuroscience and therapy. I wish I could separate trauma from politics, but as long as we continue to live in denial and treat only trauma while ignoring its origins, we are bound to fail. In today's world your ZIP code, even more than your genetic code, determines whether you will lead a safe and healthy life. (348)

As mentioned above, the diagnosis of PTSD in DSM-III refers to a single, acutely traumatic event "outside the range of usual human experience" (236), which has little relevance for situations in which people suffer in chronically traumatic circumstances, such as domestic violence or the civilian life in Kashmir discussed earlier. Bessel van der Kolk discusses a watershed moment in the PTSD workgroup led by him for DSM-IV, where a team (including Judith Herman, Jim Chu, David Pelcovitz) proposed a new trauma diagnosis for interpersonal trauma: Disorders of Extreme Stress, Not Otherwise Specified (DESNOS). To their surprise, the diagnosis that the work group had voted (nineteen to two) in favor of was not included in DSM-IV, published in May 1994. "It was a tragic exclusion," van der Kolk writes (*Body Keeps Score* 143). The DSM taxonomy tends to treat trauma sufferers as individuals susceptible to mental illness, not historical subjects for whom loss and pain are an everyday and aggregate event. "Disorders of Extreme Stress, Not Otherwise Specified" would have forced a reconsideration of the social causation of trauma instead of prioritizing universalizing neurobiological processes, giving PTSD (and the PTSD questionnaire) global currency and interdiction. In the world of fully financialized pharma, the DSM has the power to substantiate psychopathologies, which would lead, in turn, to scientific developments toward commensurate treatment. "You cannot develop a treatment for a condition that does not exist" (143).

Judith Herman called psychological trauma "an affliction of the powerless": "Traumatic events are extraordinary, not because they occur rarely, but rather because they overwhelm the ordinary human adaptations to life" (*Trauma and Recovery* 33). Trauma may be an affliction of the powerless, but the immobilization of PTSD – "my gaze is silenced" – should not be rashly translated as victimhood. Instead, building on non-dualist ideas of the physiological impact of trauma drawn from neuroscience, neuroergonomics, and developmental psycho-pathology, I propose the term "psychomattering" to describe the way in which psychoanalysis and psychotherapy can facilitate a repatterning of traumatized states. The concept revises dramatically the material-discursive logic of the trauma cure: if trauma "compromises the brain area that communicates the physical, embodied feeling of being alive" (van der Kolk, *Body Keeps Score* 3), "psychomattering" offers a way of imagining how agency and intelligibility can be restored to the shattered self.

The term "psychomattering" is adapted from the new materialist thinker Karen Barad's coinage "spacetimemattering." The ontology of the world, according to Barad, is a pluripotency, a process of constant becoming and reconfiguration. The empirical evidence of quantum mechanics shows that the ontology of the world "is not a tidy affair. A bit of a hitch, a tiny disjuncture in the underlying continuum, and causality becomes another matter entirely" (*Meeting the Universe Halfway* 233). It should be noted that she is talking about the physical world here, not the cultural or social worlds, and asserting that it has the agency to disrupt and change the latter. Barad argues that poststructuralist thought turns materiality into language too precipitately, granting forms of representation more power in determining our ontologies than they deserve. Matter is not a "passive blank site awaiting the active inscription of culture," Barad states: it is not "a support, location, referent, or source of sustainability for discourse" ("Posthumanist Performativity" 821). Barad's performative metaphysics challenges representationalism itself: instead of disjointed domains of words and things, she offers "a relational ontology that rejects the metaphysics of relata, of 'words' and 'things'" (812). The primary ontological units are not things or words but topological reconfigurings: matter is not a being but a doing, a mode of "intra-active becoming" (822).

The production of matter Barad is talking about here takes into account natural as well as social forces, in particular the "crucial intra-actions among these forces that fly in the face of any specific set of disciplinary concerns" (817). These intra-actions, these boundaries which do not sit still, cannot be easily verbalized or recorded: the ongoing flow of energy, Barad states, does not take place in space and time but in the constitution of spacetime:

> The world is an ongoing process of mattering through which "mattering" itself acquires meaning and form in the realization of different agential possibilities. Temporality and spatiality emerge in this processual historicity. . . . The changing topologies of the world entail an ongoing reworking of the very nature of dynamics. (817–818)

Barad's spacetimemattering is a dynamic and destabilizing assemblage of matter, wherein causal structures are disrupted or stabilized in space and time as well as in the making of spacetime. Agential matter comes into being through intra-actions, or differential patterns of mattering that affect ongoing reconstitution of matter. In Barad's words, spacetimemattering matters through an "inter-play of continuity and discontinuity, determinacy and indeterminacy, possibility and impossibility" (*Meeting the Universe Halfway* 182).

Commenting on Schrödinger's notorious hypothesis about the indeterminate state of a cat (whose life and death are dependent on the state of decay of an atom), Barad elaborates on "spacetimemattering" through the concept of quantum superposition, defining it as "a neoclassical relation among different possibilities":

> Quantum superpositions radically undo classical notions of identity and being.... [They] tell us that being/becoming is an indeterminate matter: there simply *is not a determinate fact of the matter* concerning the cat's state of being alive or dead. It is a ghostly matter! ("Quantum Entanglements" 251)

In this essay, published in *Derrida Today*, Barad draws on Derrida's philosophical neologism "hauntology," or a haunted ontology, in *Specters of Marx* to consider the possibility of a hauntological materialism defined by quantum superpositions and entangled phenomena. Derrida had evoked *Hamlet*'s ghost and its spectral call for justice as positing the very desire and intention driving the play's plot: "everything begins by the apparition of a specter" (*Specters* 4). Questions of agency and temporality are vexed by this haunting, which Derrida argues should be introduced into the very construction of a concept. Does one follow the ghost or is one followed by the ghost instead? And how can the future come back in advance from the past, as Derrida says? Barad calls these ghosts, encountered in the flesh, "iterative materialisations, contingent and specific (agential) reconfigurings of spacetimematterings, spectral (re)workings without the presumption of erasure": "the 'past' [is] repeatedly reconfigured not in the name of setting things right once and for all (what possible calculation could give us that?), but in *the continual reopening and unsettling of what might yet be, of what was, and what comes to be*" ("Quantum Entanglements" 264). To address the past (ghosting the present and future) is not to construct a narrative of how things were or setting the disjointed time aright. It entails taking responsibility for "the tangled relationalities of inheritance that 'we' *are*, to acknowledge and be responsive to the noncontemporaneity of the present" (264).

Studying the psychoanalytic interventions into maladies associated with disaster zones, I suggest that these are provocations wherein – and I am using Barad's agential vocabulary again –

> time and space, like matter and meaning, come into existence, [and] are iteratively reconfigured through each intra-action, thereby making it

impossible to differentiate in any absolute sense between creation and renewal, beginning and returning, continuity and discontinuity, here and there, past and future. ("Posthumanist Performativity" 815)

The matter of bodies is given a historicity: we acknowledge "matter's implication in its ongoing historicity," as Barad states (810). It is a process of becoming wherein ontological units are not things but dynamic phenomena and topological reconfigurings. Talk therapy is reconceptualized as an elaboration of matter, a dynamic production of space and time in the duration of the session. And such acts of traveling psychoanalysis become responsible, when, as in Barad's definition, responsibility amounts to "facing the ghosts, in their materiality, and acknowledging injustice without the empty promise of complete repair" ("Quantum Entanglements" 264). We will examine initiatives in which materializations of ghosts are faced, their symbolic due granted, but let us first examine the fate of the free clinic in London, one of the cities which participated in the historical movement.

Historical and Improvisatory Free Clinics

"The period after what we call World War I, but which, at the time, was thought of as having been 'The Great War to end all wars,' was a time of social idealism and progressive thinking across Europe and the West," says Penelope Crick in her address to the British Psychoanalytical Society on May 4, 2016.

> The League of Nations was formed in 1920, there was more progressive thinking in relation to women and other social class divisions. In Berlin, Budapest, "Red Vienna," Paris and elsewhere, psychoanalysts were keen to take on the social obligation to treat for free people in distress in these new psychoanalytic treatment centres.[18]

Ernest Jones, who was President of the British society, was "rather more conservative" compared to the progressive thinking of analysts across Europe, Crick states. His ambivalence about institutions such as the Berlin Poliklinik was related to long-held beliefs about a medical foundation for effective psychoanalysis, which rendered the clinical authority of non-medical and lay analysts inauthentic. "He found the recent spread of 'wild analysis' alarming," Danto also writes (63). This changed when a former patient of his, the American industrialist Pryns Hopkins, donated £2,000 to set up a clinic "for the purposes of rendering psychoanalytic treatment available for ... patients of the poorer classes" (Decennial

Report, London Clinic, cited by Crick). The new clinic opened on Freud's seventieth birthday, May 6, 1926, at 36 Gloucester Place, London W1.

In the first ten years, over 600 people were seen by either Jones or Edward Goover. They were "psychoanalytic cases," Crick states, with treatment lasting between six months and four years. By 1929, all of the members of the Psychoanalytical Society were nominated as "clinic assistants," required to treat one patient daily at the clinic (or an equivalent amount of service), an imposition which met with protests and attempts at variation of duty (such as members offering financial donations in lieu of service). During World War II, the clinic not only continued to function, it also served as an emergency center for psychological aid. The significant milestones in the next half-century were as follows: the free clinic became a part of the newly instituted National Health Service (NHS) in 1948; Wilfred Bion became Clinic Director in 1953, revising the fee structure to introduce a means-tested sliding scale of payment; there was rising disquiet in the 1960s and 1970s about the clinic's function as a training institute for students; the NHS stopped its funding of the clinic in 1990.

Reviewing this history for the twenty-first century, Crick states in her lecture that "the Clinic has a number of fantasy functions in the minds of different people." Firstly, it is expected to reflect the charitable aims of the Society of providing psychoanalysis to the poor. For the general public, the clinic has "an asylum function," Crick adds: "to contain at little or no financial cost disturbance, distress and unmanageable anxieties." Finally, for analysts in training, the clinic is expected to provide a steady stream of patients "with just the right amount of disturbance" for training needs. Today, the clinic does not invite applications for low-fee analysis but offers psychoanalytic consultations at a "reasonable fee," according to Penelope Crick, with a negotiable (lower) fee for those with limited means. The unpaid work of the candidates facilitates the relatively lower cost of psychoanalysis. Speaking of NHS services that draw on psychoanalytic training but are not in themselves psychoanalytical, Crick optimistically quotes Freud's 1919 statement about adapting therapy to large-scale applications, which, he foresaw, will "compel us to alloy the pure gold of analysis freely with the copper of direct suggestion," a speculation widely cited in scholarship to justify the transition from strict psychoanalysis to more adaptable forms of psychotherapy.[19] As this brief overview suggests, the Freudian free clinic in London would have to be located beyond the parameters of the London Clinic of Psychoanalysis.

The Soul Clinic

In the context of trauma cure, psychomattering takes the form of a translation that enfolds traumatic memory into narrative memory. If trauma is wordless and static, psychomattering sets a process in motion wherein properties and meanings are differentially enacted. To flesh out the idea of psychomattering I have proposed earlier, I will draw on case studies from my work with a couple of unique mental health services in London. The first is Nafsiyat, an intercultural therapy center in Lysander Mews, Archway: an accredited member of the UK Council of Psychotherapy (UKCP), this therapy center offers counseling to people from different linguistic and cultural backgrounds. Patients come here either through self-referral (following the information given on the Nafsiyat website), or through GP referral. Nafsiyat was set up in 1983 to provide psychotherapy to people from ethnic minority backgrounds, groups traditionally excluded from therapy or more likely to be offered medication rather than counseling (Acharyya et al.). The founders of this organization, some of them from ethnic minority groups themselves, decided to develop a psychotherapeutic service which promulgated a situated understanding of racism and cultural difference and provided support and training for others working in primary healthcare, social services, or psychiatry. Case studies from the last decade – involving Eritrean, Turkish, Syrian, Iranian, Bangladeshi, and Nigerian migrants – highlight also the failures of multiculturalism in the welfare state and the unassimilable excess of the international refugee crisis.

In a paper co-authored with Farideh Dizadji, the future Clinical Director of Nafsiyat, Dick Blackwell, from the Institute of Group Analysis, London, writes about an African client he met early in his career who was often late for his sessions:

> I explained this to myself according to the saying reported by some close colleagues, "God gave watches to the English and time to the Africans." There was thus a cultural difference about the meaning of time. One day it occurred to me that back in Africa this man had been a businessman who had regularly travelled abroad. I realized that he must be as capable as me of turning up at the airport in time to catch his flight. So at some point, God must have given him a watch too! Perhaps there was an unconscious reason for his habitual lateness? Perhaps it had something to do with my also having been late for a session with him. (6)

Blackwell, who had worked for twenty years with victims and survivors of torture and political violence sees in his own hard-bitten prejudices the persistence of the epidermal schema in formerly colonial societies, particularly in the urban ghettoes of the West, "significantly populated by the descendants of the formerly enslaved and colonized" (12). It is precisely this that Nafsiyat addresses and corrects. Intercultural therapy, according to its founder and first Director Jafar Kareem, highlights the negotiation of cultural interactions as they inevitably arise within and throughout a therapeutic relationship. It is not opposed to psychotherapy but brings additional material to its repertoire of approaches. As Kareem elaborates, Nafsiyat offers "a form of dynamic psychotherapy which is not necessarily tied to one theoretical orientation but which derives its strength from various analytical, sociological and medical formulations" (Kareem and Littlewood 16). It dislodges the colonial axiomatics of the power relationship between the "help giver" and "help receiver" (Kareem's terms, 16) by facilitating a therapeutic relationship between patient and analyst wherein both can explore each other's transferences and assumptions.

Language work is key here and is used to preempt disastrous transference relationship interpretations, the confounding of traditional beliefs with psychiatric symptoms, and a lack of awareness of differences in presenting symptoms. Cultural and emotional understanding is brought to bear on the analytic process, and a rigorous engagement with the contextual data available for each patient is compulsory. The languages on the menu include Turkish, Somalian, Bengali, and Albanian. Once a referral has been discussed at the weekly clinical meeting, and an agreement is reached that the patient is suitable for intercultural therapy, there is a subsequent assessment interview, when the Clinical Director completes a case-history form and a psychiatric symptom checklist, and the patient completes the general health questionnaire. The process is explained in detail below:

> Patients are then allocated a therapist who offers 12 50-minute sessions, usually on a weekly basis. At the end of this contract the situation is jointly reassessed and further time is offered if appropriate, negotiated in the form of a new contract for a specified number of sessions. All patients living in the borough of Islington receive therapy free of charge. Other patients are funded through their local authorities, DHAs or other agencies. In a few cases patients pay for their therapy themselves. (Acharrya et al. 360)

In a report titled "Stories from Nafsiyat," Natassia Brenman, a medical anthropologist at the London School of Hygiene and Tropical Medicine, makes an observation that was borne out by the interviews I conducted with therapists there:

Anecdotal evidence from staff at Nafsiyat told us that "recovery" is not always the most appropriate measure for the impact of their work, given the complexity of the problems they work with and the limited time they have with each client. We were therefore interested in collecting some more experiential data from clients, which could tell us about their responses to intercultural therapy at different stages along their journey.[20]

Brenman's methodology is "narrative research," which has been central to anthropological research on mental health and is also particularly well suited to capturing Nafsiyat's psychotherapeutic approach. Citing Murray, Brenman describes it as a flexible approach, "which attends to cultural scripts as well as personal and interpersonal levels of constructing stories" (4).[21] She used "semi-structured qualitative interviews following a narrative format" to collect data (5). From observations and discussions with the Nafsiyat staff, a flow chart was developed to chart the patient's journey from referral to the end of their sessions. This, Brenman states, formed the basis of the overall "narrative event" that she wanted to capture (5).

While Brenman's report is about the form, content, and temporal structure of the Nafsiyat experience, snippets of personal stories shed light on the agential ontology I am attributing to certain practices of psychoanalytically oriented psychotherapy. A cluster of testimonials revolve around the ease of communication Nafsiyat is known to foster, with or without the aid of common language. Soraya is an Iranian woman in her late fifties who experienced one-on-one therapy for the first time at Nafsiyat. She had attended group counseling at a refugee therapy center and this was her second attempt at therapy with Nafsiyat. She had arrived in 2014 with a GP referral, but says she wasn't ready for therapy then, which is why she stopped going after two sessions. While she had found the waiting time unnerving, the actual session fostered trust in her therapist and helped her to unburden her cares in a way the group therapy at the refugee centre had not. She completed therapy successfully in 2017, four years after she had first registered her illness with her GP. The experience of speaking in her mother tongue made her feel understood and, to quote Soraya, "loved" (7). As the man from Northern Cyprus, whose case Brenman documents, said of not needing a translator, "Speaking in Turkish gave me more freedom and trust, I felt understood" (10). Similarly, a Turkish patient, who had had to wait for a year for therapy to start, needing medication in the interim for depression and suicidal ideation, says she finally feels at home at Nafsiyat. Whereas, in the past, mental health workers who came to check on her twice a day (following a suicide attempt) could not talk to her because of her lack of English, she now communicated without a translator or the mediation of her English-speaking children. "Nafsiyat gave her the freedom to express herself independently" (13).

In another case study, two Bangladeshi women who are interviewed express their gratitude that intersubjective therapy did not entail a mechanical matching of clients with therapists speaking the same language. Their breakthrough came with analysts drawn from different cultures, with whom they could speak in English and speak their minds without embarrassment or fear of social reprisal: "she didn't worry about being judged," Brenman says of one of the Bengali women (13). The idea of overcoming censorship at Nafsiyat had come up with the Cypriot man as well, whose daughter had been his translator in the last course of therapy he had had elsewhere. He knew that she was holding back some of what he had said, deeming it "inappropriate," and he himself would desist from "talking openly" for fear of opprobrium. At Nafsiyat, he felt free to share his thoughts and feelings, looking forward to his Tuesday sessions. "The freedom to speak in such a way was reflected in the interview," Brenman observes, "conducted in his mother tongue and described by the interviewer as an easy, flowing conversation" (17).

The Brenman study does not dwell on the progression, in time, of the configurations of the analytic encounter, nor do we get a sense of the patient's voice in the hiatuses of therapeutic or ethnographic exemplarity. We learn very little about the nature of the maladies at the intersection of race, class, and gender that had brought these patients to Nafsiyat at the end of tortuous migrations. To understand the dynamics of intercultural therapy through the contingencies of a given case, I conducted interviews with Baffour Ababio, a Ghanaian psychoanalytical psychotherapist and clinical lead at Nafsiyat. Ababio detailed a case involving a Nigerian woman he had treated a couple of years ago, a victim of the Nigeria–Biafra war, whose parents had abandoned her and her sister in Nigeria as they fled to the United Kingdom. She spent her childhood in the bombed and famished country with an uncaring and unscrupulous aunt (the sister was in another part of Nigeria) who would pocket the money her parents periodically sent her. She sold sweets in the market for money. When she was 11, both girls were reunited with their parents in London. The father became sexually abusive. The patient was also raped by a white man in his forties when she was only 14. She terminated the pregnancy that resulted from the rape. Her subsequent relationships, with black men, were all abusive. She went on to have five children, one of whom has severe learning difficulties. Despite the adversities, N acquired graduate and postgraduate degrees. She came to Nafsiyat with acute anxiety, depression, feelings of instability, and an obsessive concern for the bipolar daughter she identified as a damaged child. Nafsiyat offered her twelve sessions: fifty minutes a session, once a week.

Ababio explains how this was a particularly tricky case in the intercultural paradigm: the relationship between black African analyst and black African analyzand was jeopardized by the ancient enmity between Ghana and Nigeria and the patient's disastrous history with black men. Naming the difference and addressing the power imbalance in the therapeutic relationship constituted the inaugural gesture, Ababio said, and it succeeded in enabling cross-cultural and elective affinities. "What is the conversation being hidden by idealisation?" The self-situating in history, both personal and political, enacted by the therapist created a "solid framework" for N's problems as she challenged – even attacked – him in the course of the treatment. The woman's history of female genital mutilation emerged in the course of the conversations, as did her transferential relationship with her ill daughter: it was clear, Ababio says, that "she wanted to look after herself in the guise of looking after her daughter." He channeled her anxiety about him – What would Baffour want me to be? Will he hurt me? – to enable her to confront the non-actualized traumas of separation and abandonment. "Her relationship with black men underwent a transformation" as a result of her therapy, Ababio states.

Recovery is not always the most appropriate measure for the impact of Nafsiyat's short-term psychotherapy, Brenman had observed. "This is only a very small chapter in [the] much broader story of their lives and long lines of different health and mental health interventions" (18). "Does it last? The effects of therapy?" I ask Ababio. "It's a journey," he replies, comparable to trauma stages. "The treatment episodes are not islands, we piece them together, and patients gradually acquire awareness." It is an iterative configuration which makes it difficult to differentiate between beginning and returning, continuity and discontinuity, the past and the future. In the Brenman study, the patients who had found Nafsiyat most effective spoke of receiving phone calls from the center just when they thought they had been forgotten. When they went back to Nafsiyat for regular, booster, or new sessions, they found that details of their lives had been remembered.

The Green Clinic

The following set of clinical case studies are drawn from my collaboration with the Tavistock Trust. The outpost of Tavistock I worked with is titled PCPCS: The City and Hackney Primary Care Psychotherapy Consultation Service, a free mental health service provided by the Tavistock and Portman NHS Foundation Trust. The PCPCS team, based in St. Leonard's Hospital in Hackney, supports general practitioners (GPs, as they are known in the UK) throughout the London boroughs of City and Hackney in the management of patients with complex needs. These complex needs include MUS (medically unexplained symptoms, which the St. Leonard's Hospital team prefer to call "medically untold stories"); personality disorders; PTSD associated with childhood abuse; chronic or severe mental illness.[22] "Because of the complexity, the needs of patients supported by PCPCS do not map onto existing structures of service provision," cite Michael Parsonage et al. (6). Historically, patients in this category have tended to resist the mental health rubric because of social and cultural stigma. As a result, they remain within primary care for treatment as long as they are able, the intractability of their problems causing stress and frustration to GPs and other practice staff. PCPCS was set up to support local GPs in the treatment of complex and chronic needs. The service has two main functions, the second eclipsing the first over the years: improving the dynamic between the GP and the patient; and offering individual treatments in the form of brief psychotherapy or psychological therapy which lasts between 4 and 16 weeks (depending on need and by agreement with patient as well as primary caregivers). It is run by a multidisciplinary team of professionals from psychology, psychiatry, psychotherapy, nursing, and social work.

As Julian Stern, Head of Psychiatry at the Tavistock and Portman NHS Foundation Trust, explains in a joint-authored paper published in 2015, "medical psychotherapy in the NHS has been predominantly psychoanalytic in orientation. Until a little over a decade ago, almost all consultant psychiatrists in psychotherapy . . . were trained in psychoanalysis or psychoanalytic psychotherapy" (Stern et al. 2). Psychotherapy in the public sector in the UK has been influenced by European psychoanalysis as well as US- and Russia-led behaviorism. With the rise of CBT and briefer forms of therapy, "designed to lend themselves to supposedly 'scientific' modes of assessing clinical effectiveness" (3), psychotherapy departments with a more psychodynamic focus have been under substantial threat, closing down as a result or forced to gravitate to brief and manualized forms of therapy with a limited number of sessions offered to patients.

> While many psychoanalysts trained within psychoanalytic institutions, and some continued working in the public sector . . . the emphasis on intensive

individual work often meant that there was a greater focus on private practice to the neglect of the public sector. (5)

Stern et al. point out that while psychoanalysis has continued to flourish in the UK, and while psychotherapists in the public sector have psychoanalytic training, the profession itself has valorized "individual, intense analytic work" (4) over giving back to the community. Consequently, practitioners trained in evidence-based medicine (EBM) such as CBT and briefer therapies could be seen in the forefront of work with marginalized and impoverished groups. As the findings of Roth and Fonagy show, by the mid-1990s CBT was the most widely used psychological therapy throughout the National Health Service, which, as mentioned above, is the publicly funded national healthcare system in the UK. Recent scholarship by Leichsenring and Rabung, Leichsenring and Klein, and Koelen et al. has not only valorized the efficacy of psychodynamic psychotherapy for complex mental disorders but also challenged the hegemony of evidence-based medicine by demonstrating how the analytical tradition (of psychoanalysis) stands up to empirical interrogation. The PCPCS interventions reflect both the popularity of EBM and the concomitant resurgence of psychoanalytically informed models. The methods are varied, including Dynamic Interpersonal Therapy, Mentalization-based Therapy, Cognitive Behavioral Therapy, Supportive Therapy, Couple Work, and Mindfulness. As Stern points out, "applied psychoanalytic and systemic concepts strongly influence the service model not only in its implementation, but also in terms of its philosophical underpinnings" (Stern et al. 13).

In Hackney, I met two Turkish psychotherapists, Ahmet Caglar and Selcuk Berilgen, who run a horticulture psychotherapy group at St. Mary's Garden. Berilgen is a psychodynamic psychotherapist, while Caglar, who is also the Community Project group therapist, is an integrative psychotherapist by training. The group of patients is Turkish: Turkish, Kurdish, Cypriot. Hackney has a well-established Turkish- and Kurdish-speaking community: the Cypriots arrived in the 1930s as Commonwealth citizens, the Turkish migrants from the mainland came to London in the 1970s and 1980s due to economic and political reasons. The Kurds, a stateless nation and one of the most persecuted ethnic minorities of our times, fled persecution in Turkey, Iran, and Iraq in the late 1980s and early 1990s.[23] According to statistics provided by the Day-Mer report, a community-based survey conducted by the Social Policy Research Centre at Middlesex University, London, in 2013, Turkish and Kurdish adults in Hackney, Haringey, or Enfield were twice as likely to be unemployed as the general population. Unemployment rates, social housing levels, and the proportion of those never having worked or in long-term unemployment could be twice as high as the city-wide average. For Turkish-born people, the unemployment rate was 7% (against 4% of the whole population) and the proportion of income support claimants 21% (more than 5 times the national average of 4%). Of the Turkish-born who were employed, the average annual income was £14,750 (against a national average of £21,250). Turkish nationals were among the ten largest groups of foreign benefit claimants in Britain.[24]

The group at St. Mary's Garden is largely female. According to the London Poverty Profile of 2015, a majority (over 80%) of women of working age born in Turkey (but living in London) are not working: this is attributed to the lack of language and trade skills, lack of access to education, child care and other responsibilities in the extended-family structure, and traditional ideas about the role of women.[25] The Day-Mer report emphasized that Turkish women, especially first-generation immigrants, could be vulnerable and socially isolated, as well as victimized by a patriarchal culture. They were more affected than men by family tensions that led to interpersonal violence. An interesting detail of the Day-Mer report was that women, disproportionately burdened as they were with not just parenting but what the report calls "bureaucratic issues," were more likely to use welfare advice and other advice services (D'Angelo et al. 41).

The regeneration of the plant world lends itself well to projects of psychic repair: as it says on the PCPCS website, "the heat and toxicity of trauma [are] moderated." The genesis of horticultural psychotherapy is often thought to be Freudian, related to the misattributed quote "Flowers ... have neither emotions nor conflicts," but the illusion of having made something happen is more Winnicottian in provenance. Winnicott, who was a paediatrician and a psychoanalyst, maintained that when there is a coincidence between something conjured up in the child's imagination and a real-life event, it fosters a sense of self-belief, which, in turn, prepares us for disappointments in later life. Moreover, in *Through Paediatrics to Psychoanalysis* (1958), he introduced the idea of "transitional space," the hyphenation between internal and external reality, which he described as a "resting-place for the individual engaged in the perpetual human task of keeping inner and outer reality as separated yet inter-related."[26]

The square-foot system of gardening makes it feel manageable, while proximity to the earth and community through shared learning provide attachment security. The therapists posit the garden as a Winnicottian

Figures 1–4 Horticultural therapy at St. Mary's Secret Garden, Hackney, London

Figures 1–4 (Cont.)

third space, "an intermediate area of experiencing" where a gradual differentiation between subjectivity and objectivity, inside and outside, may commence.[27] The program lasts for twelve months for each cohort. A day's gardening (once a week) is followed by a one-hour meeting over tea in the garden shed, when rules are revisited for newcomers, and expectations of members reiterated as required. To mobilize the group mind, it is important to maintain regularity with the timing of the meetings, including time boundaries and breaks, the therapists insist. There is no formal agenda on the table and conversation is unrehearsed, free-flowing in the best of times. "They are able to say in a group what individuals wouldn't be able to say," Caglar states. Harsher divisions of religion and culture are not apparent in the group, which is predicated on self-disclosure and interpersonal support. The seasonal variations aid the growth and maturation of relationships between strangers, many of whom have been incapacitated by the violence of familial relationships indoors. The therapists provide continuity between sessions by recalling old discussions and integrating the same with new and different outlooks. Every six months, the produce is cooked in the shed and feasted on.

As briefly discussed in the introduction, the therapy in St. Mary's Garden involves grounding, mindfulness exercises, part of the psychoeducation geared to foster embodied self-awareness in patients and an enhanced sense of being present. To restore the lost connection to their bodies, group members practice step-by-step skills to translate thinking to feeling and what Caglar terms "subjective emotional presence." They are encouraged to be aware of any positive experiences or sensations they may have. Caglar cites Ecker's opinion that, while new learning always creates new circuits, "it is only when new learning also unwires old learning that transformational change occurs."[28] The therapists take pains to create a safe space for the traumatized, troubled gardeners. This, they say, is not simply a removal of threat but draws on unique cues in the environment: how we speak, how we look, how we listen.[29] "In the group setting, therefore, we aim to recognise the patient's autonomic state, and regulate or co-regulate into their ventral vagal state, which is a safe, connected, social and resourceful state to work and communicate," the report states. The therapists also borrow from the toolkit of emotion-focused and experiential psychodynamic therapies. The report mentions Intensive Short Term Dynamic Psychotherapy (ISTDP) and Accelerated Experiential Dynamic Psychotherapy (AEDP), which work with triangles of conflict (the relationship between anxiety, defense, and feelings) and triangles of person (the relationship between analyst, analyzand, and people from the patient's past or present): in the group setting, these are deployed in interactive ways. "These modalities demonstrate how defences work … and prevent us from connecting with our feelings." The price of not connecting is the psychosomatic or medically unexplained symptom. Emphasizing the experiential aspect of this green therapy, Caglar et al. write that the focus is always on "here/this/now rather than there/that/then."

The feedback from patients in this group, facilitated by Caglar, provides new insights into this form of ecotherapy.[30] When asked if the group helped them to change the way they had hoped, the eight patients interviewed reminisced about the panoply of symptoms that had brought them to PCPCS: fainting, nervous collapses, inability to get out of the house or have social interactions, neuralgic pain, separation anxiety, and debilitating co-dependence. "I'm much better with my emotions," Patient 5 says, while Patient 7 feels "I express myself more comfortably." "It did help me. I gained self-confidence," she says. More than half of the patients acknowledge the salutary effects of working in and as a collective. "To see other people feels like family bonding," Patient 1 states, while Patient 6 says that the group has helped her self-sufficiency in that she no longer expects others to provide solutions for her problems. "I realized that I always thought of other people in my life in order not to hurt them, but I was hurt," Patient 6 reveals: "I started to think about my own needs."

The responses to the questionnaire also reveal the ambivalences group psychotherapy may generate. Patient 1 says it sometimes makes her feel worse, especially when the discussion triggers flashbacks of the children's home where she grew up. Patient 3 complains that she couldn't express herself freely as this was a cultural community and she had acquaintances in it. For the most part, however, mutual identifications among the members provide relief for feelings of isolation and estrangement: "I noticed that some people are unwell," Patient 8 says, while Patient 3 says the exposure to this group has brought her the realization that, compared to her fellows, "my situation is better than theirs." Patient 7 reveals of the group configuration that "I was introverted, I opened up more." Although her pains did not ease in the course of the therapy, Patient 7 says "the conversations in the group made me think about myself and value myself more." The group needs in relation to time-bound tasks made several patients feel they had become more organized and "tidy" in their emotion management: as Patient 5 states, "I am now doing more things during the day. I get up early. I was all over the place before . . . I can cope with my pain better." Patient 2 compared the budding friendships in the group to working in the garden to grow crops.

"Growing things is very important," Patient 8 emphasizes, echoing Patient 3, who said "the garden produce we grow is meaningful." Patient 8, who had mentioned earlier in the questionnaire that her mind was confused, prone to "forgetfulness," says "I grew vegetables for the first time and now I grow things in my garden." "The group brings some organization to my life, like being on time," she states. "To see the seeds we sow grow as vegetables gave me hope," says Patient 3, mentioning also that going out on her own once a week built her self-confidence. Patient 4 states on the questionnaire that "I was fearful with the idea of seeing a psychologist before. Speaking the same language was useful." Gardening, she muses, "made me feel I achieved something. It felt good and affected my relationship with others." "Thank you, Mr Ahmet," Patient 6 states; "I think Mr Ahmet provided a balanced group. He tries to be just and he approached us with patience and care." The victim–victimizer binary in trauma groups is defused through the movable feast of "conversation," a word that comes up again and again. The role of the therapist, the answers on the questionnaire suggest, has been to contain the projections ("I feel like [the motherless] Prince Harry"); chalk out "action plans"; work with dissociative defenses and refocus the patient on the "present day"; activate the isomorphic relationship between the divided self and the homogeneous, yet non-identical, group.

In his interviews with me, Caglar talked about a difficult patient, E. She had been in therapy with seven different clinicians for as many years. One of them described her as a "crying baby who cannot be pacified." E was so irascible that she had been banned from Turkish community groups. There is a gamut of pathological symptoms: headache, dizziness, mood changes, restlessness, insomnia, depression, anxiety. E also talked constantly about relationship troubles, her poor living conditions, and her inordinate anxiety about the health of her children. She feared in particular that her mother's psychiatric history would be transmitted to her children. E had confided in Caglar about witnessing a murder, about the violent tribulations of the trafficked journey to the UK, and the protracted process through which she was granted asylum. Her mother-in-law had been murdered; another relative had committed suicide.

"It was a big effort for E to come to the garden," Caglar says, and the transition wasn't smooth. She would moan in Turkish or Kurdish; refuse to cook, pleading a backache (she said); and the therapists were taken aback by the rage she seemed to incite in the otherwise docile group. E was eventually helped by the gardening project: the tranquil space of the garden encouraged her to become self-reflexive and confront traumatic memories of childhood abuse preceding the brutalizing period of being trafficked and languishing in half-way houses as an asylum seeker. Surprisingly enough, her disruptive presence had the salutary effect of galvanizing the group, and they found it in their hearts to reach out to her. She became capable of the projective identification Freud said was crucial to maintaining psychoanalysis – capable of transference, in other words – and the therapists were, in turn, enabled to use this analytic tool to treat the patient better.

Mrs. K is a single Kurdish woman, always well dressed, stern, and very serious. She was referred to PCPCS as her GP felt he wasn't getting through to her. She was on a cocktail of medications and had many physical complaints. One of eight children, mostly girls, she had had a very strict upbringing and practically no formal education. Her husband – it was an arranged marriage – was violent to her. Mrs. K was offered a course of brief therapy, psychoanalytic in orientation. The primary objective of the intervention was to help her to become less self-punishing and less harshly judgmental of others. In sharp contrast to her interactions with her GP, where, to his considerable vexation, she had refused to talk, Mrs. K started warming to the therapy and her therapist noticed a general softening in her demeanor.

Despite this, the therapist felt that the gains – "tiny shifts in her thinking" – were modest, and Mrs. K was offered a place in the Turkish women's horticultural project. She rejected the idea at first, fearful that her strict adherence to Islam was under attack due to the threat of potential contamination from pig manure. An intrepid PCPCS clinician approached an Imam, and, after a reassurance from him that it would be fine for her to take part in the farm community, K joined the group. The case records at PCPCS state that she went on to become a lively and engaged member of the horticulture initiative. No longer plagued by symptoms, and more physically able than ever before, Mrs. K, her GP reports, has significantly lessened her trips to the surgery. Her outcome measures, previously in the "depressed and anxious" clinical range, were now in the normal range: her mental state, the records state, is "improved."

The final case study from the Hackney garden involves a man, S, age 48, who lives in a hostel in London. It is a rare case of failure in the history of PCPCS – a telling one at that. S was raised in foster homes after his mother died in his infancy. Caglar gathers from their conversations that he joined military service after emerging from foster care around age 20, but this is unverifiable. S is filthy, reeks of alcohol, and is hopeless in day-to-day interactions. "He keeps saying 'I'm puzzled,'" Caglar states. His relationship with the horticulture group is not easy, yet S is very anxious about severing ties with the group. Caglar decides to go to his hostel to check on him when he doesn't turn up to meetings: the room is small and fetid, with no personal mementoes or pictures to be seen. S talks, for the first time, about his hallucinations (he sees a man by his bed), about the recurring pain from a hernia operation he had some years ago, and the time when he had to be hospitalized after a brutal attack on the streets. Ahmet arranges a case worker, a Turkish woman S warms to, but this does not lead to any perceivable change in his behavior – S fails to turn up to the garden, as before. His physical and psychic pain is so unprocessed, Calgar writes in his case notes, that it has impacted his capacity to attach.[31] The group feels like a family, S says, but the cookouts remind him of his wretched institutional life. S is too fragile, tormented by the fact that he was never adopted out of foster care, and suffers belatedly from the discontinuities and disorganization of a life he lacks the psychic resources to remember, let alone rearticulate. "We can't do anything for him," Caglar states, "because he is not doing anything for himself." He leaves group therapy shortly afterward. He is technically an MUS (medically unexplained symptoms) case, Caglar says, yet, look, everything is explicable: the back pain, the lack of (post-op.) aftercare, the world's withholding of an iota of love or care for S.

Roohdar Analyst

Bessel van der Kolk's *The Body Keeps Score* (2014) argues that "trauma produces actual physiological changes, including a recalibration of the brain's alarm system, an increase in stress hormone activity, and alterations in the system that filters relevant information from irrelevant" (2–3). In van der Kolk's non-dualist interpretation, the traumatized state is redefined as both a psychoneurosis and a physioneurosis, wherein changes in the brain compromise the "physical, embodied feeling of being alive" (3). By the same token, the brain can be treated to heal the body better, its neuroplasticity utilized to make survivors feel more alive, more in control of the present. Van der Kolk, one of the world's foremost experts on traumatic stress, suggests three distinct pathways of trauma cure: talking and reconnecting; taking medicines that shut down hyperactive alarm systems; and, finally, allowing the body to have experiences that viscerally contradict the immobilization and powerlessness associated with traumatized states. At the therapeutic nursery of St. Mary's Garden, the third, most recuperative stage is associated with embracing the eco-cosmopolitanism of urban living I have discussed in the previous chapter. The aim is to foster a cultural and environmental imaginary and patterns of belonging to one's body that enable a re-inhabitation in the local and national.

Discussing topographies and topologies of historical trauma, Freud had made a crucial distinction between castration trauma (and the concomitant repression) and traumatic neuroses, associated with accident victims and war veterans, which manifest less in repression than in debilitating symptoms of repetition.[32] In psychoanalytic literature, whether it is Sigmund Freud's "Nachträglichkeit" (deferred action), Jean Laplanche's dual registers of traumatic relay (between childish desires and adult lives), Pierre Janet's pathological automatisms (through which fragments of unintegrated memories surface), or van der Kolk's discontinuous cognition, trauma signifies splitting, interruption, repetition, and the sliding of signification. Trauma analysis involves translational acts which connect self with the other, autobiography with history, repetition with restitution. As Christina Zwarg states, "the strongest legacy of trauma theory is the reconfiguration of analytic interlocutor(s) in the complex temporal dyadic of the analytic method" (28). Bessel van der Kolk highlights the shamanic role of the analyst in his own innovative treatment of PTSD. Acknowledging Pierre Janet as an intellectual precursor, van der Kolk suggests that Janet, unlike Freud or Charcot, was less interested in intellectually grasping hysteria than trying to devise a cure for the patient's physical symptoms: "Janet spent untold hours talking to them, trying to discover what was going on in their minds. . . . Janet was first and foremost a clinician whose goal was to treat his patients" (*The Body Keeps Score* 178).

While van der Kolk finds narrative – "helping victims of trauma find the words to describe what has happened" – meaningful, he is convinced that "usually it is not enough" (21).[33] According to him, the aim of trauma cure is not simply generating a narrative of a belated experiencing. Nor is it predicated on the dyad of speaker and listener, as in the parable of Tasso's Tancred and Clorinda discussed by Cathy Caruth in *Unclaimed Experience*, where Clorinda's sorrowful voice speaks through the wound (and because of the infliction of the wound) that Tancred has unwittingly re-inflicted in the magic forest. The therapists and healers I have discussed in this chapter acquiesce to the sober realization that people trapped in chronic poverty and state-sponsored violence need physical rehabilitation into collaborative and socially dialogic modes of living more than what Sarah Pinto calls the "narrative-oriented therapy" (265) inaugurated by classical psychoanalysis. Treatment, in other words, is not only interpretative; it must include elaborations of care.

In *Archive Fever*, Jacques Derrida has associated psychoanalysis with an archival drive. A prosthesis of spontaneous memory, the psychoanalytic archive's will to remember is overwhelmed by the fear of forgetfulness and oblivion:

> There would indeed be no archive desire without the radical finitude, without the possibility of a forgetfulness which does not limit itself to repression. Above all . . . there is no archive fever without the threat of this death drive, this aggression and destruction drive. (19)

Perhaps the treating of trauma can benefit from the hauntology of feedback loops and nonlinear models of causation which characterize trauma. The psychic procedures of archiving associated with psychoanalysis are not merely conservational, monumentalizing the past, but are also intent on the erasure of memory. The aggression-destruction-death drive of psychoanalysis, which is its peculiar logic of supplementarity, binds it to its own finitude, its other, and to the arrival of the event. My portmanteau word "psychomattering" refers to the psychoanalytic event to come, the event which will transform the disciplinary, clinical, and cultural "archive" of psychoanalysis. It moves us away from genealogical studies of trauma toward non-teleological and experimental methods of understanding aetiology.

"Aap doctor hai kya?" (Are you a doctor?) Arshia asks Roohdar in *Haider*. Roohdar, his name meaning "spirit bearer," says "Main doctor ki rooh hoon" (I am the soul of the doctor). The spirit of psychoanalysis coaxing the memory of Kashmiri, Kurdish, or Nigerian subjects into being, making that amalgam of personal and collective history "available for immediate conscious access," to use Caruth's words ("After the End," 19), is also offering them the instrument for history's and memory's radical rewriting, overcoming, or elimination. The analyst as muse of history in disaster zones – whether in the migrant ghettoes of London or the overrun wards of war-torn Kashmir – ushers in a process whereby dreams, shock, projection, and fantasy form new conjunctions and enabling fictions. True to Barad's utopian projections, this is a posthumanist scenario, not manipulated or manageable by human intention alone, and vibrant with epistemic uncertainty and ontological indeterminacy. As in Margoob's clinic at the Psychiatric Diseases Hospital in Srinagar, we are looking at a secular ministering of souls where a 9-year-old trauma sufferer recovers functionality and capability – she goes to school and is more active at home – without being cured of her dreams.

PART II
Mumbai

CHAPTER 3

Slums and the Postcolonial Uncanny

The Bengali avant-garde filmmaker Ritwik Ghatak's 1958 movie *Ajantrik* charts a monstrous continuum of dominated life in which the machinic is humanized – "ajantrik" means non-mechanical/not-machine – and human life made to seem machine-like. Bimal is a poor taxi driver operating in the Bengal–Bihar border whose life revolves around his Chevrolet jalopy, which he fondly names "Jagaddal," or "immovable, stone-like." His undue attachment to Jagaddal makes him a butt of ridicule and opprobrium. The local Bengali club declares him inhuman – a "jantar" or "jantra" – for cathecting with a machine; children call him "paagla," or crazy; townspeople ask tauntingly if the car is his wife. The journeys taken by Bimal and Jagaddal capture the mythic no-time of provincial India, interchangeable and monotonously repetitive, as well as the linear progressive time of a town in the throes of rapid industrialization. At the juncture of both is the disappearing present of the subaltern, the Adivasi,[1] the autochthon Oraon tribal who is nameless and stateless, and who speaks in the film only in choral harmonies and the collective orgies of dance. In a key scene, Bimal watches an Adivasi procession in a drunken stupor. The striped flags and clothing of the tribe find an uncanny echo in stripes on his scarf: it would be exaggeration to speak of this as a fusion and intermingling, but there is no doubt that corollary distinctions of civilized and uncivilized, or culture versus nature, no longer dominate Bimal's world.

The cyborg, according to Haraway, is "our ontology, it gives us our politics" (150).[2] Ghatak, through the fusing of metal and man, is showing an inter-implication of the poor, hungry, battered, and outmoded Bimal's material and social worlds that can happen at a time of industrial modernization; he is also at pains to show Bimal as a possibility of resistance to the postindustrial modern. In his refusal of technological newness, and in his resolute denial of the fungibility of the objects of desire, Bimal refuses the redemptive frame of the Indian growth narrative. He will not swap out the old for the new, although he is not averse to recycling, as shown in the movie's last frame, where a child plays gleefully with the car horn.

In his short book *The Open: Man and Animal*, Giorgio Agamben, whose elaborations of the question of biopower set in train by Foucault have proved foundational for animal studies as well as posthuman theory, accepts Martin Heidegger's perplexed but ultimately privative account of the human as the discloser of being. The "bare life" – the most basic form of life – whose exclusion, Agamben argued in *Homo Sacer*, "founds the city of men" (7), is here seen as the animal. It may indeed be, as Agamben argues, that the name and being of man is always in question, that *Homo sapiens* does not designate a biological species, but rather an "anthropological machine" for the production of the human.

> Insofar as the production of man through the opposition man/animal, human/inhuman, is at stake here, the machine necessarily functions by means of an exclusion (which is also always already a capturing) and an inclusion (which is also always already an exclusion). (37)

The metaphysics of the human is a "state of exception,"[3] a zone of indeterminacy where the outside is an artificial exclusion of the inside, and the inside, similarly, is an artificial exclusion of an outside (37). Agamben follows Heidegger in defining "man" as the being that must heroically – and, it seems, uniquely – ask itself the question of its own being. "Man" is now not only the creature that is able to grasp its own essence, but the only creature that is able to experience the anguish and boredom of its lack of essence. Agamben revises and supplements Heidegger by defining this human freedom as a function of its proximity to, rather than distance from, animal life.

In his account of the machine-like process whereby the species "man" is produced, Agamben shows how identificatory characteristics emerge once the "animal" is posited as something negative in order for the human to be determined through the negation of that negation. As Adorno had stated in *Negative Dialectics*, "the equating of the negation of the negation with positivity is the quintessence of identification" (161). The anthropological machine functions, Agamben states, "by excluding as not (yet) human an already human being from itself, that is, by animalizing the human" (37). The Jew, for instance, is posited as the nonhuman within the human.

To render inoperative the "anthropological machine" that governs our conception of "man," we need not search for new, more effective or more authentic, articulations of this conception, but show instead "the central emptiness, the hiatus that – within man – separates man and animal" (*Open* 92). Agamben's positive biopolitics is a call for the human being to appropriate "his own concealedness, his own animality, which neither remains hidden nor is made an object of mastery" (80). Following Walter Benjamin, Agamben proposes a mastery of the relation between human and nature which is neither a mastery of the human over nature nor that of nature over the human.

> [I]n the reciprocal suspension of the two terms, something for which we perhaps have no name and which is neither animal nor man settles in between nature and humanity and holds itself in the mastered relation, in the saved night. (83)

The objective of such impolitical politics is not to supplant an old anthropology with the new but, as Agamben states, to expose the emptiness – "the hiatus" – between human and animal and "risk ourselves in this emptiness" (92). The literary and cultural works I will now discuss show fidelity to this condition of bare life, where the cogs of the anthropogenic machine are stopped as it tries to master not only nature but the non-man, the isolated nonhuman in the midst of humanity: "the slave, the barbarian, and the foreigner . . . figures of an animal in human form" (*Open* 37).

The human/animal distinction in Heidegger's thought, as it crystallized in the course he taught at the University of Freiberg in the winter semester of 1929–1930, is structured around the difference inherent in "the animal's relation to its environment and man's relation with his world," the animal's "poverty in the world" and the "world-forming" man (Agamben, *Open* 49–50). The animal is poor in the world, by which Heidegger means – and it is, as Agamben points out, drawing on contemporary biological and zoological studies here – captivated in its own essence. Heidegger's example of captivation is a laboratory bee, placed in front of a cup full of honey it has started to suck. If the bee's abdomen is cut away in the process, it will continue to suck honey even as it streams out of its open abdomen. The bee does not recognize the abnormal presence of too much honey, nor does it register the absence of its abdomen, so captivated is it by the instinctual activity. The animal "fundamentally lacks the possibility of entering into relation either with the being that is itself or with the beings other than itself," Heidegger concludes (Agamben, *Open* 54). The ontological status of the animal environment is open (*offen*), Agamben summarizes, but not openable (*offenbar*). This openness without disconcealment – an openness that is intimated by anthropocentric knowledge as a lack, a poverty, or a not-having of the world – characterizes also the worldlessness of the visible but unseen, animal-in-human-form population I engage with in the literary examples below.

Figures of an Animal in Human Form

"I've worked with street kids, I know where they come from, and I wouldn't refer to them as dogs even in casual parlance," said Mira Nair, whose *Salaam Bombay* (1988), a (fictionalized) narrative of street children shot on location in India, won the audience award and the Caméra d'Or at Cannes, as well as an Oscar nomination.[4] She is talking here about Danny Boyle's movie *Slumdog Millionaire*, which Indian commentators were quick to slam as "an idiot's guide to India" and "poverty porn," but which opened to noisy popular and critical acclaim in the West in 2008.[5] The term "slumdog" does not have a dictionary entry in the *Oxford English Dictionary* and seems to have gained currency after the film's release. The literal translation the movie offers, through one of its characters (played by Irrfan Khan) is "kutta," Hindi for dog: "slumdog," in the movie, refers to the feral strays who prowl the slums, including children, drug dealers, hustlers, and warlords.

Based on a novel titled *Q&A* by a former Indian diplomat, Vikas Swarup, *Slumdog Millionaire* maps the trajectory of Jamal Malik from the slums, to the orderly democratic world of a British call center, to the global playground of the game show *Who Wants to Be a Millionaire?* The film opens with Jamal Malik in police custody, accused of cheating during his appearance on the game show, and on the receiving end of "enhanced" police interrogation, which includes generous administrations of electric shocks. The police inspector wants to know how a lowly tea boy (or *chaiwallah*) from the slums could possibly know enough to reach the 20-million-rupee final round. Under interrogation, Jamal articulates the fragments of a damaged life, each of which holds an answer to the questions he faces in the hot seat. What is also articulated is a sense of a life – chronology, as well as a wealth of investigative detail. The telling of the story is both retrospective and proleptic in its ordering, with the meaning of the events and images conferred retroactively.

Setting aside the vexed question of artistic merit and specious "feel-good" effects, what one takes away from the novel and the movie is the ingenious plotting, which links what Virginia Woolf called "the lives of the obscure"[6] to the accidental triumph of a single, dominant figure. It seems, at first, to be a classic *Bildung* narrative, an Oedipal movement from the semiotic chora of the slums – mazes of corrugated-tin rooftops, the feverish business of a *dhobighat* (open-air laundromat), the dense traffic of smoggy streets, the sea of humanity that is an Indian railway station – to the reality of metropolitan arrival. "India is at the centre of the world now, bhai, and

I am at the centre of the centre," says Jamal's brother Salim, as they gaze out from a skyscraper under construction onto the landscape of their former slum. But Salim won't make it after all. And 18-year-old Jamal is in the game show for love, not money, hoping that his beloved Latika, held hostage by the gangster for whom Salim works, will spot him on screen while watching her favorite show. With the poor impulse control Jamal shows with the 20-million-rupee question, it is imaginable that he will lose the money as serendipitously as he found it. To read *Slumdog Millionaire* as what the movie itself calls a "rags-to-Raja story," or as peddling "a dated type of globalism in which the boom times are infinite" (Tyree 35) is short-sighted. Salim, Latika, and Jamal are presented as too brutalized by their hypertrophic past to lend credence to any overcoming of their melancholic mental states other than the miraculous recovery the movie holds out for the romantic pair. As Georgia Christinidis also argues, Boyle's valorization of personal relationships, while potentially redemptive, "does not represent any action or any kind of community that might challenge the structural inequalities that make it so unlikely for a 'slumdog' to succeed" (40).

"*Slumdog Millionaire* is like *Salaam Bombay* on speed," Mira Nair, the director of the 1988 film, said when questioned about obvious parallels between two movies on Indian street children. *Salaam Bombay* shares with the belated entry the portrayal of the subaltern as type, rather than figure. As Bert Cardullo points out, Nair shoots *Salaam Bombay* in medium and long shot, avoiding the close-up because she wants to show the protagonist Krishna in the context of his environment. In the course of the movie, Krishna loses his name and becomes a hand (*chaipau*, or tea delivery boy). The film is filled with high-angle shots and bars that frame faces: bars on windows, cages, or fences. In the last scene, Chaipau escapes being tram-pled underfoot in a crowd, but there is little hope for him. He stares blankly off to the right, crying, and holding, but not spinning, a tightly furled top. Similarly, the child Jamal is little more than a symptom of cultural pathology, the heartrendingly sweet face of a faceless mass which cannot be imagined otherwise. It is only after he escapes the slums and overthrows his Oedipal brother/father that his individuation can begin.

Like *Salaam Bombay*, *Slumdog Millionaire* highlights the great difficulty of the diagnosis of the pathology of cultural communities under the mark of race or class. As discussed earlier, Freud wrote in *Civilization and its Discontents* (1930) that, in an individual neurosis, the pathology of a patient needs to be demarcated and differentiated in the context of the relative normalcy of the group to which they belong – "For a group all of whose members are affected by one and the same disorder no such background could exist; it would have to be found elsewhere" (144). At first glance, it seems as if Freud, in his bid to valorize processes of sovereignty, individuation, and liberal democracy, is denying the huddled masses an unconscious as well as a collective unconscious, crammed with inherited archetypes and instincts. Rereading the passage could reveal a tone more wary than condescending. Freud is cautioning against two outcomes here: treating communal neuroses out of context, and misapplying a methodology honed for individual therapy to address a collective. As he states, "we may expect that one day someone will venture to embark upon a pathology of cultural communities" (144), but that time was yet to come.

The preferred trajectory of classical psychoanalysis is from group to self, a sovereign subject predicated on the exclusion of the group. In *Dark Continents*, her formidable study of the colonial genesis and elaborations of psychoanalysis, Ranjana Khanna describes the ethnographic interpretation of the birth of the modern individual. Reading Freud's *Totem and Taboo*, his (failed) attempt at reconciling individual psychology with social psychology, Khanna describes Freud's method as "the evolutionary progressivist one," rather than that of "the collective unconscious" (77).

> Freud posited the first evolutionary phase as one in which there is magic, primitive taboo, shame, and collective working through of contiguous relations. The second is based on animism, religious law and morality, guilt, and personal interactions. The third is structured on science, state enforcement of law, and regulation of mental health, criminality, and pathology or neurosis. (77)

Psychoanalysis is both the "symptom and the mechanism" of this creation of the modern subject where the different stages of development are analogues of successive moments in civilization (68). Khanna calls it the "calm violence" of "interpellation," through which is formed a "social contract that individualizes and individuates members of a group at the same time as it confers upon them group 'culture' or 'civilization'" (68). This is again evident in the way the slumdog leaves the entropic (and also richly relational, and transpersonal) group to become a social and psychological creature: the slums become a no-place, atopic, and constitute the hauntology of the historical being, who is now, via the call center, at the "centre of the centre."

In a blog on the "social imaginary" of the sci-fi action movie *District 9*, Ato Quayson draws attention to the portrayal of Nigerians even in this genre, its aberrant relation to reality taken for granted. The alien Prawns and the Nigerians, hungry slum dwellers both, are invaders and outcasts as far as the civil society and political order of Johannesburg (where the story is set) are concerned. For the discerning viewer, however, there are marked distinctions between the portrayal of the Prawns and of the Nigerians: the former, de-raced, group is relatively more human, possesses scientific rationality, and will eventually overcome adversities to return to their home planet; the latter is mercenary, cannibalistic, a stereotyped portrait of the aimlessness and autophagy of some postcolonial societies. Once again, "black life is depicted as somehow the bearer of an inherent moral deficit," Quayson observes.[7] In *Slumdog Millionaire*, a movie in which the slum and its dogs have become fused into a single, machinic entity by urban infrastructure, the dehumanization of these extraterrestrials is further troped through a callous stereotyping of slum habitats.

The location of the slum in *Slumdog Millionaire* is Dharavi, if the Vikas Swarup novel is to be believed, although, in the film's greedy epistemology, different slum sensoriums are rolled into a single ontology. The Dharavi of *Slumdog Millionaire*, from time to time, resembles the non-registered squatter slums near the airport: the police chase the slum dwellers admonishing it is no "private *ka* land" (it is government-owned land, in other words). The slum scenes with which the movie begins trot out the usual phobic configurations: claustrophobic density, shit, standing water, communal riots, garbage hills, bulldozers, prostitutes and pimps, drug dealers, beggar mafia who blind kidnapped children with a spoonful of acid to improve their street cred. Matias Echanove and Rahul Srivastava, two of the co-founders of Urbz, an information-sharing platform based in Dharavi,[8] call out this absurd, phantasmagoric rendition:

> Its depiction as slum does little justice to the reality of Dharavi. Well over a "million eyes on the street," to use Jane Jacobs's phrase, keep Dharavi perhaps safer than most American cities. Yet Dharavi's extreme population density doesn't translate into oppressiveness. The crowd is efficiently absorbed by thousands of tiny streets branching off bustling commercial arteries. And you won't be chased by beggars or see hopeless people loitering – Dharavi is probably the most active and lively part of an incredibly industrious city.[9]

Echanove and Srivastava see Dharavi as a "user-generated" city, its eighty neighborhoods developed organically and incrementally by generations of residents according to the needs of housing and business. They mention their participation in demonstrations in Dharavi which angrily declaimed the film's title: "The Indian media widely reported that the outrage was over the word 'dog.' But what we heard from Manju Keny, a college student living in Dharavi, was something else. She was upset at the word 'slum.' We could not agree more."

Uncanny, Nonhuman, Un-space

It will not come as a surprise that the word "slum" originates in Victorian canting speech. The convict writer J. H. Vaux in his 1819 *New Vocabulary of Flash Language* first used the term to mean "a room" (*OED*). By the 1820s, however, the word had three distinct meanings: not just a room, but one in which low goings-on took place; a street, alley, or court, inhabited by people of a low class or by the very poor; loose talk and gypsy language – slang as slum. Charles Dickens was fascinated with London's most notorious slum – that of St. Giles, the site of Hogarth's memorable etching "Gin Lane." The autobiographical fragment published by Dickens's friend John Forster testifies to this childhood fixation: "what wild prodigies of wickedness, want, and beggary, arose in my mind out of that place!" (Schlicke 360). Oliver Twist is inveigled by the Artful Dodger from Islington to Fagin's den in Field Lane. It is a labyrinthine descent symbolizing Oliver's fall from grace: "a dirtier or more wretched place he had never seen" (*Oliver Twist* 102). *Our Mutual Friend* describes the noxious rookeries of Millbank. In one of the crumbling Georgian houses around "blind" Smith Square lives the Doll's dressmaker and her drunken father. The place, Dickens writes, "had a deadly kind of repose on it, more as though it had taken laudanum than fallen onto a natural rest" (*Our Mutual Friend* 221–222). The fictional slum in Dickens's *Bleak House*, Tom-all-alone's, is unlocated, though, as Paul Schlicke observes, "it must be close enough to Chancery Lane and Lincoln's Inn Fields to allow for easy crossings between areas of prosperity to areas of dire deprivation in the novel" (361). Dickens's nightmarish slum is not peripheral but central to the nightmarish metropolis: a dark space of "tumbling tenement," these streets have

> bred a crowd of foul existence that crawls in and out of gaps in walls and boards; and coils itself to sleep, in maggot numbers, where the rain drips in; and comes and goes, fetching and carrying fever, and sowing more evil in its every footprint. (256–257)

As the urban geographer Mike Davis claims dramatically in his popular *Planet of Slums*, for nineteenth-century liberals "the moral dimension was decisive, and the slum was first and above all envisioned as a place where an incorrigible and feral social residuum rots in immoral and often riotous splendour" (22).

From Victorian London to contemporary global cities, the slum poor are routinely shunned and shamed, treated as idle, vicious, and of low worth. The Chicago School's urban theory of human ecology, which has dominated the geographic study of poverty for much of the last century, treats slums as the spatial disruption that undermines the city's intelligibility, autonomy, and inviolability; meanwhile, a Marxist geographer like Mike Davis sees in the urban poor incidences of "informal survivalism" – paradigms of self-employment in the informal and unregulated sector of the urban economy – and violent resistance (178). Yet this moral segregation of the slum from the rest of the city is not historically justifiable. The emergence of a slum like Dharavi in Bombay, for instance, is inseparable from its emergence as a colonial city from seven islands and fishing hamlets. As readers of Salman Rushdie's sensational history in *Midnight's Children* or *The Moor's Last Sigh* know, Bombay passed to the British Crown in 1661, as part of the dowry of the Portuguese princess, Catherine of Braganza, who married Charles II. It was transferred to the East India Company in 1668 but the most accelerated growth happened after 1858, when Bombay reverted to the British Crown and became a port city of consequence. The land between the islands began to be filled up by natural and artificial reclamation to form a long and tapering island city. The best infrastructural resources were reserved for areas where the British lived – the southern part of the island – while the native town extending north and east remained unplanned and poorly serviced. Dharavi was one of the six great *koliwadas*, or fishing communities, of Bombay. With the reclamation of swamps and salt-pan lands, the creek dried up, the fisher-folk left, and the marshes became home to wave after wave of migrant workers: from other parts of Maharashtra and Konkan, Gujarat, as well as Muslim tanners from Tamil Nadu, and embroidery workers from Uttar Pradesh. Entire communities of "illegals" were pushed out of South Bombay to the edge of the city. As Bombay expanded due to the influx of new industries and spilled over into the hinterland in the nineteenth century, Dharavi became more central to the city: "Ironically," Kalpana Sharma observes, "this heart-shaped settlement is now located literally in the heart of Mumbai" (19). Needless to say, the uneven development of this colonial port town continued after independence, which did little "to alter the exclusionary geography of the Raj" (Davis 97). Now the value of the land in Dharavi is estimated to be $3.5 billion, and land grab for this property – masked as environmental or social concerns – gains momentum every day.

Financial powers, backed by the state, push for forcible slum clearance. As David Harvey observes in *Rebel Cities*, though the Indian Constitution mandates that the state must guarantee rights to livelihood, housing, and shelter, the slum dwellers, many of whom are illegal occupants and cannot definitively prove their long-term residence on the land, have no right to compensation (18).

In what follows, I set out to propose a correction to the siting and sighting of the slum, an uncanny infrastructure that is both present and absent in the field of vision. Here, I use the Freudian concept of the "uncanny" in relation to the psychogeography of postcolonial Mumbai. In this definition, the uncanny is a psychological avoidance mechanism that has its dark double in the way visibility is negotiated and manipulated by the colonial infrastructure dominant in global cities. The porosities of the term "slum" – "an informal space outside of, but tightly intertwined with, formal governance institutions and property markets" (Weinstein 45) – lend themselves to the definitional anxiety constitutive of the uncanny: interstice, under-city, leftover space, urban township, tenements, shantytowns, tent cities, shit-holes. The "descriptive vocabulary," haunted still by a Dickensian aggregate of lurid fascination and dread, "loses sight," as Swati Chattopadhyay puts it, "of the political conditions that produce these slums in the present century, revealing a theoretical lag" (*Unlearning the City* xiv). However, this theoretical lag has been generative for new work on the changing urban landscape, drawing in insights from psycho-analysis in particular. Drawing into conversation the work of urban theorists, historians, and geographers, the founding premise of this chapter on slum literature is the representation of the Mumbai slum as an ambigu-ous site of the unconscious, imperfectly structured, and experienced *only* through fantasy. Reading Katherine Boo's *Behind the Beautiful Forevers* and Sonia Faleiro's *Beautiful Thing,* I examine the ways in which these genres of non-, anti-, and aberrational fiction defy the naturalistic and neo-realist documentary style generally associated with humanitarian narratives of urban poverty. These offer embodied and embedded reading practices instead, dismantling the visual culture which sees slums as urban disease.

As Sigmund Freud wrote to his friend, the Hungarian psychoanalyst Sándor Ferenczi, his big idea of "the uncanny" languished in a drawer for some years before he dug out the old paper in 1919 and started to rewrite it. The paper was published in the autumn of 1919, and no one knows when it was originally written or how much it was changed in the intervening period, although a footnote in *Totem and Taboo* shows that the subject was on his mind as early as 1913 (86). Freud scholars like to believe that the passages dealing with the "compulsion to repeat" formed part of the revision. Yet what these passages also repeat are the theories of *Beyond the Pleasure Principle* published a year later, but which Freud speaks of in the "Uncanny" essay as "already completed." *Beyond the Pleasure Principle* is Freud's radical postulation of the death instinct, and its overt and covert redoubling in the "Uncanny" essay darkens and solemnizes the latter. "For my old age," Freud wrote to Lou Andreas-Salome in August 1919, "I have chosen the theme of death" (cited in Hertz 149). He was in fact only 63 and still had some twenty years to go.

The essay "The 'Uncanny'" (1919) begins with professed unease, with Freud not quite at home in this aesthetic territory yet compelled to enter it: "It is only rarely that a psycho-analyst feels impelled to investigate the subject of aesthetics, even when aesthetics is understood to mean not merely the theory of beauty but the theory of the qualities of feeling" (217). The reason he undertakes the project, Freud suggests, has something to do with the freedom of the literary writer, with fiction's prerogative to evoke and inhabit the emotions and phantasms of the reader, and the power to lift or impose censorship. Freud would also write a theory, or even a literary myth, of this power, and he would do so by entering the scene as analyst as well as the neurotic subject of analysis.

Following the introductory remarks in "The 'Uncanny'" is a lexical and etymological analysis of the words *heimlich* (canny) and *unheimlich* (uncanny) and the now well-established assertion that the words are not simply opposites and that the concept of *heimlich* itself is ambivalent and unstable. It signifies the familiar and domestic on the one hand, and the concealed and the hidden on the other. The uncanny, Freud concludes, is not something entirely unknown or unfamiliar: "*Unheimlich* is in some way or other a sub-species of *heimlich*" ("The 'Uncanny'" 226). In Hélène Cixous's reading of the "Uncanny" essay, the words *heimlich* and *unheimlich* themselves come to life as an androgyne. They form a strange dis-identity, joining together, joining themselves, homo- and hetero-, canny and uncanny. It is worth noting that Karl Marx's *Manifesto of the Communist Party* (1848) is occasionally read alongside Freud's "Uncanny" essay for its delineation of capitalist society as a *locus suspectus*, an uncanny space. Marx posits the proletariat as the interior point of what was per-ceived as all exteriority, the hidden core of a seemingly visible and inter-pretable phenomenon – like the slum heart of Mumbai, the proletariat is the contradictory center of bourgeois society. The manifesto could be said to work like an uncanny aesthetic, bringing to light what ought to have remained secret and hidden. In *Specters of Marx*, Derrida uses Marx as a figure of uncanny haunting: "No disavowal has managed to rid itself of all of Marx's ghosts . . . Haunting belongs to the structure of every hegemony" (37). Read in this light, the uncanny is more a hauntology than a unified ontology – a bulwark, as Martin Jay observes, "against the dangerous temptations of conjuring away plural specters in the name of the redeemed whole" (24).

For Freud, the source of the uncanny is tied to the idea of being robbed of one's eyes. Here Freud turns to the clinical experience of the psychoanalyst: in dreams, myths, and neurotic fantasies, the fear of the loss of eyes seems to hide another, that of castration. In E. T. A. Hoffman's short story, "The Sandman," Freud observes, Coppelius, the "bad" father, interferes with all love relationships. He is the powerful, castrating father who supplants (kills) the good father who first protects Nathaniel's "eyes." By means of this father figure, castration is fixed and made visible, representable: all other repetitions, doublings, and splittings in the narrative are related to the self-same meaning of this composite father figure. In this literary case study, it is the castration complex as part of our infantile sexuality (genital phase) that is re-invoked by the fear of loss of the eyes. But what do those of us spared from castration anxiety make of this theory? According to Cixous, the meaning of the uncanny is "No-meaning," rather than the fear of castration:

> It is this *no-other-meaning* (*Keine andere Bedeitung*) which presents itself anew (despite our wish to outplay it) in the infinite game of substitutions, through which what constitutes the elusive moment of fear returns and eclipses itself again. This dodging from fear to fear, this "mask" that masks nothing, this merry-go-round of fear that leads to fear "is" the unthinkable secret. (26)

The uncanny is the instantiation of ontological nothingness, an agitation, a repercussion, and a movement from fear to fear without telos. "Castration complex" is the provisional term that explains the formation of identity in the field of vision: what we see, or don't see, strange unveilings and revelations. The apparatus of television, telescope, and spyglass deployed in "The Sandman" signals the activation of a predominantly optical imaginary.

In a powerful variation of Cixous's argument, Anneleen Masschelein states that:

> Like other Freudian concepts, the uncanny is a lexical concept, i.e. it is borrowed from natural language. Although Freud and numerous scholars after him have stressed that the German word "unheimlich" is

untranslatable qua form and content, more or less the same feeling can be expressed by words such as "creepy," "eerie," "weird".... Affects are, as Freud points out, highly subjective, but they are also objective in the sense that they are recognizable across different cultures and ages, independent of the words used to categorize them. Likewise, the theoretical concept of "the uncanny" refers to a construct or compound of ideas that is not necessarily limited to the word. (7)

As a concept that at the same time signifies its opposite, "the uncanny" asks the reader *both* to pare away associations to reach a burning core of meaning *and* to "expand in a horizontal, rhizomatic network of sidetracks and creative new applications of the concept ... in which associative patterns proliferate" (Masschelein 14).

The displacement of meaning associated with the uncanny's operations has had purchase for urban geography and contemporary architecture. Anthony Vidler, for instance, sees in the uncanny "a significant psycho-analytical and aesthetic response to the real shock of the modern":

> Estrangement and unhomeliness have emerged as the intellectual watch-words of our [twentieth] century, given periodic material and political force by the resurgence of homelessness itself, a homelessness generated some-times by war, sometimes by the unequal distribution of wealth. (9)

Vidler readily concedes that, faced with real homelessness, "any reflection on the 'transcendental' or psychological unhomely risks trivializing or, worse, patronizing political or social action" (13). The uncanny, however, is an unsettling concept that undermines the distinction between the metaphorical and the real, he argues. Postindustrial, post-teleological modernity, from the late nineteenth century to the present, throws up many correlates of the political uncanny for Vidler: postwar aesthetics; deserted spaces attached to bankrupt businesses; the heterogeneous crowds of a Baudelairean city; the internal limit of the Western nation posited by the arrival of the migrant and the exile. The architectural uncanny he invokes in this work is a composite of historical, psychoanalytic, and cultural analyses: "If actual buildings and spaces are interpreted through this lens, it is not because they themselves possess uncanny properties, but rather because they act, historically or culturally, as representations of estrangement" (12).

Swati Chattopadhyay draws on Vidler's discussion of the uncanny as a psychological phenomenon whereby an "original authenticity, a first burial" (*Representing Calcutta* 27) is made more potent by virtue of a return of the repressed that is out of time and out of place. She proposes that we treat the sense of the uncanny "not as an aesthetic strategy, but as an unexpected outcome of the *process of representation*" that informs the gamut of colonial publications from paintings in the Picturesque style to health maps (33). She offers as an example the Calcutta diaries of the Englishwoman Elizabeth Campbell, who traveled to the city with her husband from England in 1827 and felt a shudder of morbidity on seeing the effect of the rains on the buildings:

> The Venetian windows rot and fall out, the white or yellow walls become blackened and seem like houses destroyed by fire – the resting-place for birds and beasts of prey. The fearful familiarity of the former almost startles you. (cited in Chattopadhyay, *Representing Calcutta* 32)

A reflection initiated by the strangeness of the environment in Kolkata turns fearful not through the alienness of the image, but through the atavistic instinct it evinces. The shock of seeing Venetian windows or neoclassical architecture in the swamps of Calcutta or stumbling upon abandoned English gravestones while admiring picturesque Indian ruins, generates feelings of the uncanny in Campbell. Chattopadhyay correctly identifies "a barely concealed tropical anxiety" (33) in the use of the aesthetic modality of the picturesque in descriptions of colonial Calcutta (and India, in general). The uncanny sensation arises in the gap between the idea of India and the embodied experience of it, between the imperative need for representational mastery and the incommensurate representational apparatus at hand.

If the colonial uncanny is associated with traumatic realizations about the sinister or out-of-place nature of the colonial enterprise, the postcolonial uncanny is also about repeated failures to secure a vantage point from which to articulate cogently what Chattopadhyay calls "a landscape of difference" in her 2012 work, *Unlearning the City* (32). This anxiety manifests itself powerfully in the bird's-eye view or the master shot conferring visual and cognitive control on the chaotic conditions of slum life, whether it is a critically acclaimed *National Geographic* photograph of Dharavi, or the aerial images of melded corrugated rooftops of slums in populist "world cinema" such as Boyle's *Slumdog Millionaire*. Chattopadhyay explains further:

> Such bird's-eye views of slums, designed to capture the vast scale of urban problems in the third world, is a familiar trope to a cosmopolitan audience by virtue of the repeated use of such imagery in the popular media, from the pages of the *National Geographic* to *CNN News* and Google Maps. Such views translate the specificities of the habitations of the

marginalized in Nairobi, Rio, or Mumbai into a general pattern, thus
formulating a convenient equation between widely discrepant habitations
and historical productions. Their effectiveness, as a tool in the dominant
order of representation, resides in their ability to convey the composite
image of many small iterations as a totality: comprehension of the
counters of a vast disorder appears veritably fantastic. It is a view that
only the planner and the global consumer can have access to, and not the
dweller in the slum. (41)

The mastery, in other words, lies in making an illusory whole out of
misappropriated, decontextualized synecdoches. The violence of slum
infrastructure is adumbrated again in the planner's and global consumer's
bird's-eye view of the slums, testifying to the collusion of colonial, neocolonial, and neoliberal forces in the creation of vulnerable habitations. But is
there a way of looking, reading, and representing otherwise: a horizontal
paratactic, rather than the vertical telescopic view? And, by what other
name could we call the slum?

What Is "Beautiful"?

The value of literature, for Martha Nussbaum, lies in its possibility of
a civic or "compassionate imagination" (*Cultivating Humanity* 92), enabling a transcendence of social boundaries and ethnic nationalism through
the cultivation of sympathetic understanding. A recent crop of narrative
nonfiction works on urban India, all three with "beautiful" in the title,
testifies to this through different strategies: Boo's *Behind the Beautiful
Forevers* (2012), Siddhartha Deb's *The Beautiful and the Damned* (2011),
and Faleiro's *Beautiful Thing* (2011). If, as Gavin Jones observes, "poverty is
always intertwined with conventional literary categories such as natural-
ism, documentary realism, and autobiography" (xiv), each of these texts
pushes against the limits of these categories in the way it plays with
proximity and intimacy with the objects of inquiry. Exposing the multiple
speeds and temporalities of global megacities like Mumbai and Delhi, these
docu-novels examine the destitute as what Dipesh Chakrabarty calls "the
figure of difference that governmentality ... all over the world has to
subjugate and civilize" (56), and the figure of the nonhuman "open."
I now turn to Boo and Faleiro in some detail to show how these nonfiction
narratives, written in the decade following *Slumdog Millionaire*, also question the social purpose of the novel form, with its generic commitment to
class mobility, the redistribution of wealth and justice, and its historical
fidelity to equivocal forms of national belonging.

The February 2012 *New York Times* review of Boo's *Behind the Beautiful Forevers* describes it as a "true version of *Slumdog Millionaire* without the happy ending."[10] The title of the piece, "An Outsider Gives Voice to Slumdogs," seems to suggest "slumdog" was now common parlance, a curious move since it also acknowledges Boo's scathing critique of the Danny Boyle movie in an article which can be treated as the ur-text of *Behind the Beautiful Forevers*. Boo was a staff writer at the *New Yorker* when she wrote "Opening Night: The Scene from the Airport Slums," alluding to the Mumbai première of the blockbuster. In it, she describes the familiar landscape of class apartheid in India, here manifested in the insurmountable divide between Gautam Nagar, one of the thirty or so Mumbai slums squatting on land owned by the Airport Authority of India, and the international terminal, ringed by five-star hotels.

> The hotels charge two hundred to a thousand dollars a night and are enclosed by high walls and barbed-wire fences, so their interactions with Gautam Nagar are primarily airborne. Music from weddings and poolside parties drifts over. Ash from cow-dung and wood fire drifts back.[11]

The airborne connection stands for the intangible relations between adjacent yet antagonistic worlds: old, new, suspended, and cancelled Indias; high-net-worth and negative-net-worth individuals; the global (American) economy and a street urchin playing *Metal Slug 3* at Anna's[12] game parlor for 1 rupee a go. Sunil – one of the two Sunils Boo will dedicate the 2012 book to – is a 13-year-old boy with no academic prospects. His mother's premature death had qualified him for a private school for poor and orphaned children run by a Catholic charity, but he "played too much ... or studied too little," dropping out soon after. The missed opportunity rankles in his mind even as he calls the nun "Sister Paulette-Toilet" under his breath when he sees her in her chauffeured van, on the lookout for more promising slum children than he. Like others in his vicinity, he had been registered for classes at the local government school, but like most of the other boys and girls he had sold his school supplies for money, returning to work. "They needed rupees more than the pencil boxes," Boo quietly observes. Like the mini scavengers of *Slumdog Millionaire*, Sunil is a garbage collector, which means he forages through waste to find items of value to sell to those in the recycling trade. The downturn in the American economy had forced him into becoming a metal thief at the international airport.

In *Pen of Iron*, Robert Alter comments on Hemingway's use of parataxis for conveying a "disillusioned and unsentimental" sense of the harsh world.

> Instead of representing the world through a syntax that was a vehicle of
> qualification, analysis, and temporal, spatial, and evaluative
> complication ... he showed how unadorned sequences of parallel
> utterances ... could intimate strong feelings and fraught relation-
> ships. (162)

Boo is a master of the "paratactic rendering of introspection" that Alter
examines in relation to postwar American authors such as Hemingway or,
more recently, Marilynne Robinson (169). Her language is sparse and terse,
while narrative details abound, reminiscent of the "large gaps of motive,
feeling, intention, and meaning" Alter detects in paratactic style (159).
Morbidity, which contaminates everything in a slum named after the
8-year-old son of a scavenger who died of pneumonia after a routine
slum demolition, moves freely in this space and in familiar guises: domestic
violence, suicide, unsanitary density, malnutrition, addiction, epidemics.
While neither this article nor *Behind the Beautiful Forevers* is about mental
illness as such, Boo challenges the health paradigms that disaggregate
common mental disorders (CMDs) from common unhappiness.[13] Sunil's
favorite qualifier, when he wants to brag about work to other game-parlor
boys, is "daily": his milieu is daily acts of theft and larceny; daily "being
high" on Erase-X, the Indian version of Wite-Out; regular suicide
attempts; run-of-the-mill instances of parents trying to sell a pretty daughter into prostitution.

> While Sunil was prying tire locks from the wheels of autorickshaws, the
> woman had tried to hang herself from a ceiling fan. Someone cut her
> down. She was fine. This was dull gossip for a day at Gautam Nagar, and
> the boys did not dwell on it. Instead, they returned to Anna's, compared
> the goods found that day, and gauged which boy had displayed the most
> daring.

We learn little about the Tamil woman who tried to kill herself except that
her husband had sold the family hut in the course of a four-day binge. "She
was fine" after someone cut her down just in time.

Later in the piece, Sunil stands by Abdul, a 20-year-old Muslim scrap
dealer, overhearing his musings to a friend:

> "Like that woman who just went to hang herself, or her husband, who
> probably beat her before she did this?" Abdul said. "I wonder what kind of
> life is that – I go through tensions just to see the kind of life they're living.
> But it is a life."

There is dissociation here as well as identification: "I wonder what kind of
life is that" and "it is a life." Abdul says his mother warned him not to think

of "such terrible lives" when he shared this philosophical reflection with her halfway through a beating. The children cope with catastrophes through willed acts of forgetting. Boo writes about the death of a boy called Deepak, a death Sunil's reconnoitering for German silver (meaning aluminum, nickel, and other metals) was instrumental in causing. Deepak had been ordered by Sunil to "Go in, get that" from a compound and had been arrested: daring though he was, he was not as fast as Sunil or as alert, his mind foggy with Erase-X in this instance. The security guards gouged out his eyes and ripped a smile in his asshole with a sickle before flinging the body over the wall. This is filed away as an unspeakable thing, like dead mothers and lost children: "no one mentioned Deepak after dark. Invoking the name of any dead person after sunset increased the likelihood that his ghost would come back and haunt you."

Boo's austere self-negation as witness to these unfurling scenes functions not just to present Sunil with maximum visceral and psychological immediacy. She is not simply trying to heighten empathy and compassion in middle-class readers but straining to show us what might still be beautiful in a blighted life, or how sanity may be clung on to by those fated to endure the terrible unreason of Indian poverty. In a scene describing Sunil's visit to a construction site for strips of aluminum, we see the boy feeling momentarily free and acting his (excitable, young) age on the rooftop. He revels at the gift of height (four storys) and open space, "a rarity in his city of something like sixteen million people."

> He liked the red-tailed Air India planes flying out, and the municipal water tower with its red and white squares. He liked seeing the glow of the Hyatt sign, and trying to guess which of the dark patches underneath was Gautam Nagar. But what he liked seeing most were the people moving in and out of the terminal.... Seeing the moving people from up high made him feel close to them. He felt free to study how they did things in a way he couldn't when he was on the ground.

Arguably, Boo is using artistic license to imagine the workings of Sunil's mind, flush with a little loot and unimpeded by a Nepali watchman, in this serendipitous moment on the roof. The vantage point is not the "bird's eye view of slums" Chattopadhyay talks about earlier, the proprietary gaze of the planner and global consumer. He is telescopically connecting to his estranged social superiors in a way not allowable in life and on the ground: "There, if he stared, they would see him staring."

These beautiful moments are contrasted in "Opening Night" with the "beautified" people gathering for the theatrical launch of *Slumdog*

Millionaire. The glittering center of the city, Boo observes, not breaking character yet, is also the site of the "cat-infested t.b. sanatorium where his [Sunil's] mother and neighbors had been treated before they died." Later, she ponders the reasons why the British film might not be "universally admired" in India, as evidenced in lawsuits and effigy burnings to protest against the comparison of human beings with dogs. Educated, affluent Indians disliked the film too, Boo notes, because they thought it slighted "the increasing affluence and prominence" of their booming economy. The West does tend to fetishize the Indian poor, Boo concedes, even when the poverty rate had fallen from 36 to 27 percent in a decade. However, it wasn't simply national pride that made prosperous India skeptical of *Slumdog*-type representations of the squalid postcolony: the jitters, Boo reckons, came from a deepening alienation with the very city the gated properties had sought to segregate and protect themselves from. What if a denizen of this unseen outlying city realized, one fateful day, that "a shot of rare Scotch consumed in ten minutes at the Sheraton's ITC Maratha cost exactly as much as he earned in seven hundred fourteen-hour days picking up aluminum cans and used tampon applicators" ("Opening Night")?

Behind the Beautiful Forevers is a correction of the illusion, perpetuated by movies such as *Slumdog Millionaire*, that a child's perilous trajectory through slum life could provide the very tools for its overcoming. While Sunil, had he seen the movie "that ends with an airport-slum boy finding money, love, and fame," would have probably agreed with the movie's conceit that deprivation gives one street smarts, the other conceit "was the lie" ("Opening Night"). This is not to say *Behind the Beautiful Forevers* is defeated or defeatist. In fact, as its concluding Author's Note claims, *Behind the Beautiful Forevers* attacks the image of slum dwellers as "mythic," "passive," and "pathetic" (249). Boo, a Pulitzer prize-winning investigative journalist, who spent four years in the Annawadi slum of Mumbai, says she wanted to "honour their experience and their complexity" so that "readers could make a connection that was more blooded and sophisticated than that of pity" ("Q&A with Katherine"). Instead of viewing Annawadi, a squatter slum located between the Mumbai International Airport and the five-star airport hotels, as negative space, she shows how it is the liminal, interstitial quality of this endangered space that allows it to thrive. From the "smogged-out, prosperity driven obstacle course up there in the over-city . . . wads of possibility tumbled down to the slums" (xii). If the subjugated race, as Albert Memmi argues, usually bears "the mark of the plural," forever condemned to an "anonymous collectivity" (129), here we have singular lives: Abdul, Fatima, Zehrunisa, Sunil, Kalu, Meena, Manju, Asha. If "Opening Night" revolved around a Hindu boy, Sunil, here a Muslim youth of indeterminate age called Abdul is the life to be documented: the two friends are not interchangeable ciphers, and Boo tenaciously engages with the subcultures of religion and community that define and differentiate each. Annawadi is shown to be a reclaimed space, solid land summoned from a bog – "a snake-filled brushland across the street from the urban terminal" (*Beautiful Forevers* 3) – by migrant Tamil workers. And, despite their habitat being used as a waste bin by the upper city, the inhabitants find ways to turn bog into land and 8,000 tons of garbage into "vendible excess" (xii). If the colonial maps of Bombay showed slums as dark patches marked by "ZP" (*jhopadpatti*, or slums), Boo's narrative eloquently follows the "broken-toothed, profit-minded Santas [who] darted after crumpled cigarette packs tossed from cars with tinted windows [and] dredged sewers and raided dumpsters" (xii).[14]

The spatial diffusion and extensiveness of global markets and media give rise to a sense of belonging to a borderless, shared world, when the reality is that such developments lead instead to greater polarization and division of nations and regions. The slum Boo writes about is, once again, located near Mumbai's international airport. Unlike the Gautam Nagar of "Opening Night" (which turns out to be a particular section of Annawadi), the phenomenological border in this space is not between the slumdogs and the lucky 1 percent in the five-star hotels that loom over Annawadi, but within Annawadi itself, a slum community comprised mostly of migrants fleeing a crisis-ridden agricultural sector only to find themselves as the surplus of cheap labor in Mumbai. "For every two people in Annawadi inching up, there was one in a catastrophic plunge" (24). True to Mike Davis's characterization of the divisions between "the more advantaged poor," the poor, and the "poorest of the poor" (43), the struggle unto death in Annawadi is between the poorer and the poorest. Abdul Husain, a key character in the narrative, gains his sense of upward mobility by contrasting his lot with that of less fortunate neighbors, those miserable souls "who trapped rats and frogs and fried them for dinner," or "ate the scrub grass at the sewage lake's edge" (6). It is the construction of a solid wall between two hovels by Abdul's family that precipitates the calamity that destroys both families. One-legged Fatima, Abdul's belligerent neighbor, spitefully sets herself on fire. The protest comes to nothing and does not better the life of Fatima by falsely implicating her neighbors in criminal activity, as she had intended. A small crowd gathers but does nothing. "The adults drifted back to their dinners, while a few boys waited to see if Fatima's face would come off" (70). Trying to take Fatima to the hospital, her husband finds himself rebuffed by autorickshaw drivers, worried about the potential damage to seat covers. The poor, Boo writes, "blame one another for the choices of governments and markets" (254), and she documents, with unsentimental intimacy, how the poor compete with and undermine one another whilst the remainder of one of the world's most unequal cities soldiers on in relative peace.

The "beautiful" of the book's title refers to a hoarding over a concrete wall that repetitively uses the words "beautiful" and "forever" to advertise Italianate tiles, and that conceals the sprawl of the shantytown from view of the international traffic shuttling up and down the airport road. As usual, the slum poor are peripheral to the existence of the city, the surplus population utterly deprived of social goods or services despite providing the labor critical to the functioning of the service sector in advanced and growing economies. Boo's third-person fictional narrative forgoes the first-person perspective, as before, to privilege historical figures with no voice or agency in their own life dramas. This technique informs Boo's portrayal of Abdul, who sells the trash of Mumbai's rich to recycling plants for profit. "People have learned to respond in creative ways to the indifference of the state – including having to set up a highly functional recycling industry that serves the whole city," Echanove and Srivastava argue in "Taking the Slum out of 'Slumdog.'" However, despite the fact that it was "a fine time to be a Mumbai garbage trader" (6), Abdul wants to escape an identity indistinguishable from the trash he sells – "some called him garbage, and left him at that" (6) – and dreams of not only survival but full civic participation. "He wanted to be better than what he was made of. In Mumbai's dirty water, he wanted to be ice" (218).

Behind the Beautiful Forevers captures a moment in Annawadi's history when its inhabitants dared to dream of a better life, "as if fortune were a cousin arriving on Sunday, as if the future would look nothing like the past" (11). Despite only 6 of the 3,000 people living in the slum having permanent jobs, this was a time of economic liberalization, and the informal, unorganized economy of Annawadi was not only managing to stay alive, but wanted more. Abdul's brother dreamed of working in uniform at a luxury hotel; Asha wanted to be a slumlord; Meena wanted freedom, not the drudgery of an arranged marriage; Sunil (yes, the main character of "Opening Night") wanted to eat enough to start growing; One Leg, a.k.a. Fatima, wanted to be seen and desired despite her crippled body. Zehrunisa, Abdul's mother, dreamed of a hygienic home, a shelf on which to cook "without rat intrusions," a small window to vent the cooking smoke "that caused the little ones to cough like their father," and ceramic tiles on the floor "like the ones advertised on the Beautiful Forever wall" (62). The advertisement is a fitting façade of what Ashis Nandy calls the doctrine of "secular salvation" (*Intimate Enemy* x), the visual bait to a good life legitimizing the greed and violence of urbanization. Zehrunisa wanted "tiles that could be scrubbed clean, instead of the broken concrete which harbored filth in each striation" (82). Abdul himself, a Muslim of "garbage-related provenance" (22), wanted to leave the slum for a home in Vasai, outside Mumbai, where Muslim recyclers had a sizable community, and for which he had paid an installment. "If life and global markets kept going their way, they would soon be landowners, not squatters, in a place where Abdul was pretty sure no one would call him garbage" (23). Their dreams turn to dust in the wasteland behind the wall. Abdul and his family are falsely incriminated by Fatima. Even if she hadn't done so, he would inevitably be raided by the local police officers, who would extort money for his thriving unlicensed business, a bribe which would not ensure any protection. The devastating truth was that "to be poor in Annawadi, or in any Mumbai slum, was to be guilty of one thing or another" (12).

Boo does not extrapolate from the short-lived insouciance of characters like Abdul, Zehrunisa, or Fatima a polemic about the moral resources of the most resource-poor. Her task here is to make the unintelligible life recognizable, if not intelligible.[15] An unforgettable section of the book is where Fatima – irrepressible, impossible One Leg, cuckolding wife, and bad mother who looked gender and disability prejudices in the eye, and who had set herself on fire as a stupid stunt – loses her unique voice.

> "The neighbor family set me on fire," Fatima told her mother, and then she told a different story of what had happened, and the mother became confused. Fatima was confused herself by now, and didn't want to explain it all over again. Her job was to heal (104).

There is no healing in store for Fatima, we know, and ignominious life ends in ignominious death in a public hospital. The duty doctor reuses her soiled bandages, (free) medicine is out of stock at Cooper Hospital, and the nurses avoid touching patients to apply soothing burn cream. She is asked to hydrate but her husband can no longer afford bottles of mineral water after spending borrowed money to buy the ointment. A thumbprint coerced from the dying woman by Poornima Paikrao, Special Executive Officer of the government of Maharashtra, validates a drastically revised victim statement. In the absence of incriminating evidence against the

Husains, the statement now reads like a suicide note, allowing the police authorities to extract money from the Husains, named in the document, for incitement to suicide.

> Fatima's file was tied up in red string and sent to the records room of the morgue, where feral dogs slept among the towering stacks of folders on the floor, and birdsong came through the window. A flock of spotted doves had colonized a palm tree outside, the *croo-croo-croo* of one bird overlapping the call of another. (114)

This is an extraordinary passage in an overwhelmingly extraordinary work. The red string speaks to the banal red-tape-ism and bureaucracy which carry out violent genocides. The overlapping bird calls, the stacks of unread folders on the floor, the unclaimed lives of the bodies in the morgue in Boo's paratactic style add up to the tonal flatness of post-grief states. Nothing new is expounded here, followed by explanatory clauses. As we have come to expect, the state exculpates itself every day through rewriting the deaths of its poorest wards. When Fatima dies of an infection, the doctor changes the record to avoid culpability: 95 percent burns instead of the 35 percent that covered her body upon admission. When Kalu is found murdered outside Air India's red-and-white gates, his eyes gouged out and a sickle up his ass, the inspector in charge, in collusion with Cooper Hospital pathologists, declares it a death from TB as photos of the corpse vanish from the files at Sahar station. The body of a well-known scavenger is declared "unidentified" by police and sold off as cadaver to B. M. Patil Medical College in Bijapur. Sanjay Shetty's desperate suicide, which follows the terror of his witnessing Kalu's murder, is registered as a heroin death.

If the narrative mode of "Opening Night" was free indirect discourse, *Behind the Beautiful Forevers* combines it with immersive reportage. To optimally convey the plot twists of these obscure lives, to bear testimony to subjects who work silently, sorting trash, for most of their lives, Boo attempts the impossible task of representation as presentation. As she has said in interviews, she resists metaphorical appropriation or the allegorizing impulse when it comes to representing the poor.

> I've been waiting years to run into a representative person. Sadly, all I ever meet are individuals ... [and] qualities that transcend specificities of geography, culture, religion, caste, or class. My hope, at the keyboard, is to portray these individuals in their complexity – allow them not to be Representative Poor Persons – so that readers might find some other point of emotional purchase, a connection more blooded than pity.[16]

Boo captures this complexity by means of an almost mechanical transcrip-
tion of the voice, or the unscripted voice consciousness, of subaltern figures
like Abdul. This difficult feat is achieved by cross-checking the parapher-
nalia of written notes, audio tapes, video recordings, photographs, and
hundreds of interviews with thousands of public records, and a team of
translators.

> When I describe the thoughts of individuals in the preceding pages, these
> thoughts have been related to me and my translators, or to others in our
> presence. When I sought to grasp, retrospectively, a person's thinking at
> a given moment . . . I used paraphrase. Abdul and Sunil, for instance, had
> previously spoken little about their lives and feelings, even to their own
> families. I came to my understanding of their thoughts by pressing them in
> repeated (they would say endless) conversations and fact-checking inter-
> views, often while they worked. (Author's Note 250)

With overworked people, especially boys like Abdul or Sunil who spent
the bulk of their days working silently with waste, "everyday language
tended to be transactional," Boo states (250). Besides imagining interior
monologues to personalize her case studies, Boo chronicles symptoms of
the insidious trauma suffered by the Annawadians. In a brilliant "Freud in
the slums" scene, Manju, daughter of the slumlord Asha, and pipped to be
the first female college graduate to emerge from the slum, copes with her
life by "by-hearting [learning by rote] her psychology notes," and practis-
ing the textbook denial they teach. "Young men have mostly ambitious
wishes. Young women have mostly erotic ones. The ordinary person feels
ashamed of his fantasies and hides them" (179). She blocks out painful
subjects like her corrupt, ruthless mother, and a failed love affair. Boo
prides herself on being present on the scene at the time of events, or
reporting them soon afterward, for slum dwellers could change their
testimony under pressure from the police. She notes also how
"Annawadians rearranged narratives for psychological solace: giving themselves, in retrospect, more control over an experience than they had had at
the time" (252). Their relationship is impersonal yet mutually trusting: the
populace warms to her, Boo thinks, because of her concern about the
distribution of opportunity in twenty-first-century India. And, "When
I wasn't dredging up bad memories, they liked me fine" (253).

Sonia Faleiro's "notebook-pencil" approach to reporting is different
from Boo's obsessive audio and video recordings, but she too treats her
three years shadowing her subject as "research." In circumstances involving
risky social interactions where she was not able to take notes, "I wrote an

obsessive amount when I returned home."[17] The journalist Faleiro's *Beautiful Thing* (2011) traces the entangled lives of bar dancers, bar owners, sex workers, transvestites and transsexuals (also known as *hijra*), pimps, gangsters, and the police. Faleiro befriended a young bar dancer for intimate access to the netherworld of Bombay's dance bars. "Only she could teach me what I wanted to know," says Faleiro of Leela, the native informant seven years younger than she: "the truth about a world that fascinated me, intimidated me, and as I came to know it better, left me feeling frustrated and hopeless" (6). A sassy, devil-may-care bar dancer at the Night Lovers club, Leela is a *picaro*-figure who has escaped conditions of grinding poverty, domestic violence, and sexual exploitation in her hometown. The narrative charts her financial ruination and descent into dangerous sex-trading, traversing the run-down but middle-class neighborhood of Mumbai's Mira Road through to the dangerous slum settlement of Cheetah Camp in Trombay, waving off Leela as she embarks on the perilous journey across the Arabian Sea to the Dubai underworld.

Beautiful Thing, in the writing of which Faleiro conducted "hundreds of interviews across Bombay" (224), is about two nations, the Bombay rich and the Bombay poor. While Faleiro hails from South Bombay, with its heady mix of old money and new money, regal colonial relics and aspirational cafés that bake thirty kinds of fudge brownies, her new friend lives where "there were no domes, no pillars, no sushi restaurants" (7). Leela and her co-workers, who bring in hundreds – sometimes thousands – of rupees every night, cannot be classified as the Bombay poor or the Indian poor, but their livelihoods are hazardous and their lives perishable. While the bar dancer is higher in the street hierarchy than, say, the street prostitute or the waiters of "silent bars" (where drinks come with hand-jobs), the income of even the highest-paid worker in Night Lovers amounts to very little. Once the bar owner, landlord, police, pimp, drug peddler and folks back home – in Leela's case, the parents who had sold her virginity to the local police to punish her for refusing to make pornographic movies – have taken their cuts, there is hardly anything left for the bar dancers. Bar workers are, therefore, frequently forced to sell sex to supplement income, a choice often accompanied by the forlorn hope of finding a rescuer in the sea of punters, someone who will whisk them away to the suburbs or Dubai, as in the Hindi movies.[18] Faleiro also sheds light on the plight of the transgender sex workers, who are plagued by the high mortality rates of shoddy castrations, paid less than half their cis female counterparts (200 rupees for every 500 rupees a cis female sex worker would demand for a "shot" or a sexual service), and twice as likely to be violently beaten or raped. "Bijniss" (business) is neither safe nor steady, and turns downright dangerous after the Bombay Police Act of 2005 banned performances in all establishments rated three stars or less. Needless to say, dancing continued in high-end luxury hotels even after the Police Act. Additionally, there is the ever-present threat of sexually transmitted diseases, HIV in particular.

Faleiro's testimony enjoins us to rethink the lexicon and temporality of trauma and its cure. "The limited experiences of the line [profession] and the extreme nature of these experiences – adult, violent, sexual, and highly stressful – created a lonely and lasting trauma that made bar dancers feel constantly vulnerable" (118), she writes. The psychic malady that *Beautiful Thing* anatomizes is not post-traumatic stress disorder (PTSD) but continuous traumatic stress (CTS), marked by a daily exposure to violence and trauma and an absence of safe places to escape from danger or threat. CTS was first proposed by anti-apartheid mental health activists in the context of the political violence and state oppression of 1980s South Africa, and revived in the scholarship of South African clinical psychologists, especially Gillian Eagle and Debra Kaminer. Trauma exposure in the dancers of Mira Road or sex workers of Kamathipura cannot be decisively located in the past, although each of the characters has had a traumatized childhood: trauma is concurrent and to be anticipated for the near future. Clinical or social interventions into these modalities of traumatic stress are often very difficult to achieve, giving another meaning – that of an interminable process – to the descriptor "continuous."

Faleiro carefully notes the symptoms of traumatic states without trying to frame diagnostically these with the label of "disorder": Priya, Leela's best friend and fellow bar dancer, is literate but refuses to read; Leela tries to expunge images of dead babies in trash cans, abandoned by hapless young mothers, which had she convinced herself at the time were hallucinations. The girls talk about gang rape as if it were a professional hazard, feigning deafness to Faleiro's well-meaning suggestion of a rape counselor. Leela exhibits conditions of pathological bondage to persecutory figures like the married bar owner (and her lover) Shetty, stimulated no doubt by her forced interaction with, and dependence upon, such a person. With CTS, the temporal focus of therapy shifts from the past (and after-effects of past trauma) to the present, and the ongoing effects of traumatization. The task in these cases, as Eagle and Kaminer would argue, "is to prepare for future traumatization and to develop the ability to discriminate between stimuli that might pose a real, immediate, or substantial threat from other every-day stimuli" (91).

Faleiro's *Beautiful Thing* is a realistic appraisal of the prolonged and ongoing psychic violence faced by the precariat of the metropolitan sex industry. Refusing the lure of an accusatory narrative that pits victims against perpetrators, Faleiro exposes the infrastructure of economic exploitation and the perpetuation of a permanent underclass instead. Her self-positioning is not unlike that of an analyst perfecting her tactics of listening: "Although I was shaken by their stories, I tried never to be discouraging. Sometimes it felt that simply by listening I was helping out" (104). Faleiro has spoken in a *New York Times* interview about her father entering national politics when she was very young: "I saw up close how people with power are treated in India. That early experience of privilege is pretty much why I write about the poor. If I can make their voices heard, I will." If there's one misconception she tries to dismantle, it's that the poor are defined by their poverty. Strongly echoing Boo's view on the subject, she comments that "people seem to believe the poor are one-dimensional":

> [It is as though] they don't lead lives as rounded and complex as those who are better off, [as buoyed by dreams,] as rich with plans, ideas and humor. Poverty is a wretched thing, and being poor has enormous implications on every aspect of a person's life, but there's much more to the average poor man or woman in India than just their poverty.[19]

Faleiro admires from afar the affinities that bind together the mixed and multicultural community of bar dancers and sex workers, and works hard to gain its confidences. At a birthday party in Bombay's most notorious red-light district, she lets the *hijras* sit close to her, stroke her hair, peek into her blouse: "That night, the pinching and prodding by Maya (one of the eunuchs) and her friends made me feel on the in" (103). The girls treat her like a paparazzo, asking her to take snapshots of special moments when they are not taunting her for what they see as her unrelenting will to know: "Come, come. Have your fun. Take foto" (98). These moments act as the text's traumatic core, lying outside the sharable codes of the official text, comprised of the investigative journalist's notes and interviews: there are no photographs in either the book or the webpage devoted to *Beautiful Thing*. In sharp contrast to Boo's willed absenting of herself from the diegetic plot, the critical or analytical distance between Faleiro and her objects of inquiry is slowly obliterated in the course of the project. The author weeps, frets, scolds, curses, and finally mourns. Cognition in *Beautiful Thing* becomes increasingly non-verbal and embodied, the

affective charge lending a mythic intensity to Faleiro's realistic representation of banal and brutal events.

Affects, Fredric Jameson reminds us in *The Antinomies of Realism*, are
bodily feelings, different from the category of "emotions" in that they are
not conscious states or sensory perceptions that can be captured in language. Emotions have objects and can therefore be named, while affect is
a bodily argot. By positing emotion as the binary opposite of affect per se,
Jameson says he is insisting on "the resistance of affect to language, and
thereby on the new representational tasks it poses poets and novelists in the
effort somehow to seize its fleeting essence and to force its recognition"
(31). Evocatively, third and first persons merge confusedly in the final
section of *Beautiful Thing*. Leela, the bar dancer, is flying to the Middle
East in search of a better life, and Faleiro is her unlikely chauffeur to the
airport. Their voices merge indistinguishably as the narrative rages, outside
quotation marks, against the pimp, "Sharma," who has facilitated this trip
to Dubai's sex industry: "He was a khabru, a cunt, a failed crossing away
from being a chamar chor" (Faleiro 222). Faleiro's depiction of this charged
scene reveals both her momentary identification with and irrevocable
estrangement from Leela's life, displaying what Jameson calls the "antinomies" of the realist mode, wherein affect militates against and sometimes
defeats the seductions of narrative. *Beautiful Thing* perfectly captures the
social worker's or investigative journalist's sense of immobilized terror
when faced with victims subject to situations of prolonged and ongoing
danger. The narrative succumbs to Faleiro's melancholic sense of the
futility of preventive and curative measures in the situations of endemic
poverty and sexual violence she details.

Boo's "beautiful account" (to quote Amartya Sen's endorsement on the
book's cover) of the precarious and the powerless in urban India is similarly
chastened by her stark realization of the easy disposability of such lives and
dreams. The delusion Annawadians tended to succumb to was that "a
difficult-to-raze house increased the odds that a family's tenure on airport
land would be acknowledged by the relocation authorities" (Boo, *Beautiful
Forevers* 89). In reality, the upward-mobility narrative of these slum dwellers promises no social or economic betterment: more often than not, it is
a bleak, pathetic account of how they invest their meager capital and
threadbare resources in building up what would be systematically razed
to the ground. Despite the tragic undertone of these works, however, the
ways of seeing promulgated by Faleiro and Boo demonstrate a questioning
of the processes of repression by which the familiar and well-established
have become unfamiliar, uncanny, and enemy. If the upshot of the

"Uncanny" essay is that space is a projection of the psychical apparatus, which confounds inside and outside, or self and other, the authors discussed here rescue vulnerable habitations and subaltern spaces from being subsumed by this characteristically modern nostalgia. Instead of co-opting the topos of the uncanny to cultivate paranoia and anxiety for the metropolitan subject, the authorial, artistic, or archaeological persona, in each case, undergoes a salutary unhoming. In Vidler's words, the subjectivity is rendered "heterogenous, nomadic, and self-critical in vagabond environments that refuse the commonplaces of hearth and home in favour of the uncertainties of no-man's-land" (xiii). Freud had identified the "uncanny" as an aesthetic, adding the qualifier that aesthetics was "not merely the theory of beauty" but an anatomy of the qualities of feeling ("The 'Uncanny'" 217). Not narrowly limited to "what is beautiful, attractive, and sublime," the capacious aesthetic mode of the uncanny also represents "the opposite feelings of repulsion and distress" (217). Through the prism of the *unheimlich*, the violent infrastructural impacts of Mumbai's stark inequalities and divisions are at once exposed in plain sight and yet hidden. The singular contribution of the humanitarian fictions discussed above lies in their unflagging commitment toward making what Boo calls "invisible individuals" (*Beautiful Forevers* 254) visible, and the uncanny a perplexity of the beautiful.

The favorite motif of the uncanny, Vidler reminds us, is that of besieged domesticity – its seemingly hermetic entity breached by alien presence – and its psychological corollary, where the other seems to be a replica of the self, "all the more fearsome because apparently the same" (3). It is "the quintessential bourgeois kind of fear: one carefully bounded by the limits of real material security and the pleasure principle afforded by a terror that was, artistically at least, kept well under control" (4). Faleiro and Boo are frank to the point of self-deprecating in declaring their staggeringly different backgrounds and formations from the slum dwellers or sex workers they briefly rub shoulders with. "To Annawadians, I was a reliably ridiculous spectacle," Boo writes in the "Author's Note" with which the narrative ends (*Beautiful Forevers* 251). She concedes, however, that she sees herself in the people she writes about – in Fatima's fury at being defined by a differently abled body, or Asha's self-justifying, or Abdul's fear of losing the little he possesses. There is no safe distance, no safe haven in this writing where the terror of the unhomely can be sublated to and contained as a thrilling reading effect. "What would I do, under these circumstances, if I were Asha or Sunil or Meena? That's what I'm always asking myself."[20] If the labyrinthine twists of Leela's life do not provoke uncanny feelings, it is also because nowhere does she return as a replica of the author's self, an *unheimlich* double, even when the first- and second-person voices become jumbled in the intensely non-semantic sections of the book, implicating the absorbed reader as well. When asked about her favorite part of *Beautiful Thing*, Sonia Faleiro's response suggests she doesn't think she has invented *all* of it: "Any part in which Leela speaks."[21]

Psychoanalysis of the Oppressed, a Practice of Freedom: Free Clinics in Urban India

In *Pedagogy of the Oppressed*, first published in Portuguese in 1968, the Brazilian educationist Paulo Freire turns his attention to what he, in later works, calls the "culture of silence" of the dispossessed.[1] In the years immediately before, Freire, Professor of History and Philosophy of Education at the University of Recife, had conducted his early experiments with the teaching of illiterate populations, an initiative considered so radical that he was imprisoned for seventy days after the military coup of 1964. Freire left for Chile soon after his release, working with UNESCO and the Chilean Institute of Agrarian Reform. *Pedagogy of the Oppressed* was published during Freire's decade-long exile from Brazil, while Freire was a consultant at the School of Education at Harvard.

For Freire, the world is not a given reality but a problem to be worked on. The human inhabitants of this world have the "ontological vocation" to be a subject (66). Education can either be coercive, forcing younger generations to conform to the status quo, or it can be "*the* practice of freedom," fostering radical creativity, criticality, and liberation. Axiological definitions of humanization must take into account the "ontological possibility" and "historical reality" of dehumanization (43). Dehumanization concerns not only those whose humanity has been stolen or stunted, but the perpetrators guilty of the "*distortion* of the vocation of becoming more fully human" (44). It is the condition of being less human which leads the oppressed to struggle for the emancipation of labor or the overcoming of alienation. Freire cautions against a struggle which makes the disenfranchised "the oppressors of the oppressors" (44), or acts of false charity on the part of the dominant classes which perpetuate the dependency of the historically marginalized.

> True generosity lies in striving so that these hands – whether of individuals or entire peoples – need to be extended less and less in supplication, so that

more and more they become human hands which work and, working,
transform the world. (45)

Freire offers two valuable insights here: the lesson and this apprenticeship
for true generosity must come from the oppressed themselves; and that the
oppressed will not gain liberation by luck or chance "but through the praxis
of their quest for it" (45). Freire's pedagogy of the oppressed is a pedagogy
that is "forged *with*, not *for*, the oppressed (whether individuals or peoples)
in the incessant struggle to regain their humanity" (48). The central
problem, however, is this, Freire notes: "How can the oppressed, as
divided, inauthentic beings, participate in developing the pedagogy of
their liberation?" (48). How can the depersonalized, the colonized, and
the subjugated race inaugurate libertarian praxis? "The colonized is never
characterized in an individual manner," Memmi had gloomily observed in
The Colonizer and the Colonized: "He is entitled only to drown in an
anonymous collectivity" (129). How are masses, then, to reinstate individual rights and collective freedom, in a process that also restores the
humanity of the oppressor?

The libertarian pedagogy Freire envisions has two stages: in the first, the
oppressed demystify the world of oppression and actively work toward its
transformation. In the second stage, where oppression is no longer the
dominant reality, pedagogy "ceases to belong to the oppressed and
becomes a pedagogy of all people in the process of permanent liberation"
(54). Freire invokes terms such as "critical and liberating dialogue," and the
"reflective participation" of the oppressed in the same to overcome the
inauthenticity and abjection they have internalized over time (65). This, he
insists, is not merely "armchair revolution" but a call to action, one which
has trust in the oppressed and "in their ability to reason" (66).
Revolutionary leadership, mobilized within and across class lines, must
be dialogic and "co-intentional," Freire insists (69). If, for Freire, political
action on the side of the oppressed is necessarily pedagogical, could we
venture another modality – the psychoanalytical – of emancipatory action,
not *for* but *with* the oppressed. In this chapter, we look at psychoanalysis
and psychoanalytically oriented psychotherapy in the Indian context,
examining its "committed involvement" – another Freire term for the
revolution-to-come, in relation to the urban poor (69).

Around the same time that free clinics were cropping up in Europe in
the 1920s, psychoanalysis had a promising start in India. Girindrasekhar
Bose (1885–1953), a Calcutta-based physician who later obtained
a doctorate in clinical psychology, an autodidact therapist often referred

to as the "father of Indian psychoanalysis," founded the Indian Psychoanalytical Society in 1922.[2] Bose was a student of Brojendra Nath Seal, George V Professor of Mental and Moral Philosophy, who designed the first independent course in Experimental Psychology at Calcutta University in 1905.[3] Bose experimented with a psychological method of treatment as early as 1911, going on to formulate theories of "opposite wishes," repression, homosexuality, and infantile wishes. "Though he might have heard of psychoanalysis as early as 1905–6, his interest in it was first stimulated around 1909 by articles published in various periodicals," Ashis Nandy points out (*Savage Freud* 93). It is possible that when Bose started his psychoanalytic writings, he had not read Abraham Arden Brill's English translation of selected Freud papers. Bose developed a depth psychology of his own that was culture-specific, often at variance with that of Freud's. The two entered into a correspondence with each other when Bose's doctoral thesis was published as *The Concept of Repression* and he sent a copy to Freud. For nearly two decades (1920–1937), they discussed theoretical notions and developed a strong, if also ambivalent, relationship.[4]

In 1940, the Indian Psychoanalytical Society (IPS) was instrumental in instituting Lumbini Park, a non-profit mental hospital aimed at alleviating the sufferings of the mentally ill. At the time, the government was running a few hospitals that complied with the Indian Lunacy Act, but none of these focused on restorative and rehabilitating measures. Lumbini Park was a result of discussions in the early 1930s between Girindrasekhar Bose and his close associate, the psychoanalyst T. C. Sinha, and was approved by the IPS council in 1938. The name, "Lumbini Park," the birthplace of Gautama Buddha, was a tribute to Rajsekhar Bose, noted Bengali satirist and brother of Girindrasekhar, who had not only fund-raised for the hospital but donated a house (of the same name) for it. Lumbini Park started with three indoor beds, with no financial assistance from the government, its first years benighted by the epochal trauma of a World War, a refugee crisis (evacuees from Burma), Japanese bombing of Calcutta, the Bengal famine, and, finally, the Partition in 1947.[5]

The similarities between Lumbini Park and the free clinic model are uncanny, especially since these interventions were co-synchronous but in non-adjacent and non-corresponding sociocultural spheres: there is no mention of the "free clinic" in the Bose–Freud correspondence. Both Lumbini Park and the free clinic movement place equal emphasis on scientific and humanitarian work. On the occasion of the silver jubilee of Lumbini Park hospital in 1966, Anna Freud congratulated the Indian

Psychoanalytic Society "for devising mental methods of therapy" to address "human suffering and human conflicts" (*Lumbini Park Souvenir*). The founders aspired to build a teaching and research center for students of psychological medicine and abnormal psychology, and the plans included the foundation of a child guidance center. Lumbini Park was to be a non-profit organization with a voluntary fee structure where the best psychiatrists in Calcutta worked with limited resources and no public support, and in active collaboration with social workers, occupational therapists, and nurses. At a time when, in India, thousands of psychotics lived behind prison bars, and the stigmatizing word "lunacy" persisted in anachronistic enactments such as the Indian Lunacy Act, Lumbini Park hospital offered a systematic psychological as well as physical appraisal of each individual case, a clean and tranquil environment, and the promise to align mental health with general health and human rights paradigms.

Ashis Nandy makes the intriguing suggestion that psychoanalysis had a significant presence in India during Bose's lifetime not despite, but because of, its "near-total isolation from the day-to-day culture of psycho-analysis in Europe and North America" (*Savage Freud* 132). In Nandy's persuasive argument, the contradictions which structured the elaboration of psychoanalysis – the metaphysical versus the empirical, the clinical versus the experimental, the aesthetic versus the rational (132) – and influenced Freud's singular self-definition as analyst did not constrain the Indian psychoanalyst. Bose, for instance, extrapolated ideas from the heuristic traditions of the Vedas and Upanishads as well as the positivist science of contemporaries such as Jagadis Chandra Bose. Moreover, for the non-Western scholar or practitioner of psychoanalysis, Freud, Nandy states, "could be used as a radical critic of the savage world and, at the same time, a subverter of the imperial structures of thought that had turned the South into a dumping ground for dead and moribund categories of the Victorian era" (*Savage Freud* 136). Therefore, even though psychoanalysis arrived in India as part of the colonial Enlightenment project, retooling Indians into mimic Europeans, the other Freud (literary, philosophical, Easterner, Jew) survived "in the cracks of the modern consciousness" (*Savage Freud* 138). Nandy argues that, in a similar way to Freud, Girindrasekhar Bose did not claim he had discovered the unconscious: especially in his Bengali-language psychoanalytic writings, he used, albeit with mixed success, Indian cultural texts and categories to reimagine psychoanalysis in the framework of Indian cognitive approaches. Unlike Freud, however, Bose did not feel the need to go beyond hypnosis or the methods devised by experimental psychologists. He saw Freud's departures from these techniques as professional quibbles. He was able to be creative in his method – and invent a more methodologically adventurous Freud for India – perhaps because "he had more freedom as a *bhāsyakāra*, a traditional commentator on texts partly cut off from the modern West, than a formal psychoanalyst" (*Savage Freud* 144).

The focus of this chapter is not the travails of European psychoanalysis in contemporary India, or a long-historical review of structural factors that disallow this metapsychology from including non-Western theories of subject constitution. It does not trace the different stages of psychological thought in the subcontinent; nor does it document how psychoanalysis was painstakingly disaggregated from its civilizing mission by Indian sympathizers.[6] As Gayatri Chakravorty Spivak states in her essay "The Political Economy of Women as Seen by a Literary Critic," an examination of the insertion of psychoanalysis in "Third World" countries may well expose institutional forms (of psychoanalysis) to be "a latter-day support" of "epistemic violence" (226).[7] What the chapter aims to do, instead, is to examine the panlexicon derived from psychoanalytically oriented psychotherapy and deployed in the community to see, hear, and talk to poverty-stricken India. In that sense, the chapter could be about the travails of Freud in India – the mature, war-weary Freud of the free clinics he inaugurated in Budapest through that speech act of 1918. As the psychoanalyst Honey Oberoi Vahali points out in the Fourth Freud Memorial Lecture (2017) at the India International Centre, New Delhi:

> historians of psychoanalysis, including psychoanalytic clinicians themselves have forgotten [this] Freud who fed his patients, took care of their economic needs, and the one who gave an equal place to inner psychic forces and structural and politically-induced inequality.[8]

As a frequently quoted World Health Organization (WHO) study (2001) outlines, there are 4,000 psychiatrists in India, which represents a ratio of approximately 1 psychiatrist for 250,000 people. In rural areas and less developed states, the ratio would rise to 1 psychiatrist for more than a million people. The treatment gap (determined on the basis of prevalence of mental illness and the proportion of patients who get treatment) is 70 percent.[9] The central budget allocation for mental health in a country where 10 crore (1 crore = 10 million) people suffer from mental illness, with about 1 crore needing urgent hospitalization, is 1.03 billion rupees approximately, less than 1 percent (0.83 percent, according to the WHO report) of the total health expenditure. Commenting on the WHO report, Soumitra Pathare, preeminent psychiatrist and Director of the Centre of Mental

Health Law and Policy in India, states that, "in spite of the high burden of mental disorders and the fact that a significant portion of this burden can be reduced by primary and secondary prevention, most people in India do not have access to mental healthcare due to inadequate facilities and lack of human resources."

> India has 0.25 mental health beds per 10,000 population. Of these, the vast majority (0.20) are in mental hospitals and occupied by long-stay patients and therefore not really accessible to the general population. There is also a paucity of mental health professionals. India has 0.4 psychiatrists, 0.04 psychiatric nurses, 0.02 psychologists and 0.02 social workers per 100,000 population. To illustrate the level of under-provision, Indonesia, a low-income-group country from the Asian region, has 0.4 beds per 10,000 population and 0.21 psychiatrists, 0.9 psychiatric nurses, 0.3 psychologists and 1.5 social workers per 100,000 population.[10]

Despite mental health disorders making up a sixth of all health-related disorders and accounting for one-sixth of all health-related disability, they are grossly underestimated and overlooked by the Indian health system. Pathare's paper recommends the following action: increasing allocation to mental health in the health budget; integrating mental health services in primary care; legislative and policy changes which will allow health professionals other than psychiatrists to prescribe psychotropic drugs, without which, Pathare argues, the primary care integration will not work; increasing the number of mental health professionals through expanded training programs; intersectoral collaboration between private, public, and third sectors; community services (greater involvement of community members in the delivery of mental health services, as well as improving access to mental healthcare in the community).

The Mental Healthcare Act (MHCA) of 2017, which Pathare co-drafted with Keshav Desiraju, the former Health Secretary, Government of India, changed human rights jurisprudence in India by making access to mental healthcare an enforceable right. There are echoes of Freud's Budapest declaration in the text of the MHCA, as cited in this report by Pathare and Arjun Kapoor:

> Maintenance and improvement of public health have to rank high as these are indispensable to the very physical existence of the community and on the betterment of these depends the building of the society of which the Constitution makers envisaged.

"For the first time in the history of India's health governance, a law has statutorily recognized the *right* of *all persons* to access mental healthcare and treatment from services run or funded by the government without discrimination on any basis," Pathare and Kapoor write.[11] The MHCA mandates that the government meet, by the year 2028, the international guidelines on the number of mental healthcare professionals required to address the needs of a given population. *Unseen City* is written in the interim between the MHCA of 2017 and 2028, when we will see its transformative potential realized. The National Mental Health Survey of India of 2015–2016 estimated that 10.7 percent of the adult population (an estimated 150 million) suffers from some form of mental illness: of this number, a shockingly high 70–92 percent, which is the equivalent of 105 to 138 million people, do not have any access to treatment and care from the public health system (Pathare and Kapoor). According to the eleventh five-year plan, which covers the years between 2007 and 2013, the training infrastructure produces 320 psychiatrists, 50 clinical psychologists, 25 psychiatric social workers, and 185 psychiatric nurses per year, "a gross deficit . . . buttressed by the absence of adequate infrastructure, mental health facilities . . . and budgetary allocations" (Pathare et al.). When I last checked (in January 2021), the Indian Psychoanalytical Society, with headquarters in Kolkata and chapters in Mumbai and Delhi, enlisted only 32 full members, and a mere 40 candidates in training.

Environmenting: Barefoot Research

My search for free clinics in India began with notable NGO interventions in slum communities. In the summer of 2014, I got in touch with PUKAR (Partners for Urban Knowledge, Action and Research), a research collective and urban studies center in Mumbai founded by Carol Breckenridge and Arjun Appadurai and run by Anita Patil-Deshmukh, a Harvard-educated neonatologist.[12] Patil-Deshmukh, who served as Faculty Director of the Neonatal Intensive Care Unit at the University of Chicago for twenty-five years until she joined PUKAR in 2005, calls herself "a self-taught developmental worker." I emailed her outlining my project and the response was prompt: "I am afraid and ashamed to say that we have not come across any service delivery or psychotherapeutic interventions so far in the slums where we have worked . . . and we have worked in a large number of slums." Patil-Deshmukh agreed to talk to me at the PUKAR headquarters in the Municipal Tenements of Shivaji Nagar, Bandra East. While PUKAR was not focusing on mental health per se, they had just completed a study on "The Psychological Toll of Slum Living: An Assessment of Mental Health, Functional Status, and Adversity in an

Unregistered Mumbai Slum" in the Kaula Bandar (KB) slum, with 4 separate instruments and 521 respondents.[13] The researchers had used GHQ (General Health Questionnaire-12, a screening tool for mental disease used extensively in India), WHO's DAS (Disability Assessment Schedule 2.0, which serves as a cross-cultural measure of disability resulting from illness, cognitive disorders, and physical impairments), and the Slum Adversity Quantitative Index, based on a sequential, mixed-methods design. These were complemented by in-depth, randomized interviews of people. The purpose of the study was to ascertain the prevalence of common mental disorders (CMDs) and to identify slum-related stressors that might increase the risk of mental illness. Survey data were collected by PUKAR's "barefoot researchers," local youth, many of whom lived in KB. They had been trained beforehand by a clinical psychologist and two physicians about CMDs, non-judgmental interviewing techniques, research ethics, and administration of the quantitative survey. Interviews were conducted in Hindi, Marathi, and Tamil.

According to the United Nations, a community qualifies as a slum if it meets at least one of the following criteria: overcrowding, poor structural quality of housing, insecure residential status, inadequate water access, inadequate sanitation access. As explored in the last chapter, the slum poor are peripheral to the existence of the city, a surplus population deprived of social goods or services despite providing the labor critical to the functioning of the service sector in advanced and growing economies. Mumbai has the largest slum population of any city in the world: more than half of the city's population live in slums on less than 9 percent of its land area, making its slums some of the highest-density settlements on earth. Kaula Bandar translates as "roof dock": the name refers to roofs constructed in Gujarat and Mangalore and shipped to Mumbai's port area. KB is a slum of about 12,000 people located on a wharf on Mumbai's eastern waterfront. While the first waves of migrants were from Tamil Nadu, KB has recently seen an influx of migrants from Uttar Pradesh and Bihar. The land is owned by the Mumbai Port Trust, which bans its use for residential purposes. As a non-notified slum, Kaula Bandar is not entitled to any local government services, such as municipal water, sanitation infrastructure, and electricity, and is particularly vulnerable to slum adversities – chronic stressors (lack of access to water, electricity, and sanitation, poor food security, and debt) and traumatic events (eviction, home demolition, home fires).

In the study, 23.2% of individuals were seen to be high-risk for having a CMD, and 73% as having some form of disability (25% had severe disability). The qualitative findings substantiated and enriched the quantitative results by showing how specific adversities caused severe stress, which in turn precipitated adverse mental health outcomes. To give an example, exposure to rats repeatedly emerged as a major chronic if not traumatic stressor, as seen in this women's focus group discussion:

WOMAN 1: Rats eat everything, even wooden cupboards.
WOMAN 2: They eat matchboxes, money, everything.
[All talking excitedly at once]
WOMAN 3: When we're making rotis they steal them from under our noses.
WOMAN 4: On the bed we find left-over apples and other things they've eaten . . .
WOMAN 2: They've even damaged vessels made of German steel. [Group laughs]
WOMAN 5: They eat our clothes . . .
WOMAN 1: They've even eaten our electrical wires in several places.

Of the population sampled, 51% testified to the adverse impact of rats in day-to-day life. Of this population, 33% showed a high risk for CMDs. That is a good 10% higher than the average risk of CMDs (23.2%). Needless to say, rats here are markers of structural deprivation – household density, poor hygiene and sanitation, proximity to solid waste dumps, poor-quality housing, intra-slum inequality – and one of many factors in the complex interplay of stressors.

The evaluation of disability, a structural feature of the study, provided the investigators with a unique insight into psychological distress, which seemed to contribute more to the overall burden of disability than specific physical deficits. The much higher WHO DAS scores among individuals with CMDs, when compared to those without CMDs, highlighted the loss of function associated with mental illness in this social context. The investigators respond with a resounding "yes" to the question, "Does living in a slum take a psychological toll?" A drawback of population-based studies on slums such as the one discussed here is that they are cross-sectional, and do not involve a time series analysis, which would give a sense of how relevant the stressors were over a period of time. A cross-sectional analysis also makes causality difficult to ascertain. Do CMDs cause disability or is it the other way around? The study identifies "sleeping sitting up or outside the home due to a lack of space" as one of the slum adversities associated with high CMD risk: is it possible that individuals with CMDs were being singled out to sleep outside the home? The PUKAR report recommends "structural interventions" addressing poverty and slum adversities: "the high burden of CMDs in the context of a severe shortage of trained psychic personnel in India, highlights the need to explore community-based expansion of lay health worker-driven psychiatric interventions."

Elizabeth Povinelli argues that the "statistical imaginary"[14] has long allowed state-controlled production of knowledge of its population, in particular the knowledge of its health, malaise, and mortality. "By transforming the invisible, dispersed, and uneventful into the visible, compact, and eventful, statistics obliterate the very nature of death," Povinelli claims (153). The voices of women fixated on the rat menace sound out wider implications of the event captured by the statistics, and the relationship of the subject's life and death to the social structure in which she is incorporated. Framed by the poverty alleviation effort of the PUKAR initiative, the rest of this chapter will outline the workings of three "community-based" and "lay health worker-driven" initiatives (recommended by PUKAR), the case material drawn from the dusty fringes of three Indian hypercities: Bengaluru, Kolkata, and Chennai. A study such as PUKAR's, with its call for improving access to and the outreach of mental health services, seems to endorse Martha Nussbaum's capabilities approach, which insists that, to secure mental health rights, what is needed is "affirmative material and institutional support, not simply a failure to impede" ("Poverty" 55). In the absence or failure of national welfare states, traditional rights talk has ignored mental health issues, structured as it is on the traditional distinction between a public sphere, which the state regulates, and a private sphere, which it must leave alone. Nussbaum argues that fundamental entitlements are not secured by prohibitions against interfering state actions alone: there is urgent need for affirmative action to determine "what obstacles there are to the full and effective empowerment of all citizens," and to "devise measures that address these obstacles" (55). It is to such modes of affirmative action, which not only address the inequity of the state's mental health provision but actively champion redistribution and substantive equality, that we now turn.

The barefoot researchers, the lay counselors, the community-based mobilizers of this chapter offer new definitions of the "vulnerable" expert that Sudhir Kakar saw the psychoanalyst to be (*The Colors of Violence* 3). According to Kakar, the core of the analyst's sensibility is empathy, not expertise – an empathy that strategically mobilizes the analyst's objective and impassioned selves, allowing them to "understand with [their] bodies" (4). Of the three examples of free clinics cited here, two (Janamanas and NALAM) force us to consider the body of the analyst made vulnerable not just by the physical and epistemological intimacies of the therapeutic encounter but by poverty, socioeconomic and gender inequality, interpersonal violence, and psychosocial disability. It is a psychoanalysis of and for the oppressed, and, in two cases, by the oppressed: an untold story of the listening ears and seeing eyes of a mass-mobilized people's psychiatry and psychotherapy.

Abbreviating: "We Don't Go to Childhood Experiences Because There Is No Time"

In Bangalore, I met Dr. Srinivasa Murthy, Professor of Psychiatry at NIMHANS (National Institute of Mental Health and Neurosciences), retired, and a notable historian and critic of Indian and global psychiatry. Dr. Murthy has long championed the need for psychiatrists to practice psychotherapy. Like Venkoba Rao and S. Reddy before him, Murthy traces psychoanalysis in India to the days of the *Mahabharata*. In an article of 2010, he wrote that the Bhagavad Gita demonstrates how "Krishna functions as Arjuna's teacher and psychoanalyst. Krishna's analytic (thera-peutic) function is not interpretive per se, but he functions as an object that facilitates the development and maturation of Arjuna's ego (psychic)" (159–180). Murthy sent me to his former colleague C. R. Chandrashekar's free clinic, the Samadhana Counselling Centre in South Bangalore. The for-midable Chandrashekar, a.k.a. CRC, who was once described as the "rock star of psychiatry," turned out to be a soft-spoken and unassuming man in his late sixties. He has the steely cheerfulness and can-do-ism of social reformers who not only initiate historical change but find themselves in the unenviable position of singlehandedly preserving its momentum. Chandrashekar, who, in his heydays, treated up to fifty patients a day, is deeply invested in two causes: raising social awareness around mental health issues and furthering mental health education, and counteracting the commodification of mental illness in lucrative pharmacotherapy.

A psychiatrist at NIMHANS for forty-four years (retiring in 2013), Chandrashekar has tirelessly translated his vast medical experience in one of India's foremost public-sector mental hospitals into public lectures, public education initiatives, ambulatory care in villages, and, finally, the rehabilitation centers and free clinics he has set up with his private funds in the city. Recurring expenses are met through workshop fees and voluntary donations made to the trust created in the name of Dr. Chandrashekar's parents, B. M. Rajannachar and S. P. Sarojamma. CRC reaches out to 150 villages around Bangalore – to those people, he said, who did not have the 50 paisa (less than 0.25 pence) bus fare to the city – and has published over 150 popular books on mental health matters, some of which have been translated from the original Kannada to Urdu, English, and Gujarati. In addition, he has authored 20 books in English. He receives letters from patients in Karnataka and the adjoining states, describing various mental problems, every day. "So far, I have replied to more than 40,000 letters," he says smilingly in an interview.

It was his interest in Kannada literature that drove C. R. Chandrashekar to psychiatry, particularly the way in which human behavior was anatomized in the novels of Triveni and the books of Dr. R. Shivaram. However, mental healthcare, he says, is not only about delving into the conscious and subconscious minds: it is also about addressing the psychiatric health of society. The Samadhana Counselling Centre is run by lay counselors, trained by CRC and a team of psychiatrists/psychologists over 25 to 50 sessions. "We primarily teach counselors how to be empathetic," Chandrashekar says, showing me a diagram that outlines the basic tenets of counseling in thought bubbles arranged around the term: listening; understanding; being non-judgmental; being responsive; keeping confidences; making a change. The counselors are volunteers, mostly white-collar professionals with two or three languages. Take Castelino Patrick, an English teacher at BGS National Public School, Hulimavu, for instance. "I deal with people between 16 and 60 years of age, who are loners or are depressed. We are taught to lend a listening ear to people without passing judgments. It goes a long way in helping them vent suppressed emotions, solve problems and feel lighter," she said.[15] One of the counselors I interviewed, Gayathri Devi Prasad, has degrees in clinical psychology and education, and volunteers once a week at the Centre. The counselors and psychotherapists do not follow any school of treatment as such, and methodology tends to be eclectic. It can best be described as supportive psychotherapy, a combination of psychodynamic, cognitive-behavioral, and interpersonal conceptual models and techniques. With rural and poor populations, the task of the counselor often begins with removing ignorance and addressing misconceptions, superstitions, and unscientific belief around mental illness. The worst offenders are the following: bad alignments of planets or the rogue Saturn; defects in the horoscope; the envious attitude of others; spirit possession; black magic done by enemies; and fears around masturbation and intercourse outside marriage. Chandrashekar recounts how, on a visit to a Dargah (a shrine, usually built over the grave of a Sufi saint) where mentally ill patients were chained to the wall and in the throes of spirit exorcism, he went up to the priest and said: "This is schizophrenia, boss. Send this man to NIMHANS."

Patients at the Samadhana Counselling Centre start with an initial psychiatric evaluation, carried out by CRC, and the pathological cases are instantly despatched to NIMHANS or the nearest government hospital that has trained psychiatrists. The counselors decide over the course of the sessions whether the patient requires medicine, therapy, or both. They devise pragmatic, workable, and time-driven sets of strategies. "Through rapport building, we allow the patients to find their own resources," Gayathri Devi said. Unlike psychoanalysis, the course of treatment is short, sometimes lasting for just two to three sessions, and outcome-oriented, and the goal is the alleviation of symptoms – not necessarily helping the patients to know themselves or their desire. The Centre is designed to look not so much like an analyst's chamber, or a set of doctors' chambers, but a place of active commerce, where messages are received, decoded, and recoded. The hallway is divided into makeshift rooms made by temporary partitions. Patient X in cubicle 1 can easily hear Patient Y in cubicle 2. It is also not uncommon for sessions to be interrupted, by CRC himself or by a member of the volunteer group wanting to consult the senior therapists on matters arising.

As in the NIMHANS Centre for Wellbeing, which I visited, Samadhana is programmed to receive people not likely to do one-to-one therapy. The questionnaire handed out at the portals of the counseling center is filled in by family and friends, and the counselors said they drew heavily on family background as well as relying on leads and feedback from family members. The most common forms of mental disease the Samadhana counselors treat are depression, anxiety, learning difficulties, neuroses related to family issues – pride of place being taken by mother-in-law/daughter-in-law problems – and alcohol addiction. The duration of each session is 30 minutes: counselors try to understand the nature of the problem (guilt? loss? anxiety?) while also addressing immediate physical manifestations such as sleep deprivation, loss of appetite, low self-esteem. "We don't go to childhood experiences because there is no time," Gayathri Devi Prasad states matter-of-factly.

Case 1

The case records of Samadhana Counselling Centre are reproduced in CRC's many DIY books, such as *You Too Can Learn the Art of Counselling*, from which the following is taken. There is the 40-something Mrs. Pratibha, who has, for eighteen long years, suffered from incontinence when under stress. The stressors seem at first to be money-related – job loss, debt, the fear of financial ignominy – but in the course of treatment (six sittings, approximately eight hours), the counselor learns that the problem first started at age 14, when she had a physical relationship with a male classmate. The therapist in charge, Mr. A. Srinivasamurthy, adopts three key strategies: he enjoins the patient to treat the urinary problem as psycho-somatic (and treatable through therapy), not a physical disorder; works at removing guilt around adolescent sexuality; recommends practical, com-monsense measures such as consuming less fluids before a journey or informing colleagues about the medical condition. The counseling sessions are supplemented with a consultation with CRC: "He prescribed medicines to take for some time and instructed them [Pratibha and her husband, who has attended all the sessions] to come for weekly follow-up sessions to report the progress" (166). Three months after the sixth session, Pratibha is rid of the problem altogether. "Now she comes to Samadhana once in 2–3 months just to recharge herself" (167). She has stopped taking medicines and the problem has not recurred, the case record states.

Case 2

In this case, narrated to me by CRC himself, Ms A, a 23-year-old account-ant, suffers from headache, palpitations, chest pain, and insomnia, which started during the onset of her mother's terminal illness, and which continue to plague her when "bad thoughts come to her mind." Here, too, there are lurking money worries and episodes of unedifying sex. "A" had become overly dependent on her colleague, Mr. S., who helped her emotionally and financially during her mother's recent hospital stay. There was no question of marriage – they were not in love with each other and were from different castes, a social deterrent she does not challenge – but there was a sexual relationship. The counselor advises A to eat fresh fruits and green vegetables; get adequate sleep and maintain good hygiene; take walks; meditate. CRC prescribes her anti-anxiety drugs. The counselor asks her to write down her experiences with Mr. S, which she does. Ms A is fascinated by the subconscious mind and discusses Sigmund Freud during her sessions. The therapist has a breakthrough during session 5, when he asks her to enact life events using chairs scattered about the room (as if they were people). "She cried and showed her father's anger, mother's helpless-ness, her colleagues gossiping about love and sex." CRC increases the dose of the anti-anxiety drug. Five sessions over, "Ms A felt comfortable and left the Centre with a smile."

The key issue that arises from a perusal of case records at Samadhana Counselling Centre is the lack of transparency regarding the role played by pharmacotherapy or psychotherapy (or both, when the delivery of these is integrated) in the course of a given treatment. The interviews I conducted were not clarifying either. While CRC clearly had oversight when it came to the counselors, the medical practice of the "people's psychiatrist," as CRC is fondly called, was not monitored or even documented in the records. The volunteer counselors at Samadhana say optimistically that the Centre has a 100 percent success rate. The urge to reintegrate people with psycho-social disabilities back into the society and their families is admirable, but in the absence of follow-up exercises, this claim is unsubstantiated. Finally, the methodology of the lay counselors seemed too extemporaneous and eclectic to set solid precedents. C. R. Chandrashekar is the engine room of Samadhana (and Prasanna, a related organization) and it is difficult to imagine the centres running at all without or after him.

Karnataka has 250 psychologists and around 100 psychiatrists – of which number, Bengaluru has less than 50.[16] CRC's voluntary training of lay counselors – 5,000 so far, and 2,000 teachers in student counseling – toward the free treatment of mental disorders is therefore a monumental contribution to the deficit in mental health services. I remembered afterward that the female patients in the two case studies had both insisted on absolute confidentiality. They were middle-class women, struggling to make ends meet, and neither was troubled by the hunger, the inequality, or the wide gap between financial predicament and the prevailing standards of necessities that we associate with acute poverty. This too was a definition of a free clinic I would have to acknowledge – a safe haven where women would, under the cover of anonymity and immune from social discrimination or moral censure, be allowed to talk freely and be heard, and acquire the capability (that Nussbaum term) to liberate themselves from destructive neuroses.

Tele-communicating: "Moner Kotha" Relays

My next sustained collaboration was with Anjali, a mental health rights NGO in Kolkata whose aim is to establish mental illness "within the mainstream health paradigm of India."[17] Anjali works with three public-sector mental hospitals in West Bengal: Pavlov, Lumbini Park, and Bahrampur. It provides institutionalized patients with a package of health-care services and therapies which supplement the treatment they receive in

Figure 5 Lay counselors at Janamanas, an initiative of Anjali, Kolkata

government hospitals. Anjali's is a form of caregiving that corrects the "coercive and non-participatory forms of treatment" prevalent in state-run institutions, and these are its aims: the full rehabilitation of psychiatric patients to family and society after the course of treatment; removing stigma around psychosocial disability by encouraging civic participation in this rehabilitation; upholding the human rights of each patient by enlisting their consent in all decisions impacting their lives.

Within Anjali, I focused on a program titled Janamanas, a community mental health initiative, which involves the training of lay counselors – the very foundation of the free clinic edifice – for deployment in mental healthcare kiosks. The collaboration began in 2016, with my attending a leadership and organizational skills training session that focused on personal growth and domestic violence. The participants, drawn from lower-middle-class and resource-poor households, were asked to share their sociocultural understanding of domestic violence, as well as personal experiences of the same, if any. All six women had experienced brutalizing experiences of physical or psychological torture within the nuclear family: in half of the cases, the violence was endemic, the perpetrator still in an intimate relationship with the victim, and while the latter had coping mechanisms in place, there was clear evidence of residual rage and guilt and unresolved trauma. The participants were eloquent and presented linear narratives. The session was expertly moderated by the facilitator, a trained counselor, who parsed and consolidated insights. Common features and causes of domestic violence were recognized, and its debilitating physical and psychological impact dwelt on. The facilitator then offered ways in which, through introspection and esteem-building, the difficult task of regeneration and self-empowerment might begin.

The participants I shadowed in this training workshop run Anjali's Janamanas program. Translated as "the psyche of the people," Janamanas strategically uses the city's extant municipal corporation system to train volunteers in therapeutic techniques. Ratnaboli Ray, the founder of Anjali, says "community could be the entire civil society."[18] Janamanas is led "for, by, and with the people, particularly women": the kiosk operators, Ray points out, are not just "stakeholders" in the project but also the community (41). In a detailed, day-long interview I conducted in November 2017, all the counselors present recounted painful, poverty-stricken childhoods (Manika Mazumdar, who has counseled more than 2,700 patients, specifically mentioned 17 years of trauma blighting her early life); domestic violence; the lack of educational opportunities; dead-end, low-paying jobs. They said this *doinondin koshto* – the quotidian struggle – made them the caregivers (*porisebak*) they were. The 7 lay counselors all mentioned their commitment to not just mental health but social equality: one remarked that this social work was not a hobby but a livelihood, a mobility story that lifted them from violent, deprived, precarious living conditions. It made them feel valued where they had felt valueless before: "mulloheenke mulloban kore deoa."

Janamanas, funded by the Innovative Challenge Fund and the Hans Foundation, was taken over by the Rajarhat-Gopalpur municipality in 2011, which means staff salaries are now paid by the municipality. I visited the Rajarhat-Gopalpur kiosk, initiated by Anjali in 2007, where the all-woman team of lay counselors engaged with the local population in the form of dialogue and counseling at the kiosk, street corner meetings, awareness camps, door-to-door leafleting, and home visits. The kiosk is open five days a week and is a nodal point in a network of community stakeholders committed to the identification of persons in need of mental health assistance: outreach workers, health workers, local self-government institutions, the municipality, partner NGOs. Nussbaum's capabilities approach considers different definitions and social aspects of poverty and touches on a key opportunity – or what she terms "capability" – that can counter it: "Having the social bases of self-respect and non-humiliation;

being able to be treated as a dignified being whose worth is equal to that of others" (*Hiding from Humanity* 79–80). The relay of psychotherapeutic diagnoses in the Janamanas program is built on the conviction that for this capability to be secured, therapy, alongside general policies in the area of social and economic entitlements, would have to play a crucial role. As Balagopal and Kapanee observe:

> Due to the interaction between mental health and poverty, the kiosks emphasise on the social aspects of mental illness such as gender, sexuality, livelihoods, access to basic services, citizenship, etc. Consequently, the women who lead the *Janamanas* programme go beyond just counselling. They extend their help in facilitating public–government interface. (58)

Rajarhat, where the lay counselors work, is a straggling and unevenly developed suburb of Kolkata. According to the 2001 consensus, the Rajarhat-Gopalpur municipality has a population of 271,811. Of this number, 39,916 are Muslim and 50,634 Bahujan.[19] In the municipal area, 9 percent of the population lives in slums: the percentage of people below-poverty-line (BPL) is 15.51. Once a part of the wetlands of East Kolkata, Rajarhat used to be a thriving center of agriculture and fish cultivation: according to a 2000 report cited by Ishita Dey et al., 17,000 workers depended on recycling waste and recovery systems through fish cultivation and vegetable cropping in the wetlands (*Beyond Kolkata* 6). The authors point out that Rajarhat is not connected to metropolitan Kolkata but to Sector V of Salt Lake City, which is located in the North 24 Parganas district in the Indian state of West Bengal. Its real trade is with Baguihati, a dingy bazaar which is also a bus and cycle-rickshaw depot, a site of sundry stalls, and a waiting room for large numbers of day laborers waiting to be hired. Baguihati is one of the fringes of Kolkata where farmers, fishermen, vegetable growers and sellers, boatmen, and agricultural labor, now robbed of livelihoods, provide cheap labor, transportation, or vegetable supply to the newcomers of Rajarhat, who live in Newtown. Sprouting cities such as Newtown are "exterior to the city proper": those who live in the high rises in Newtown and/or work in the e-firms, hospitality industry, malls, and companies in the area have little to do with "dirty marginal places" like Rajarhat or Baguihati – or with Kolkata, for that matter (*Beyond Kolkata* 9). The New Town agenda, which the authors of *Beyond Kolkata* describe as an urban "dystopia" (11), and the conversion, over two decades, of agricultural land to non-agricultural use has created "an extremely low-cost subsistence economy" and a "fragile environment":

with the new town coming up, the waste-recycling system would break down, waterlogging in suburbs would increase, economic rehabilitation of those dispossessed and deprived of livelihoods would become difficult, social unrest would grow, biodiversity would be lost, and the city would be deprived of fish, vegetables, and other agricultural products. (8)

Around 28% of the population of the North 24 Parganas, where Rajarhat is located, live in slums. In the specific community Anjali targets (through Janamanas), 33% of households were run by precarious, day-laborer family members. Examining evidence on an indicator of deprivation – namely, disability – from the Socioeconomic and Caste Consensus (SECC), Balagopal and Kapanee point out that the North 24 Parganas has a higher share (than the state average of 47%) of households with one or more disabled members and no household adult. Moreover, the share of households with no deprivations is lower than the state average (43–44%). The political turmoil in Bengal has meant that when the Rajarhat-Gopalpur municipality was dissolved, the threadbare resources of the kiosk served all the mental health needs in the neighborhood. With the dissolving of the municipality and the escalating of political conflict, the kiosk had to shut down for a brief period when there was a murder at its doorstep. The clients either come by themselves or are brought to the kiosk by concerned family. "Muslims tend not to come by themselves," one of the counselors observes. Sessions are usually one-on-one and the duration is 30 minutes for new registrants. The monthly caseload is around 20. While the services are free, clients are encouraged to drop 1 rupee into a drop box if they can spare it.

Roughly half of the clients have a psychiatric history and are already receiving some form of psychiatric treatment: in many cases, the treatment had been facilitated by Anjali workers. At Rajarhat-Gopalpur, they refer around five cases a month to Pavlov hospital – cases which need urgent medical attention. The roster of illnesses considered by the kiosk workers includes paranoid schizophrenia, depression, OCD, bipolar disorder, dementia. Talk therapy at the kiosk addresses symptoms in the compassionate way pills can't: fanatical cleanliness (*shuchibaayu*); insomnia; domestic violence; lack of personal hygiene; pyromania; suicidal thoughts. Most of the clients from the community (72 percent) utilize the kiosk to address interpersonal issues, and there is counseling for non-psychiatric symptoms. The kiosks provided services for 2,545 clients during the 2011–2012 period, ensuring the most vulnerable sections of the slum populations – women and those in the lowest income group – could access mental health services (Balagopal and Kapanee 61).

The Janamanas kiosk is also an ambulatorium in the sense that the counselors go knocking on doors, armed with introductions and handbills, and the offer to discuss mental health problems. "Moner kotha" is the term they use: a heart-to-heart would be the most accurate, if not literal, translation, and I would claim it as a vernacular alternative for the Freudian term "transference." In *The Post Card*, Jacques Derrida wordily described the Freudian notion of transference as "correspondences, connections, switch points, traffic, and a semantic, postal railway without which no transferential destination would be possible" (383). In Freudian literature, transference is a salutary form of resistance: in the "Uncanny" essay, he describes it as wandering about "in a dark, strange room, looking for the door or electric switch and collid[ing] time after time with the same piece of furniture" (237). If, in the Freudian prototype, the dark, strange room is the site of repetition of an unknown ur-event, the analysis of resistance in the Janamanas kiosk takes place not on a temporal axis but a spatial one: the unanalyzable returns not from the primordial past but through a mobilized intertextuality between the lay analyst and analyzand in the present. As I have remarked elsewhere, Freud's anxiety about this kind of telepathy between strangers had something to do with telepathy's association with pseudoscience: "he also saw it as a leakage, an occult transmission between analyst and analysand that bypassed the protocols of proper analytic interaction" ("This Traffic of Influence," 59). Transference is indeed a clairvoyant process, and, as Derrida shows in his essay "Telepathy," telecommunications are "encrypted within psychoanalysis, as an autoimmune process that threatens the latter's claim to rationality and coherence" ("This Traffic of Influence," 59).

In the process of "moner kotha," the counselors encounter paedophilia, marital rape, interpersonal violence, addiction, depression leading to loss of function. The counselors make notes on the families that are particularly afflicted. "Why should I talk to you?" someone once asked Manika. "Because I will listen with full attention," she replied readily. The wives are more responsive to these home visits, the counselors observe. The home visits and word-of-mouth work as excellent publicity for the kiosk, where there are two counselors for each patient, 30- to 40-minute sessions, and four or five sittings a month for six to eight months. I will now offer a few case studies to demonstrate the improvisatory ways in which counseling, to quote Manika, "helps [our] patients express pain, resolve dilemmas, diffuse family and mental pressures, get clarity." As another counselor stated, "we work hard to make sure it is not branded as *pagoler kaaj* (the treatment of madness) but is, instead, an opportunity for those oppressed by silence to talk."

Case 1 (eight sessions)

A young man comes to the kiosk saying he suffers from crippling low self-esteem. He is disoriented, can't take decisions, can't even make eye contact with his interlocutors. He is a traffic policeman and with his sleeplessness and periodic amnesia, combined with a developing alcohol addiction, the situation is literally an accident waiting to happen. He has married a village girl and seems to be fixating on her lack of educational qualifications (she only has the secondary education 10th-class exams to her name). The counselors suspect he is seeking their approval to embark on an extramarital affair, so they respond frankly. "Help your wife to come up in life instead of opting for a new woman," one of them advises. These are not smartphones – Nokia or Reliance, she says with barely concealed pride at the cunning metaphor – which can be swapped or upgraded. The man continues to come to the kiosk despite the reprimand, and says, in one of his monthly follow-ups, that he could not have talked to relatives about any of this.

Case 2 (sixteen sessions)

Tanaya always aced her studies. Her family, while not affluent, was supportive and spared no expense in her upbringing. She wanted from an early age to be a schoolteacher and was well on her way to achieving her goal when she was admitted to a B.Ed. (Bachelor of Education) program, which she would stay in a hostel to pursue. Tanaya's life changed dramatically one day when her mother died of a mysterious disease. Unable to emotionally connect with her father, and sinking into depression, Tanaya starts visiting a psychiatrist and is put on medication. Just as her life is beginning to fall into place, her father announces his second marriage. To make matters worse, her boyfriend leaves her. She has graduated with dazzling results and the coveted job of schoolteacher is finally hers, yet she feels empty inside.

Tanaya learns about the Janamanas program from a newspaper. Though dubious at first, she contacts the team, carefully gathering information about the work of the organization. She starts counseling, talking about the different phases and aspects of her personal life: her love for her mother; the expectations she had of her stepmother; her sense of betrayal with her father. "Tanaya wanted to be a spectator of these relationships," the Janamanas coordinator writes in her case study, and Janamanas provides her the "distant place" from which to critically assess. She decides to stay in rented accommodation, spending only weekends at home. She manages to have a meaningful conversation with her stepmother. After attending ten sessions at Janamanas, she knows herself and her needs better. Tanaya's life feels less tortured and when she comes to the counseling sessions now, as she does regularly, she talks about her future.

Case 3 (ten sessions)

She (unnamed patient) came with her mother to say she felt insignificant and useless at home. The Janamanas team figured out soon enough that her interactions with the world outside – her friends – was fine, it was the domestic space that was proving impossible to negotiate. After five sessions, the team recommended she contact a psychiatrist, when the mother revealed the girl had been in treatment for the last three years. She had turned to Janamanas only when, in the two preceding years of psychiatric consultation, her troubles had escalated – this coincided with her discontinuing her medication in the second year of treatment, resuming it fitfully in the third. The Janamanas team ask her to not discontinue the medication under any circumstances. They decide on a home visit and talk to her parents, with whom she lives. They find the household conflict-ridden and dysfunctional, with parents disagreeing on everything. When the Janamanas team point out the impact this constant conflict is having on their client's mental health, the parents soberly accept the recommendation that they change their behaviors. The woman begins to feel more at home, helping with household chores, working with her father at his shop. During her most recent Janamanas trip, she mentions a marriage proposal that is bothering her. The team decide on another home visit but are happy she no longer feels insignificant and useless.

Case 4 (four sessions)

She (name withheld) came to the kiosk with depression. She had divorced her first husband thirteen years ago, remarrying three years back. She has a 13-year-old son. She works at a government office. The immediate problem she approaches the team with is her severe lack of compatibility with her mother, whom she blames for the failure of her first marriage. The mother suffers from OCD and schizophrenia. The team learn that their client too had been diagnosed psychiatrically and prescribed medication for depression. They advise her to maintain boundaries with her mother and create her own space in order to live life on her own terms. She loses her father in a road accident in the course of her engagement with Janamanas, which causes a mental breakdown. The team support her through this traumatic time. The notes from the last follow-up session state that she is better, keeping herself busy with work. She has just returned from a vacation and is setting up her new home.

(Self-)Mobilizing: "Our Best Teachers"

On her way to college – the Women's Christian College in Chennai – Vandana Gopikumar, a Master's student of Social Work, saw a semi-naked woman, her body battered, hands filthy and hair matted, running from one end of a crowded street to another. She remembers being shocked by the fact that, while there were many onlookers, no one broke their stride to help. With the help of college authorities, Vandana and her friend Vaishnavi Jayakumar tidied the woman and got her admitted to an NGO. To their dismay, they found shortly afterwards that the woman had fled the shelter and could not be traced. This is the oft-cited beginning of a historical journey the two would embark on to get mentally ill women off the streets, an intervention which was formalized when, in 1993, they rented a flat and started living with rescued women. The Banyan Emergency and Recovery Centre was thereby founded on the principle of providing an "alienated and hypersegregated" group the opportunity of leading an independent and fulfilling life.[20] "Our focus was to restore self-esteem and work on their life beyond mental illness," the duo emphasize.[21] It soon grew in size to house 100 inmates. Today, the NGO Banyan is an internationally renowned mental health charity with three growing regional chapters and five multi-pronged projects that has transformed the lives of more than 5,000 people.

One of the first lines one reads on the Banyan website (thebanyan.org) is: "1 in 4 people are [*sic*] living with a mental health condition: it could be you." Banyan recognizes the pervasiveness of mental illness and the psychosocial precarity it engenders, a precarity which can "fall into" poverty and homelessness. Moreover, common mental disorders are twice as frequent among poor communities: those from the lowest socioeconomic backgrounds have a risk 8 times higher (than those with higher socioeconomic status, or SES) for schizophrenia. Mental illness impairs an individual's ability for self-care and familial or social bonding, besides impeding gainful employment and household duties.[22] Integral to the Banyan approach is poverty alleviation through addressing the mental health needs of homelessness. Vandana Gopikumar has been forthright about her own troubled mental health history and how this affliction, suffered across the considerable class divide, informs the otherwise asymmetrical power relationship between care provider and patient at Banyan. The impactive "Banyan model" can be divided into four overlapping stages: experimentation; course correction based on field experiences; collaboration with state governments, NGOs, community-based organizations, universities; and integration of multiple approaches as a bulwark against the prevalent overmedication route.

NALAM, the project I will be examining in this section of the chapter, belongs in the present phase and is described as "a multi-interventional model that approaches mental health from a wellness perspective." It is in the forefront of Banyan's community mental health activities and works in juxtaposition and cooperation with a range of governmental and non-governmental organizations (Department of Health, Panchayat, Corporation, Colleges, and the State Training and Resource Centre). NALAM has two facets: Urban and Rural. NALAM Urban serves low-income areas in Chennai city, namely Mogappair, Padi, Padiputhunagar, KK Nagar, Jafarkhanpet, West Saidapet, Choolaimedu, Santhome, and Teynampet. NALAM mobilizers in the city address the chronic trauma of unemployment, alcoholism, child labor, interpersonal violence, and sexual abuse in these communities, offering integrated clinical and social care. They conduct awareness programs and focus groups to identify and address mental health needs. Banyan has also initiated a diploma in lay counseling at Stella Maris College, a structured training course which builds capacity in trainee volunteers for counseling and the emotional support it demands.

NALAM Rural offers services in the Kancheepuram and Nilgiris districts of Tamil Nadu, with the mobilizers addressing mental health needs of clients in cooperation with local NGOS, youth groups, Primary Health Centres (PHCs), and governmental initiatives. The outreach is a sizable 140,000, with 600 clients utilizing the services every month, and 30 new clients each month. The case studies below are drawn from NALAM'S work in villages, and show, once again, the complex engineering of psychotherapeutic principles, local systems of healing, and practical wisdom I have described earlier as *jugaad*. While these pose an exception to the metropolitan mental health interventions I have recounted in this and other chapters, Banyan offers services to poor populations through

Figures 6 and 7 Community mobilizers at NALAM, a rural initiative of The Banyan, Chennai

grassroots workers (or lay counselors) in rural geographies alone. The mobilizing stories are also incomplete without the world city's framing of the stories as a horizon of opportunity, modernity, education, and progressive politics.

Case 1 The Story of G and S

G was 14 years old when she married a man fifteen years older than she and with whom she went on to have four children. Loss and mourning were familiar themes in G's life. Her parents had died when she was a teenager, and her eldest child succumbed to an illness at age 3. When G was 56 years old, her husband died. It was after this that G recalled feeling extreme affliction, attributing this to the problems her children were facing (as grown-ups). Her second son was an alcoholic who refused to get sober or take care of his family (a wife and three children). Her younger daughter was facing social and familial ostracism because of her childlessness. She was also struggling to repay a debt undertaken to build a home. G had to pawn the little jewellery and land she owned to help the daughter pay the crippling interest on the loan.

This sequence of events compelled G to seek out services at the Banyan. Soon after, her older daughter died from a kidney ailment. Her son-in-law turned alcoholic and neglected his motherless children. It was at this point that she met S (a NALAM mobilizer) who started visiting her regularly at home. This is how G narrates their encounters:

> I feel relaxed whenever I meet S. She has been instrumental in my recovery. She has been with me from the time of my daughter's illness, when I was utterly helpless. She even mobilized blood donors and accompanied me to visit my daughter in hospital during her last days. The way she talks to me makes me feel better ... I can see my dead daughter in her. I share my feelings and worries; she gives me practical suggestions to move ahead in my life at this age.

S encouraged G to create local networks in the community and helped her to enrol with the MGNREGA[23] scheme, so that she could both earn a living and enjoy human company during the day. G says:

> There are a lot more people who have problems in their life not unlike me in my village. When I go to work, I can listen and relate to them. This makes me feel less alone. Also, the earnings and my husband's pension are my only source of income – it cannot be denied that it helps me tide over in everyday life.

When G's daughter died, S stayed connected on the phone for follow-ups. She continues to provide lay counseling to G's son and son-in-law to help them to understand G's mental health needs. There was a period when G's son attributed his mother's condition to her "need for attention," dismissing it as "plain acting." S took this as a challenge and started regular home visits to speak with him and his wife and help to change their attitude. Moreover, S negotiated with G's younger daughter (who doesn't have children of her own) to parent her late sister's children. There was a brief period when, unfortunately, G's son-in-law, who had initially consented to this arrangement, changed his mind, refusing to send his children to their aunt's place. It was S who mediated this situation as well and helped matters to come to an amicable close. The Banyan stepped in to provide the children educational support, and this has motivated the father (G's son-in-law) to send the children to school regularly.

Case 2 The Story of P

P had a troubled first marriage. When his wife, who was having an affair, chose to leave him, he struggled to come to terms with it. He recalls being socially withdrawn and having low self-worth in the aftermath of this forsaking, sinking into severe depression for the next fifteen years. Attributing his malady to black magic, his mother and other family members introduced him to faith healing, which made no difference. P speaks of wasted years, visiting one miracle worker after the other, in desperate search for a solution to his anguish. In the process, he was forcibly subjected to abusive rituals, which included his being tied to a tree and being flogged.

Over time, his mother decided that a second marriage might help to turn the course of events. After the marriage, P found himself overcome with irrational fears, which intensified during periods of stress. Despite his wife's best efforts to help, an overwrought P refused to listen. As he became increasingly averse to being in public spaces, he started to avoid people, including his family, and went to extreme lengths to safeguard his isolation. His panic levels impeded on familial roles – as husband, son, and father – and he isolated himself in his home, the only safe space for him. P started accessing localized clinical and social services after a NALAM worker initiated a dialogue with his family. They patiently and persistently addressed P's consuming anxiety and built a relationship with him that gave him the confidence to step out. The mobilizer also addressed the social stigma and superstitious customs around mental health, such as black magic, and traditional healing practices. Apart from follow-up services to build on the initial conversations, the worker facilitated family support, helping P to get a job as a daily wage worker at a construction site. Writing in 2020, Lakshmi Narasimhan from the senior management team at Banyan reports to me that, for the past year, P has not been taking medications as they were deemed unnecessary by his psychiatrist. P now lives an ordinary life in his village with his family – he continues to work as a daily wage worker at a construction site and contributes to sustain his family's wellbeing.

Case 3 The Story of E and S

E hails from the marginalized Irular community, a Scheduled Tribe, in Kottamedu. She was 25 years old when her husband, unable to pay a debt of INR 18,000 (£192, $247), committed suicide. This was the breaking point of a life devastated already with violence, abuse, and poverty. Her parents-in-law started to blame her for their son's death and began controlling her life choices. People in the community, instigated by the in-laws, also turned against her. E started getting threats from the moneylender, but her marital family refused to let her go to work, fearful that she would start a new romantic relationship there. E states that she managed to feed her three children because of the livestock in her possession. With each day's existence becoming impossible, E's mental health took a turn for the worse and she started accessing services at The Banyan's NALAM clinic.

At NALAM, E met S, a mobilizer. S decided to call upon the local leadership for support. She first met the *Panchayat* (village assembly) leader and requested his intervention to stop the harassment by the moneylender, as it was this phenomenon that had triggered E's husband's suicide. S started to regularly visit the in-laws to help them to understand the dire situation from E's point of view. As E states:

> Having S as my friend feels good as I can share my feelings without any anxiety. She is not different from me: she has led a tough life too. She convinced my in-laws and made them regain their trust, they treat me better now. They say now I should go ahead and marry someone because I am young. However, I don't want to since I have three children who need my full attention and support. I am happy to live with them.

Additionally, S arranged for E's children to receive a "stay at school" scholarship from The Banyan, which provided much financial and mental relief. She significantly helped E to reclaim her agency by enrolling in MGNREGA and preparing herself better to confront adversity. E is now supporting her family with her income and lives an independent and dignified life.

Case 4 The Story of a Mobilizer Mobilized

G grew up in a middle-class family and went to school up to the 8th grade. She married at the age of 17 and has a daughter who is now in the 12th grade. She pursued tailoring as a full-time vocation from home until she started working as a NALAM mobilizer. She had chanced upon the work done by The Banyan in Kovalam when she was visiting on behalf of a self-help group she was involved with. She initially started contributing as a volunteer for three months, after which she was invited to join the team. To begin with, she involved herself in group activities with clients, children, and carers at the health center, graduating to home visits from these duties.

Her life experiences have helped G to connect with clients, shared histories enabling her to forge relationships based on mutual trust and respect. She recalls the trauma her family underwent when her father, unable to repay a loan, went underground for a few days. They were verbally abused by loan sharks and accused of colluding in his disappearance. G helped to tide her family over this period, taking the initiative to locate her father and help him to confront reality. She credits her NALAM work for initiating transformational personal change. As G states: "I used to make all the decisions for my daughter based on normative expectations of the society. Now I enable my daughter to make her own decisions and give suggestions when needed."

Recently, G has decided to build a house on her own, with modern facilities including an attached toilet. This is especially significant to her as she has experienced difficulties sharing a community restroom. She has taken a loan to construct the house despite not having financial resources or family support. When she was not able to repay the loan on time, her friends and peers at work came to the rescue, standing by her and motivating her to find optimal resolutions to the crisis, which she did. At NALAM, G is now a senior case worker and a supervisor of the mobilizers.

Case 5 Story of K

K, a married woman, had two children by the age of 20. She had wanted to pursue higher education but her father forced her to get married as she was the eldest daughter. Her husband, ten years her senior, was abusive physically, emotionally, and sexually. K's life was a relentless struggle for her as she was the sole provider for her children. Although she found it daunting to separate from her husband, she was unable to withstand the torture and went ahead with the legalities. Soon after, she started working at the Banyan as part of the housekeeping team, after which she became a community worker. Working in the community was a challenge at the beginning, triggering traumatic memories as it did, but K was motivated by peers to overcome this. K expressed strong interest in client work and was promoted as a coordinator for the clinics. As she states:

> I spend most of my time working with broken families and help them emerge from the difficulties with the help of our interventions. Some clients come to the clinic just to spend some time together as they see this as a safe space to unburden their sorrows or indulge in mindless chat. This is especially true for elderly people and for women in abusive marriages, with whom I don't hesitate to share my past. Out in the community, I have been a witness to these diverse lives and stories, which helped me reshape my personal perspectives as well.

The NALAM work allowed her a viable opportunity to enter the public sphere, travel independently, and build formidable community resources. The mobilizers observe that none of this self-affirmation could have come from her natal family, patriarchal and misogynistic in its beliefs, or any man in her generation (K has no brother and is separated from her husband). Her social and cultural awakening at work has motivated her to encourage her children, regardless of gender, to learn to drive a car and participate in all activities equally. When her daughter scored low marks in her board exam, K says she did not lash out at her as would be the expected response. Instead, she encouraged her daughter to choose subjects she showed some aptitude for. The daughter is now training to be an economist. K works as supervisor and senior case worker at NALAM.

The three improvisatory free clinic structures – third-sector and inter-sectoral, grounded and ambulatory, peri-urban and rural – I have detailed in this chapter address the treatment gap in India as well as gaps in community mental healthcare. With the Janamanas and NALAM mobilizers, we see another emancipatory phenomenon: the peer supporter, a peer-modeled provision of services to persons with mental illness by those who have experienced mental illness or psychosocial disability themselves. These are Kakar's "vulnerable" experts, as mentioned above, whom Ritsuko Kakuma et al. call "affected individuals."[24] Citing research on clinical recovery by M. Slade and others, Pathare, Kalha, and Krishnamoorthy point out that the (Indian) state's mental health policy is predicated on clinical recovery, which primarily entails the removal of symptom and the restoration of social function. Internationally, however "there is increasing focus on *personal recovery*, which is seen as a unique personal journey including the development of new meaning and purpose for one's life despite mental illness" (2).[25] Peer support supplants a hierarchical doctor–patient relationship with mutual sharing, and its lack of infrastructure, while not an advantage in itself, allows it nevertheless to challenge the predominance of the medical model. It has, therefore, proved crucial for personal recovery in the socioeconomic contexts discussed above.[26] Whether it is the white-collar volunteer at Samadhana, the all-women municipality workers at Janamanas, or the NALAM mobilizers drawn from the very communities they help to heal, the objective is to create a transferential circuit that leads to what Paolo Freire, in *Pedagogy of the Oppressed*, called "conscientization" – the painstaking building of a critical consciousness for the marginalized, for those in the struggle for social equality, and ultimately for society itself (35). The actual term Freire uses is *conscientização*,[27] a word he did not coin himself but adapted, and which came to mean a process of (self-)awareness-building, which moved from the primary apprehension of reality to a critical engagement with it, leading to reform politics. Conscientizing is a dynamic process, its stages leading to an expansion as well as a deepening of conscious awareness. It transforms the subject from a sufferer of unjust and oppressive reality to the creator of a more humanized and agential future. "Mulloheenke mulloban kore deoa," as the community social workers at Janamanas say: making the hitherto disvalued valuable. For Freire, who imagined conscientizing in a liberation pedagogy frame, it was education as a tool of liberation for students as well as teachers, a denudation of prejudice and privilege for the latter that would, curiously enough, allow them to be more. Vandana Gopikumar, the founder of Banyan, lends further credence to Freire's hard-won insights when she states the following:

> Through the years, those whom we cared for, our best teachers, taught us what it meant to be poor, sad, alienated, hopeless. Their insights guided us as we developed a whole array of services and demonstrable models that helped reduce or alleviate distress.[28]

PART III

New York

CHAPTER 5

Open, Closed, and Interrupted City

In *Self and Emotional Life* (2013), their influential work on affect, Adrian Johnston and Catherine Malabou talk about Jean-Luc Nancy's departure from a tactilist or haptocentric metaphysics in his work *Corpus*. As Jacques Derrida observed in *On Touching*, if the (Western) metaphysics of touch can be characterized by "[c]ontinuity *and indivisibility*" (cited in *Self and Emotional Life* 23), for Nancy, touch is parting, partitioning, discontinuity, and interruption. The writer, Nancy speculates, "doesn't touch by grasping" but touches by way of sending themselves to the touch of something outside, "hidden, displaced, spaced" (*Corpus* 17). Their very touch is, in principle, "withdrawn, spaced, displaced" (17), and writing about the body outside is an "exscription," not inscription (18). Following Derrida, Johnston and Malabou find the medical term "syncope" – a temporary loss of consciousness experienced by a drop in blood pressure or a blockage of the blood to the brain – apt to describe a non-metaphysical touch that is also an expression of loss (discontinuity, interruption, syncope):

> An affect touches me but I don't know what "me" means. The interruption between me and myself appears to be a "spacing," which is the genuine spatiality of the breached affected subject. . . . Because the primordial affect (the affect of the self for itself) is always interrupted by the intrusion of alterity, all particular affects (love, hatred, joy, sadness, wonder, or generosity) are also constantly syncoped, interrupted, and discontinuous. (24)

In Jean-Luc Nancy's corpuscular philosophy, community is not enclosed, circling back to itself: not only is touch interrupted and divided between self and other, it is ungrounded between "me" and "myself." With this performative contradiction of shared yet parted contact in mind, this chapter examines narratives that function as interruptions, often inventions: acts of heteroaffection that are syncoped and discontinuous. It is interruption as breaking apart, breaking off, and also breaking into.

In his influential essay, "Walking in the City," Michel de Certeau examines "foreign" practices which disrupt the "'geometrical' and 'geographical' space of visual, panoptic, or theoretical constructions" (*The Practice of Everyday Life* 93). Written in 1984, this work has had an enduring life in cultural and urban studies for its nuanced readings of urban semiotics and the utopianism it vests in quotidian acts of walking, whereby the legible city space becomes ambiguous, personalized, a leaderless mass movement. In the three novels I discuss – Teju Cole's *Every Day Is for the Thief* and *Open City*, Rawi Hage's *Cockroach* – the "archive of the unconscious"[1] is the postcolonial and global city. Here, we find urban walkers who are analysts and analyzands, not city planners or cartographers. The narrators of the Cole novels are Nigerian-born psychiatrists (in training) living in New York, while Rawi Hage presents an Arab neurotic, an unsettled immigrant in Montreal. De Certeau does not address migrant workers and walkers explicitly, but his acute observations on the interruptions to imaginary totalities are trenchant for the out-of-place voyeur and *flâneur*[2] in these novels. Hage's 2009 novel is set in Montreal, while Cole's novels navigate postcolonial Lagos and multiracial, post-9/11 New York, respectively. All involve the restive figure of the city walker. The narrator of *Open City*, Julius, forensically examines the obscure, forgotten, or buried lives of the migrant city: the bodies of slaves interred near Wall Street, the Moroccan clerk at an internet café who could have been an intellectual, the Liberian refugee stranded in the waiting room of history at a detention center in Queens. The unnamed narrator of *Every Day Is for the Thief*, a psychiatrist-in-training and aspiring author, has returned to the begrimed streets and oppressive sitting rooms of Lagos after fifteen years in New York to chase a "spot of sun that moves over the house walls and slips over the unaware forest of flickering faces" (10). The narrator of *Cockroach* is not psychiatrist but a psychiatric patient: forced to be a confessing subject for a state-assigned therapist, he digs up his past and present in libidinal, larcenous, and murderous city escapades. I would argue that, in these novels, "a *migrational*, or metaphorical, city" interrupts "the clear text of the planned and readable city," to quote de Certeau (93).

The Nigerian author Teju Cole's drone stories on Twitter combine first lines of classic tales with drone imagery: "Stately, plump Buck Mulligan came from the stairhead, bearing a bowl of lather. A bomb whistled in. Blood on the walls. Fire from heaven." There are others, presented as short stories on Twitter:

1. Mrs Dalloway said she would buy the flowers herself. Pity. A signature strike leveled the florist's.
2. Call me Ishmael. I was a young man of military age. I was immolated at my wedding. My parents are inconsolable.
3. I am an invisible man. My name is unknown. My loves are a mystery. But an unmanned aerial vehicle from a secret location has come for me.
4. Someone must have slandered Josef K., for one morning, without having done anything truly wrong, he was killed by a Predator drone.
5. Okonkwo was well known throughout the nine villages and even beyond. His torso was found, not his head.
6. Mother died today. The program saves American lives.

Cole's choice of texts to bomb deserves attention: Virginia Woolf's *Mrs Dalloway* (1925), Herman Melville's *Moby-Dick* (1851), James Joyce's *Ulysses* (1922), Ralph Ellison's *Invisible Man* (1952), Franz Kafka's *The Trial* (1925), Chinua Achebe's *Things Fall Apart* (1958), Albert Camus's *L'Étranger* (1942). The canonicity of each involves much more than the event of its publication. Melville's work did not become a classic until the 1920s. The Camus novel wasn't even translated into English until 1946, when Stuart Gilbert, a friend of James Joyce's, published it as *The Outsider*.[3] The Gilbert "Mother died today" translation of *L'Étranger*'s "Aujourd'hui, maman est morte" has generated conflicted interpretations and misreadings of Meursault, of Camus, and of the text, traces which constitute its diachronic entity. Not only is this great book not allowed to exist, with it goes future histories of the book, future debates on the relative merits of autonomous or corpus-based, instrumental or hermeneutic modes of translation. Turning to *Mrs Dalloway*, there would be no "indescribable pause" on page 4 – and, arguably, no Clarissa Dalloway – if a signature strike finished the florist's on Bond Street. A drone attack is indeed a "tumbling" of the city (*Mrs Dalloway* 4), but not in the sense Woolf means it: it wrecks the city, instead of "creating it every moment afresh" as *flâneurs* do in their singular interactions and fabrications (4). Woolf's valorization of the fragmentary, the spasmodic, and the obscure has been compared to Einstein's theory of relativity, where, as Katherine Hayles observes, "the world is made partial and contingent . . . Relativity implies we cannot view the universe from an Olympian perspective" (49). The drone's, however, is an Olympian perspective, its killing strategic and targeted, even when the victims are innocent civilians.

"Quoting a text implies interrupting its context," Walter Benjamin has said (*Understanding Brecht* 19). Cole's citations from the canon use an improvisatory grammar that baffles metropolitan accounts of revisionism as a writing or talking back to the silences and strategic omissions in the classic, the precursor text. Nor are they marked by the familiar anticolonial or postcolonial self-loathing associated with being "Greco-Latin Negroes" (Fanon's angry term in *The Wretched of the Earth*), Hellenized against themselves in the coercive power/knowledge networks of the European humanist project. The emotional resonance of these extrapolations builds from the taxonomic use of classics – and the repetitive force of citing them in this way – in a series of 140-character messages, referring, for example, to Joyce's (and Homer's) *Ulysses*. In this instance, Cole mourns the loss of banal, stultifying days in the midst of modern perpetual war by quoting the inaugural lines of a literary classic which had monumentalized the banal and the stultifying. *Ulysses* is killed off by a drone attack before it has properly begun, like other unborn classics, and in this interruption lies the pity and the poetry. Similarly, *Moby-Dick*, the Great American Novel, is not allowed its constitutive self-estrangement, pluck, and survivalism as its hardy narrator dies prematurely. The assumed name – "Call me Ishmael" – lies unused and unmourned as his death in a meaningless act of state violence is marked privately.

A Million Untold Stories

The idea of unborn classics haunts the narrator of Cole's first novel, *Every Day Is for the Thief* (published in Nigeria in 2007). The unnamed narrator is a New Yorker who has returned to Lagos after fifteen years to find himself irked by the endemic corruption in Nigeria, from the consulate in Manhattan to the yahoo yahoos (who studiously perpetrate a notorious internet crime, the advance fee fraud, in fluorescent-lit cyber cafés) to the unemployed "area boys" spreading menace. The sense of shame and guilt is less civic than personal, the narrator unnerved by the realization that, like the nightly electric outages, he finds it oppressive because he's "no longer used to it" (19): "I have taken into myself some of the assumptions of life in a Western democracy – certain ideas of legality, for instance, certain expectations of due process – and in that sense I have returned a stranger" (16–17). Like any Western tourist, he wants to take public transportation – more specifically, the *danfo*, passenger buses his uncle and aunt call a den of thieves and voodoo. America has softened him, they say, so it hardly matters that he rode these in his high school days. "The degree to which my family members wish me to be separate from the life of the city is matched only by my desire to know that life" (35), the narrator states in all earnest. When he does hop on the people carrier, cell phone and digital camera in the front pocket of his jeans, shoulders "dropped back," face "tensed" and eyes "narrowed" (37), the plan of immersing in the demotic Lagos life, "creative, malevolent, ambiguous" (35), goes awry. He is distracted to find a woman passenger reading a Michael Ondaatje work. Given the low literacy rate and the relative paucity of high-brow English literature, why is someone of her social standing on this bus at all, he wonders. He wants to say to her, "with the wild look common to all those who are crazed with overidentification, 'We must talk. We have much to say to each other. Let me explain'" (43).

This and other cultural phenomena elicit curiously amplified responses to predictable facets of quotidian Lagos life. The national museum in Onikan, fallen into disuse and disrepair, is meager, lacking, withholding for the visitor, his "appetite" whetted by acquisitive paradigms of imperial curation and classification in metropolitan centers:

> My recent experience of Nigerian art at the Metropolitan Museum in New York was excellent. The same had been true at the British Museum, as well as at the Museum für Volkerkunde in Berlin. A clean environment, careful lighting, and, above all, outstanding documentation that set the works in the proper cultural context.... The West had sharpened my appetite for ancient African art. And Lagos is proving a crushing disappointment. (74)

The Musical Society of Nigeria also evokes an extreme, if opposite, reaction: "Each time I am sure that, in returning to Lagos, I have inadvertently wandered into a region of hell, something else emerges to give me hope" (87). When he is not feeling sorry for his doctor friend's paltry 70,000 naira a month, the "repressed violence" (111), as he calls it, of heavy furnishings darkens his mood in bourgeois living rooms.

The narrator is not Teju Cole, though his too is a "journey of return" to Lagos from New York (119), his travelogue audaciously illustrated with photographs Cole has taken. We learn more than halfway through the novel that he is a psychiatric resident in New York, not an author or photographer, yet in the novel he is presenting stylish and witty vignettes of Nigeria, from its fratricidal wars in the eighteenth and nineteenth centuries, its "shared sin" of transatlantic slave trade (115), to its dubious reputation, in the international media, of having the happiest people in the world. "The air in the strange, familiar environment of this city is dense with story, and it draws me into thinking of life as stories. The narratives fly at me from all directions," he says in a moment of short-lived euphoria

(64). He evokes the analyst's listening, which enables the associative yet "unpredictable" flow, when he says "All I have to do is prod gently, and people open up" (64). At other times, he aspires to be the "recording angel," transcribing details redolent of Gabriel García Márquez novels (65). "Life hangs out here. The pungent details are all around me," the narrator says (65) while daydreaming about Vikram Seth's or Márquez's risky authorial gambles as they wrote their masterworks like monads, "in monk-like solitude" (64).

The vaunted ambition of analytic listening or setting up a talking shop are, however, interrupted by practical concerns, such as questions of professional development, Nigeria's failures of governance and infrastructure, its inept social services and poor distribution of amenities, its infernal power cuts. The three noisy diesel generators in the family compound, a luxury only a few city dwellers enjoy, evoke paroxysms of despair in the narrator:

> The noise, the dark gray plumes of the diesel smoke are foremost in my mind: the moment there is a power cut, my evening is finished.... It is impossible to hear myself think. I would prefer, on these evenings, to sit in silence with a candle, but that is not a decision I can make for the eighteen other individuals in the compound. (67)

He is filled with admiration for anyone who can sustain creative work in the country, in the chasm between "the wealth of stories" and "the rarity of creative refuge" (68). The lack of reading culture he had pondered earlier in the novel begins to make sense: people are so depleted by a Lagos day that "mindless entertainment" (68) is preferable to high-cultural alternatives. By this account, long-form literature would be absurd and impossible in this dragging city, with its "ten-minute journeys that take forty-five minutes, the rarity of places of refuge, the constant confrontation with needs more abject than your own" (68). The narrator sees venality when he is not overwhelmed by the elemental vitality of the place and its people: there is no middle ground, no compromise formation, between the helplessness and hopelessness of people's troubles and the incessant talk that bespeaks resilience, humor, survivalism. His mind, unsurprisingly, is torn between "I am not going to move back to Lagos. No way. I don't care if there are a million untold stories" and "I am going to move back to Lagos. I must" (69).

Similar to the narrator of *Every Day Is for the Thief*, Julius in *Open City* is a psychiatrist-in-training in Manhattan, his research project a clinical study of affective disorders in the elderly. Curiously unperturbed himself by what is clearly a stressful profession – at least one of his patients is suicidal – and seemingly unaffected by the recent break-up of a serious relationship, he walks around New York (and, later, Brussels) gathering stories, plumbing depths, and sounding shallows. "The walks met a need: they were a release from the tightly regulated mental environment of work, and once I discovered them as therapy, they became the normal thing, and I forgot what life was like before I started walking" (7). If work was a regimen which allowed neither improvisation nor human error, the streets were a "welcome opposite" (7), beckoning its denizens to aimlessly linger, get lost and remain lost, and experience, for once, the inconsequentiality of choice in a state of true freedom. It is a proliferating as well as palimpsestic cityscape Julius inhabits, although the layers of the palimpsest are built on the erasures, not viable traces, of successive ethnoscapes. Standing where the obliterated twin towers once did, he recalls the network of little streets – Robinson Street, Laurens Street, College Place – destroyed in the 1960s to make way for the World Trade Center buildings.

> Gone, too, was the old Washington Market, the active piers, the fishwives, the Christian Syrian enclave that was established here in the late 1800s. The Syrians, the Lebanese, and other people from the Levant had been pushed across the river to Brooklyn, where they'd set down roots on Atlantic Avenue and in Brooklyn Heights. And, before that? What Lenape paths lay buried beneath the rubble? (59)[4]

If it is a "written, erased, rewritten" city, Julius sees his relationship to multitudes in terms of urban morphology: he is, he says, "one of the still legible crowd" (59).

"[F]or a young doctor completing a fellowship, he seems to have an awful lot of free time to wander the city at night, and to go to museums and concerts," Michiko Kakutani wrote in her *New York Times* review.[5] Kakutani sees Julius as "melancholy and dyspeptic," not the disinterested man of science his profession has prepared him to be. Sometimes in dandyesque high spirits, and benumbed and melancholic at others, Julius resists easy and lazy affiliations. The reader pieces together this character serendipitously, interpreting disavowals, denials, and estrangements as though these constituted a confessional. He must be an African, we say, when, watching a film set in Africa, he prepares to be angry again ("Africa was always waiting, a substrate for the white man's will, a backdrop of his activities," 29). He is wary of Western(ized) liberals, or he must be, for, during a visit to a detention center with a church group, he snipes at "that beatific, slightly unfocused expression one finds in do-gooders," of whom his girlfriend is one (62). He cringes when the postal clerk, in unsuspecting solidarity with another "black" man, shares a poem about "silenced voices" (187), making a note to avoid that postal office in the future; when the black cab driver is offended by his demonstrable lack of camaraderie, Julian airily says he feels in no mood "for people who tried to lay claims on me" (40). He is more at home with fleeting, no-strings-attached, even wordless encounters with strangers in the elite spaces where he engineers accidental social inductions: the disembodied voices of European radio hosts in his sparse apartment; the exiled Berliner in a Munkácsi show at the International Center of Photography; the tastefully dressed Dr. Maillotte with her "measured voice" and copy of Joan Didion's memoir (87) on the flight to Brussels; the all-white, middle-aged audience at a Mahler concert in Carnegie Hall.

Julius's race is confirmed when he cites Yoruba cosmology, and when, bemused, he is recounting an Indian-Ugandan doctor's rant on Idi Amin and the Africans. He is as covetous of other people's stories as he is withholding of his secrets: his Nigerian past; his estrangement from his mother; the lost German grandmother, to find whom he goes to Brussels (only to spend time reading high theory in his room or debating it with Farouq, an argumentative Moroccan at a local internet café); the unresolved issues with Moji, a girl he knew in Nigeria, and who accuses him of sexual assault when they were young. Caught between the metonymic proliferations of event and detail attaching to his peregrinations, and the stasis and repetition compulsions of his private self, "what moves the prose forward," James Wood comments, "is the prose – the desire to write, to defeat solitude by writing." Julian does not, in the end, rigorously analyze the emigrant and immigrant lives he has compulsively collated. Nor is there auto-fiction or a meaningful record of auto-analysis. What he does most tenaciously is put the city on the couch. Pompeii, in the Wilhelm Jensen story, the city whose ruins were miraculously preserved after the eruption of Vesuvius in AD 79, gave Sigmund Freud "a perfect analogy for the condition of repressed wishes, at once buried and alive, at once past and done and actively impinging upon the present," as Rachel Bowlby puts it (163).[6] In Teju Cole's *Open City*, Julius is the outsider whose excavations – excavating both in the sense of retracing steps and that of digging deeper and deeper – help the city to confront its repressed history and begin to mourn the bodies. One such secret story is the Negro burial ground between Duane Street and City Hall Park, where 15–20,000 slaves were unceremoniously interred.

In the Wake (2016), Christina Sharpe's haunting account of the legacy of chattel-slavery "necropolitics"[7] in contemporary USA, argues in the introduction that the personal anecdotes with which the complex argument of the book is inaugurated function to connect a specific, singular family's being in the wake to those of all black people in the wake: "to mourn and to illustrate the ways our individual lives are always swept up in the wake produced and determined, though not absolutely, by the afterlives of slavery" (8). Quoting Saidiya Hartman, who states that the autobiographical example is "not a personal story that folds onto itself," Sharpe valorizes the personal as a window into social and historical processes – a mode of witnessing which entails not passive sufferance, but countering what Hartman calls "the violence of abstraction" ("Fugitive Dreams" 7) with the contingent personal. The scene where Julius chances upon the memorial for the African burial ground, a site of 6 acres in the seventeenth and eighteenth centuries now reduced to a perfunctory monument on a tiny plot, is framed with a shakily personal narrative of trauma. Julian had been beaten violently and mugged by two young black men just two weeks before – "brothers" with whom he had exchanged a nod of solidarity minutes before the assault. Now, in lower Manhattan, his bruises healed but for a nagging ache in his left hand and surrounded by imposing federal buildings with snaking lines of immigrants, Julius is, as Sharpe describes it, "in the wake," the semiotics of the slave ship continuing "from the forced movements of the enslaved to the forced movements of the migrant and the refugee, to the regulation of Black people in North American streets and neighbourhoods" (21). Sharpe had used "wake" in three senses: coming to or becoming awake; a vigil for the dead; the track left on the water's surface by a ship.[8] "I had no purchase on who these people were whose corpses, between the 1690s and 1795, had been laid to rest beneath my feet," Julius thinks at first (220). He had, effectively, desecrated the dead already as he wound his way through buildings, shops, diners, and pharmacies built over the burial ground. He recounts how the repressed had returned to claim its symbolic due when construction of a building on Broadway and Duane in 1991 uncovered human remains. The bodies of slaves had been buried in white shrouds in coffins pointed toward the east. The skeletons showed signs of disease – arthritis and rickets but also syphilis – and brutalization. The black-on-black violence of diasporic modernity is traced here to the original sin of slavery as the oneiric reality of the chapter gives way to Julius's coming-to-consciousness in the shared time of the wake. Julius feels a sharp pang, ancient and recent blunt traumas becoming one, as he steps into the security island and touches the grass.

> What I was steeped in, on that warm morning, was the echo across centuries, of slavery in New York. At the Negro Burial Ground, as it was then known, and others like it on the eastern seaboard, excavated bodies bore traces of suffering: blunt trauma, grievous bodily harm. (221)

In distinct and unmistakable ways, *Open City* is a doppelgänger of Cole's *Every Day Is for the Thief*. Like the narrator of the first novel, Julius has visited Nigeria after a gap of fifteen years. Both protagonists are mixed race; fatherless, with white mothers they no longer speak to, both are on aspirational, self-fathered trajectories in the new world. Each makes an "unexpected connection" (*Every Day* 112) to slavery: one stumbling upon a forgotten burial ground north of Wall Street, the other on a national secret in the middle of a traffic jam in Lagos, "dense with rapidly moving human bodies" (112). At the artery of the CMS junction, the nameless speaker of *Every Day Is for the Thief* has a vision of the "chain of corpses" (112) connecting Lagos with New Orleans across the Atlantic. He ponders the complicity of the fratricidal Yoruba wars in drawing slave ships to the river mouths of the Niger Delta for 300 years, and even after the British ban on the slave trade in 1808. The vanquished tribes were brought from the interior to the coast and sold to the people of Lagos, who then arranged auctions with English, Portuguese, Spanish, and Brazilian traders. The calm waters of the delta let the ships dwell as long as necessary to load up on the human cargo: consequently, there are no forts here, and little for tourists to see. In the absence of a national memory culture, is the text of the novel meant to be the monument that will wake Nigerians from their dogmatic, dreamless slumber?

> This history is missing from Lagos. There is no monument to the great wound. There is no day of remembrance, no commemorative museum. There are one or two houses in Badagry that display chains and leg-irons but, beyond that nothing ... in Lagos we sleep dreamlessly, the sleep of innocents. (*Every Day* 114)

The unnamed narrator and Julius are also shrinks, a profession Julius associates explicitly with the politics of strategic seeing and unseeing. "The practice of psychiatry is partly about seeing the world as a collection of tribes," Julius observes (205). The medical practice of psychiatric seeing, however, is jeopardized, by the way in which it organizes the "normal" and the "mad" as control groups with major differences between and minor differences within the categories. "In my duties as a medical school graduate and psychiatric resident, I was licensed to be the healer, and nudged those who were less normal toward some imaginary statistical mean of normalcy," Julius frets (206):

> what are we to do when the lens through which the symptoms are viewed is often, itself, symptomatic: the mind is opaque to itself, and it is hard to tell where, precisely, these areas of opacity are ... I have felt that most of the work of psychiatrists in particular, and mental health professionals in general, was a blind spot so broad that it had taken over most of the eye. (238–239)

Why then, is the shrink the stand-in for the author in both novels? Can these figures, standing at the spreading edge of psychiatry and psychoanalysis in global cities, see otherwise?

If psychiatry is an optical knowledge which presupposes correspondences between "external Signs" and "internal realities" (238), Julius offers the corrective of seeing in the darkness, viewing each patient as a dark room. For the speaker of *Every Day Is for the Thief*, the analyzable text flies from everywhere, even when it lies hidden in plain sight or the strategic forgetting of neocolonial states. Julius, in *Unseen* City, assumes analytical stances, if by analytical stance we understand "a scopic and gnostic drive" related to what Michel de Certeau describes as "this lust to be a viewpoint and nothing more" (92). He is self-conscious of the elevation and estrangement of his exclusive vantage points, whether it is a glassed-in terrace overlooking the Hudson or a perch 70 feet above street level on the "unlit side of Carnegie Hall." Similar to the psychiatrist's treatment of the patient *as* a dark room, "[i]n the darkness, above the sheer drop, I could see" (255), he says, describing a high-wire act between the monadic intelligence and the un-actualized worlds beckoning from the crowds below. Again, it is the author as analyst in *Every Day Is for the Thief* whose free association, functioning as self-analysis, helps us to uncover the purposive links between the shared sin of slavery and the informal economy on Lagos Island or police brutality in New Orleans. The last chapter of this fictional travelogue, which, we are told, is written from New York, goes fitfully back to old Lagos. It is the spectral authoring Gayatri Chakravorty Spivak evokes in "Ghostwriting," which is "not only a *revenant* (a returner, the French for 'ghost') but also an *arrivant*, one who arrives" (71). While "people are hard at work" in perfectible time,[9] "I alone wander with no particular aim," the narrator says, waking to a labyrinthine dream of mindlessly returning and arriving (*Every Day* 159).

"The Doctor, Like the Sultan, Is Fond of Stories"

Sharpe's *In the Wake* describes a "living in and with terror in that in much of what passes for public discourse *about* terror we, Black people, become the *carriers* of terror":[10]

> This is everywhere clear as we think about those Black people in the United States who can "weaponize sidewalks" (Trayvon Martin) and shoot themselves while handcuffed (Victor White III, Chavis Carter, Jesus Huerta, and more), those Black people transmigrating the African continent toward the Mediterranean and then to Europe who are imagined as insects, swarms, vectors of disease; familiar narratives of danger and disaster that attach to our always already weaponized Black bodies (the weapon is blackness). (15–16)

Rawi Hage's *Cockroach* forcefully revises critical thinking about dispersed populations – black and brown bodies recast as mutant, viral carriers of infection – "insects, swarms, vectors of disease" – in a historical moment made sleepless by the greatest refugee crisis the EU has known, the greatest since World War II. In 2015, around 205,000 Europe-bound refugees had entered Greece via the outlying Aegean isles. The vast majority were Syrians (69 percent) fleeing war and the brutal occupation of their homeland by Islamic fundamentalists, Afghans (18 percent), Iraqis, and Somalis fleeing conflict in their countries.[11] A UN report of December 8, 2015, states that more than 911,000 refugees and migrants had arrived in Europe since the start of that year; 3,550 lives had been lost in the journey.[12]

Cockroach is about a migrant who has fled the decade-long Lebanese civil war (and a personal trauma) to arrive in Canada, and who imagines himself half-cockroach: wretched, driven underground, hungry and scrounging. In one of his hallucinations, a cockroach doppelgänger says: "We are ugly. But we always know where we are going. We have a project. A project to change this world" (102). Hage's ugly and wily cockroach chidingly reminds the reader of the erstwhile British Prime Minister David Cameron's description of migrants trying to reach Britain as a "swarm." "He should remember he is talking about people and not insects," the Labour Party's Harriet Harman had said in the chorus of condemnation that followed.[13] This was in the context of Calais in 2015, where hundreds of migrants had tried to enter the Channel Tunnel overnight, and thousands had been trying to reach the UK from Calais. According to the UNHCR (the United Nations High Commissioner for Refugees), the UN refugee agency, 2,500 people had died that summer trying to cross the Mediterranean to Europe: 9 had died attempting to cross the Channel.

Cameron's exact words, uttered during a tour of South East Asia, were: "a swarm of people coming across the Mediterranean, seeking a better life, wanting to come to Britain." Britain should not be treated as a safe haven for migrants in Calais, Cameron thundered, adding that the French had deployed additional police and the UK was investing in fencing and security measures. The leader of this imperial nation told the BBC that "everything that can be done will be done to make sure our borders are secure and make sure that British holidaymakers [in Calais] are able to go on their holidays."

Hage's 2009 novel asks to be read and revisited in the glare of the images of the tragedy unfolding on the shores of Europe in and since September 2015: hundreds of migrants piled up in the nineteenth-century railway station, Keleti, in the Hungarian capital, while European leaders bickered over who should take responsibility for these unwanted arrivals; hundreds taking off from Budapest on foot; the image of 3-year-old Aylan Kurdi face down on a beach in Turkey, killed with his brother Galip and mother Rehana while attempting to enter the Greek island of Kos illegally, the family fleeing Syria to seek refuge with relatives in Canada. Read alongside Teju Cole's *Every Day Is for the Thief* and *Open City*, the Lebanese-born Hage's *Cockroach* throws up a mess of images and postcolonial themes constellated in the figure of the migrant as city walker. If Cole's protagonists are the city's analysts (in training), Hage's insect-like protagonist, scuttling around for food and love, is the swarming unconscious of the icy city. The global city becomes an "urban 'text,'" to quote Michel de Certeau – a manifold fiction produced by the very act of walking, a text the walkers write "without being able to read it" (93). In these novels, peregrinations and disconnected conversations (a narrator posing as analyst, the other defaulting as analyzand) stand in for (absent) plots. For every written city, there are many unapparent, unwritten cities.

In *Cockroach* we meet the walker-writer at the outset, learning that he had tried to commit suicide, was sectioned briefly, and is now ordered by the state to visit a therapist, Genevieve, every week. The narrative comically alternates between the hallucinatory reality of the protagonist's waking and dream lives – his memories and traumas, his thieving and larceny, his sexual fantasies and sexual shenanigans, his ragtag socioeconomic milieu, comprised of *émigré* hustlers and con artists (Iranians, Albanians, Algerians, Lebanese) – and deadpan exchanges with an uncomprehending therapist in a barely furnished public health clinic. The narrator, unnamed, has fled his Middle Eastern home (identifiable as Beirut), for a modern city (identifiable as Montreal, which Hage once described as "a large military industrial complex"). It is also a frozen city in northern terrain:

> nothing here exists; there is no queen, there are no seals, no dancing bears, moose, cabins, high trees, bonfires. Descriptions of these are all a ploy, an illusion, a conspiracy. There is nothing but that which freezes, and the only way to escape it is to dig deep holes, dig and sail under it. (250)

The Quebec of *Cockroach*, like its historic counterpart, is racially diverse – and racist.[14] If, by the end of the nineteenth century, the vast majority of the inhabitants of Montreal (98 percent) were of British or French descent, the influx of Eastern European Jews in the 1910s and 1920s, the Italians in the 1940s and 1950s, Haitians in the 1960s and 1970s, and the Vietnamese in the late 1970s and 1980s reduced the number of inhabitants with French or Anglo-Celtic descent to one third of the population. As Susan Ireland and Patrice J. Proulx note, "the term 'ethnic,' which had previously been used to designate French Canadians, began to be applied to those of non-French-Canadian origin" (2).[15] The government, the narrator of *Cockroach* observes, is open for business when it comes to Christian, French-speaking Europeans:

> The Québécois, with their extremely low birth rate, think they can increase their own breed by attracting the Parisians, or at least for a while balance the number of their own kind against the herd of brownies and darkies coming from every old French colony, on the run from dictators and crumbling cities. (27–28)

In stark contrast, the narrator is not settling in nicely but being a pest, transmogrifying into a detritivore invasion. "All nature gathers and invades" (210), he says, as snowflakes, gusts of wind, and the words that fly from people's teeth, all make him think shudderingly of the force field of little particles: "Little creatures that seem insignificant and small are murderous in their sheer vast numbers, their conformity, their repetitiveness, their steady army-like movements, their soundless invasions" (209). In "Walking in the City," de Certeau asks us to analyze the "microbe-like, singular and plural practices which an urbanistic system was supposed to administer or suppress, but which have outlived its decay":

> one can follow the swarming activity of these procedures that, far from being regulated or eliminated by panoptic administration, have reinforced themselves in proliferating illegitimacy, developed and insinuated themselves into the networks of surveillance, and combined in accord with unreadable but stable tactics to the point of constituting everyday

regulations and surreptitious creativities that are merely concealed by the frantic mechanisms and discourses of the observational organization. (96)

If the language of power is urbanizing, de Certeau follows out the swarming, proliferating life that threatens any such organization. The act of walking in the city is a speech act, "a process of *appropriation* of the topographical system on the part of the pedestrian" (97). In *Cockroach*, the "swarming activity" and "surreptitious creativities" of the protagonist may well be the enunciatory act of unlimited illegitimacy de Certeau locates in such practices, but the narrator shows little interest in subverting surveillance (or the panoptic administration of which it is a tool). He wonders how he might explain this, his disinterest in belonging to or mobilizing a (radical) collective, to his therapist.

> How can I tell her that I do not want to be part of anything. . . . I am part roach now and what if my instincts make the best of me and lead me to those armies of antennae, hunched backs, and devouring teeth that are preparing from the underground to surface and invade? (210)

The protagonist of *Cockroach* is a character dreamt up by Kafka (Gregor Samsa) and Burroughs (*Naked Lunch*). He is a visionary, like Dostoevsky's Underground Man; and he represents the "anonymous collectivity" (Albert Memmi's term)[16] of Ellison's *Invisible Man*. A thief, anarchist, and a social satirist made ill by his own bilious observations, he jogs memories of Céline, Rimbaud ("The Drunken Boat"), Camus, Genet, Cronenberg. Nouri Gana, among other critics, sees similarities between the transmuting part-roaches of Hague's novel and the Egyptian playwright Tawfiq Al-Hakim's *Fate of a Cockroach*. The protagonist's mental troubles can be traced to the death of his sister, fatally attracted to a violent man: we gather that it is his unwitting complicity in the sister's tragic death that has driven him to Montreal. Here, he falls madly in love with Shohreh, a beautiful and willful Iranian woman who uses him for sex but doesn't love him back. His suicidal thoughts are precipitately forgotten when he becomes embroiled in Shohreh's perilous reinvention of herself from victim to perpetrator of violence after she bumps into an Iranian politico – the one who raped and tortured her in Iran – in the restaurant where the narrator works as a bus-boy.

Unlike fiction we have come to identify as diaspora literature, with the "ex-centric communicative circuitry" (Paul Gilroy's phrase in *Against Race* 129) of their patterns of power, communication, and conflict, Hage's novel takes little interest in dismantling the colonialist center–satellite binary that continues to polarize postcolonial geography. Its prime focus is not on transforming metropolitan space for dispersed populations to – and I quote Gilroy again – "converse, interact, and . . . synchronize significant elements of their social and cultural lives," but on finding a room without light where the narrator can have his breakdown in peace. He is scathing on the question of assimilation or embourgeoisement, as seen in his attitude toward Reza or the Professor, experts at playing "the fuckable, exotic, dangerous foreigner" (199). He abhors the affluent French Canadian women who fall for his 'noble savage' act and whom he subsequently robs. He can live in filth and hunger if Shohreh will sleep with him, he insists:

> I can tolerate filth, cockroaches, and mountains of dishes that would tower above our heads like monumental statues, like trophies, testifying that we value lovemaking and a hedonistic experience, and that all else can wait! (52)

Becoming animal, however, is not simply an escapist fantasy in *Cockroach*: metamorphosing though he may be into an alien organism, he can hardly suspend his deliberations on personhood and identity. It is a sensation of feeling "heavy" as well as "light and fleet," exfoliated and "weightless" as well as "sad": he is the last human on the planet and the first post-apocalypse invertebrate (118). His ruminations testify repeatedly to the quandary, pain, and mortality of raced subjects: "I was split between two planes and aware of two existences, and they were both mine" (119). Although the narrator jokes about enjoying a spot of "anti-imperial loot- ing" (251), helping the janitor's Russian wife steal from an old lady in her care, whose British officer husband – according to the janitor's covetous wife, anyway – "stole everything from the Indians, or the Chinese" (41), *Cockroach* is about a deterritorialization without the emancipatory promise of reterritorialization. It is about coming undone, but without a transformative vector, and it is about a protagonist who rejects alike the seductions of archaism and futurism (Deleuzian terms, similar to territorialization). The narrator seems to suggest that his psychotic epi- sodes are, in fact, involuntary acts signaling a nonconformity with power, which is inherently corrupting and predatory. "How can I tell her [Genevieve] that I do not want to be part of anything because I am afraid I will become an invader?" (210).

What Rawi Hage's *Cockroach* shores up, by way of urban text, is the underground, laying claim to a psychiatric culture that had hitherto denied the colonized, the by-products of coloniality, and the wretched of the earth the civilizational benefit of possessing an unconscious. Echoing Freud's there is no "no" in the unconscious, Hage writes: "The drain swallowed everything, nothing was filtered, recycled, tossed away" (156). However paranoid and restrictive the immigration policy of the world above ground, "All was good, all was natural, all was accepted by the underworld" (156). The novelist and poet James Lasdun's *Guardian* review of *Cockroach* associates an uncensored muchness with Hage's prose:

> While your average British or American writer would opt for a single, precise image to illuminate an object or idea, Hage (who writes in English) likes to throw in all the alternates and variants he can think of, good and bad alike, as if he is constitutionally unable to forgo any possibility of deepened or extended resonance.[17]

This reminds the reader of the rich, teeming sewage Hage describes in *Cockroach*, "nothing . . . filtered, recycled, tossed away": the style is processual, a becoming, which eschews "any possibility of deepened or extended resonance" – the possibility of existentialism, in other words. "The nomad exists only in becoming," Deleuze and Guattari stated, thinking of Bedouins, Eskimos, and the wanderers of the Asian steppes (475).[18] Figurative representations of nomad theory and poetics have to capture constant movement and what Milovanoff calls a non-dualist "museal world,"[19] not immobilized states. The death-dealing episteme is counteracted in effluvial fantasies of digging and sailing under the icy city. It is here, with the "crickets, crocodiles, muddy rivers . . . and troops of roaches receiving signals, conspiring to take over the world," that the ambulatory poetics of *Cockroach* is at its most giddying:

> All that exists, all that will ever exist, shall pass through this passageway under the ice, the dead corpses when they turn to dust, the big happy meals, the wine, the tears, the dead plants, the quiet settling storms, the ink of written words, all that falls from above, all that ascends, all that is killed, beaten, misused, abused, all that have legs, all that crawl, all that is erected, all that climbs, flies, sits, wears glasses, laughs, dances, and smokes, all shall disappear into the underground. (250)

In his critical interpretation of "Delusions and Dreams in Jensen's *Gradiva*," Sigmund Freud's psychoanalytic critique of Wilhelm Jensen's novella, the French critic Sylvère Lotringer argues that the hero Norbert Hanold's interest in Gradiva is not a fetishistic fixation on a woman's foot, as Freud suggests. Jensen's story is about an archaeologist who is obsessed with the bas-relief of a walking woman that he has seen in a museum in Rome. He names her "Gradiva," or "she who walks in splendour." He procures a plaster cast of this relief and is plagued by dreams of this woman coming to life among the scenic ruins of Pompeii. Norbert's obsession

takes him to Pompeii, where, in a "strangely dreamy condition," he sees his
Gradiva walking on lava stepping stones. She turns out to be his childhood
sweetheart, Zoe. The joke is that he is attracted to the sculpture in the first
place because it is an exact likeness of his childhood sweetheart, and it will
be up to Zoe to reinstate him to the truth and attainability of his desire.
According to Lotringer, what attracts Norbert to Gradiva is an image of the
freedom of walking, a movement of the body. "Nomadic form, without
specific territory, and from no definite epoch: transhistoric" (cited in
Wright, *Psychoanalytic Criticism* 172).[20] The archaeologist is moved not
by formal beauty but by the representation of someone in motion in the
Gradivan gait. Where Freud saw fetishistic fixation on the unobtainable
ideal in Norbert's feelings for Gradiva, Lotringer sees the flow of libido,
a movement of desire (Wright, *Psychoanalytic Criticism* 74). The Gradiva
case study shines a light on Hage's *Cockroach* and the Teju novels discussed
above, all of which use, as their leading characters, active, not passive,
subjects, who refuse to be immobilized or rooted to a spot. Like the living
woman in *Gradiva* or the runaway cockroach, they slip quickly away from
edification, containment, control, identification, and predation (in its
different forms). The unnamed narrator in *Cockroach* likens his therapist's
epistemic greed to that of the Sultan in the *Arabian Nights*, which he will
baffle with pseudo-narrative in every wily exchange. Here's a snippet of
that conversation:

> Who is Abou-Roro?
>   My mentor. A thief in the neighbourhood.
>   Genevieve nodded. She looked intrigued but held her composure Her
> pen made its way inside her lips, and I could see her breathe in a steady,
> regular motion, in time to her heartbeat. The doctor, like sultans, is fond of
> stories, I thought. (102)

In interesting contrast, in the Teju Cole novels, where the figure of the
analyst or psychiatrist is a migrant, the role is associated with obsessive but
not appetitive truth-seeking: this is a quest which leads to doubling and
equivocation, not positivist knowledge. In this re-arrangement (or
derangement) of the novel's epistemology lies its analytic breakthroughs.
Back in snow-covered New York, the narrator of *Every Day Is for the Thief*
is haunted by a memory which "stands out of time" (158). He sees himself
in the area around St. Paul's Anglican Church. The city, with its hodge-
podge of architectural styles, has become "trackless as a desert" (158).
People are hard at work while he wanders aimlessly. Little streets entwine
confusingly, and on house after house is painted the directive "not for sale."

Losing his historical and geographical bearings, the narrator connects at last to the returning and repeating city, Lagos in New York, "as pure place" (159).

Parasitism

"I am not going back there. They won't find me," says the narrator of *Cockroach* to his shrink (286) as he categorically rejects her offer of a psychiatric referral. He seemingly has no faith in treatment at the hospital or subsequent social rehabilitation: he is headed underground. The analytic scene, at its most intense at the very moment of its dissolution, reminds us that touch can be parting and partitioning. In the Teju Cole and Rawi Hage novels, the interruption appears in the form of the canonical, urban, communal, and cultural texts. The author is posed as both *arrivant* and *revenant*, interrupting cultural memory and cultural amnesia or being rumbled and breached himself by his returns to a strange and estranging past. And, as Hage's *Cockroach* dramatizes so poignantly, interruption is the affected subject's desire for touch – "I just wanted to be invited in" (286) – but it does not lead to homogenistic community.

"Mass displacement is the product of modern violence and oppression," Lyndsey Stonebridge writes in *Placeless People*: "to humanize the inhuman is to lend dignity to a condition that by robbing people of citizenship – of the right to exist in a community – has deliberately denied them dignity" (11).[21] She cites Edward Said's 1984 essay, "Reflections on Exile," written in the aftermath of the massacre of Palestinians in refugee camps in Beirut. It is the "age of the refugee," Said had said of late-twentieth-century mass immigration, sounding a cautionary note at the same time that to think of the corresponding literature of exile as "beneficially humanistic" was to "banalize its mutilations" (cited in Stonebridge 11). The parasitism of *Cockroach* refuses to "concede the political experience of mass displacement to literary humanism," to quote Stonebridge again (12). It brings together the nonmetaphysical touch of the interruptions I have described with the fractal selves resulting from interruptions in para-sites of the global city. Derrida states in *Limited Inc.* that the parasite "is never *simply* external, never simply something that can be excluded from or kept outside the body 'proper,' shut out from the familial table or house" (90).[22] The parasite is inside, outside, beside ("para"), the very logic of supplementarity that makes deconstruction what it is. Derrida uses the metaphor of the parasite as an unlikely characteristic of iterability (not to be mistaken for repetition). Iterations, from their very inception, are "parasited, harboring and haunted by the possibility of being repeated *in all kinds of ways*, of which theater, poetry, or soliloquy are only examples" (90). In *Limited Inc.*, Derrida offers a deconstructive reading of the binaries (and hierarchies) of language in J. L Austin's *How to Do Things with Words*: successful and unsuccessful, happy and unhappy, normal and serious versus peculiar and parasitic. In certain circumstances, Austin states, language may be used in way that is parasitic to its normal use, to be classified under the "*etiolations* of language" (22). In Derrida's interpretation, the parasite is part of so-called normal language, not extraneous, and "it is part of it *as* parasite" (*Limited Inc.*, 97).

In *Strangers to Ourselves,* a work which seems to espouse a critical parasitism wherein the figure of the stranger is discovered *within* one's sovereign self,[23] Julie Kristeva turns to *L'Étranger*, one of the canonical texts whose drone deaths on Teju Cole's twitter began this chapter. Meursault is not a typical Frenchman among Arabs, Kristeva argues, but a borderline "case," or "a quasi-psychotic, rather than . . . a prototype of the foreigner" (25). He is as alienated from the pieds-noirs as he is from Arabs. Kristeva's reading of Meursault as the prototype of the stranger or foreigner unwittingly reveals xenophobic attributes that she readily ascribes to the figure: a state of mourning; lost consciousness; an "anaesthetized indifference"; a lack of "innerness"; adrift relationships and loyalties (27). We are to extrapolate, from the neutralized first words ("Today mother died") with which *L'Étranger* begins, a hollow man who "remains outside conversation, outside communication, outside action, outside passion" (28). Consequently, his murderous act in the novel is indifferent and insignificant. In Kristeva's eloquent interpretation, we have someone from the dominant class in Algeria who is also the expedient representative of an inner exile. Controversially, Kristeva insinuates that this strange European's act of murder is innocent of motive and tantamount to shooting at shadows: as she states with conviction, "whether French or Maghrebian, it matters little" (26). If Meursault the benumbed colonial is the uprooted person, what happens to the uprooted colonized persons – such as the unnamed Arab he kills – who are denied speaking parts in this absurd theatre, or the prerogative to kill with impunity? If the foreigner is within us, and if this introjected foreigner makes of us the split and schizoid subject of enunciation, perhaps no real foreigners need apply. "Freud does not speak of foreigners," Kristeva asserts, "he teaches us how to detect foreignness in ourselves" (191). The novels by Teju Cole and Rawi Hage I have interpreted here, with characters whose intranational displacements stop short of the cosmopolitical, espouse a different ethics of transnational psychoanalysis, one that refuses to meld the identities of host and guest, analyst and analyzand, in shareable codes of strangeness. "I just wanted to know you. . . . I just wanted to be invited in," the narrator of *Cockroach* tells his shrink before severing all contact (286).

Postscript: Clinical Interruptions

Aisha Abbasi's *The Rupture of Serenity* elaborates on how interruption – her term for it is "intrusion" – can strengthen the core of an immigrant psychoanalysis. Pakistani-born Abbasi moved to the US in 1987, completing a residency in psychiatry at the Henry Ford Hospital (Detroit, MI). She later trained to be a psychoanalyst at the Michigan Psychoanalytic Institute, where she now works. "This book was written as a life is lived," begins Abbasi, comparing psychoanalysis to a meandering path to be walked, not a theory to be swallowed whole (xv). The most trenchant intrusions upon clinical space she records occur in the last section of the book, written in the shadow of 9/11: they chronicle dangerous conversations that occur between the patients and their immigrant Muslim analyst, focusing on their sadistic feelings in the transference.

The events of 9/11 made her work life take a catastrophic turn, Abbasi writes, leaving her struggling to find her own precarious balance while helping her patients to find theirs.

> The devastation caused by the terrorist attacks had breached the necessary boundary between fantasy and reality to a shocking degree, and the "as-if" quality of my patients' transferences toward me was temporarily shattered. They vacillated between imagining, on the one hand, that I was a reliable analyst toward whom they could have destructive wishes, *feeling* that I might retaliate but at the same time knowing, on a deeper level, that I would not, and on the other, feeling that I was an unreliable and dangerous person who came of dangerous stock, and that their hateful feelings toward me might actually cause me to hurt them: after all, look at what my people had just done. (119)

Abbasi writes about an Indian patient from Bangalore – Mr. Gupta – an IT expert whom she had evaluated a few years earlier during one of his professional stints in the US. Ten years later, in February 2009, he rings Abbasi, requesting to begin a course of analysis a decade after she had recommended it. Abbasi agrees to work over the phone, wondering why he had contacted her when he did and feeling sorry that his travails had persisted over the years. She learns that he is still struggling with his homosexuality and that his "narcissistic vulnerabilities" (127), stemming from feelings of being unloved by his father, continue to pose setbacks. Gupta mentions a host of reasons for contacting the analyst, including the Mumbai terrorist attacks of 2008, which had coincided with a period of acute professional and romantic frustration (he had felt overlooked by his boss and suspected he was being emotionally manipulated by a man he liked).

When Gupta mentions the traumatic fallout of the Mumbai attacks, Abbasi ponders the coincidence that the terrorists were, like herself, Pakistani Muslim. She wonders if, overwhelmed by shame and rage, he had made of her a figure of abandonment (when, in reality, it was Gupta who left America to return to India). They begin a telephone analysis five times a week. Abbasi narrates the following session, which takes place a year into the analysis, and just before a ten-day break requested by Abbasi, which Gupta had known about for six months. Gupta starts by saying he had seen a movie, *My Name is Khan*, where the eponymous hero, an autistic man, overcomes the hysterical and lethal Islamophobia of the post 9/11 months to prove that Muslims weren't all terrorists. Gupta next turns to the biopolitical regime unleashed on Muslims, including body scans and body-cavity searches that were now compulsory for residents of certain Muslim countries at airport security checkpoints in the US. Abbasi hears this as an "indirect, ominous threat . . . his wish for me to be viciously intruded upon and humiliated" (129). Gupta continues to speak provocatively, turning on his analyst now with allegations that she was volatile and hot-headed: he speculates that she could get very angry if he insisted the terrorists belonged to an outfit called Lashkar-e-Tayyaba, located in Pakistan. Abbasi calls out his ambivalence toward her, noting that, while he thought it was "cool" to have a Muslim analyst, he also found it "very dangerous" (130). Gupta next talks about his recurrent fear of abandonment and rejection, now focalized through his vexed social interactions, flaring up at his analyst's interjection that he humiliated people in retaliation for the acute humiliation he himself felt.

"I am wondering how it is for you now in America?" Gupta says. "Do people think you might be crazy, like a terrorist?" (131). Abbasi records feeling the full onslaught of this retaliatory attack: "He had tapped into the most primitive anxieties I had felt after 9/11" (131). Collecting herself, she asks Gupta what he thinks this cultural moment might entail for her, to which he says in a "matter-of-fact" way that she would be "wiped out professionally," left bereft of any patients (131). Abbasi sees through the punitive fantasy, gaining "more stable analytic ground":

And that would serve me right, wouldn't it? ... For leaving you. It's satisfying for you when you imagine I might be subjected to having my bodily orifices intruded upon and violated, or that I might be wiped out professionally – and you speak about it so calmly. (131)

Gupta claims he is not calm at all, but agitated and hurt, fearful that she had taken him on only because she wanted to make money, and because no one else wanted her as their analyst. "I heard his comment," Abbasi writes (132), the hurt and pathological insecurity that made it impossible for him to believe he could be valued or loved for himself. She tells him that if that were the case – and he was to be her only patient – he would be "very very special" to her in the fantasized scenario (132). "I would really want you. Not like the way you felt with your parents" (132). Gupta relents, admitting that in the throes of "so many real disappointments and rejections," he probably imagined people mistreating him even when they were not, "people like you who are actually trying to help" (132).

Drawing on Jean-Luc Nancy's *Corpus*, Johnston and Malabou use the idea of nonmetaphysical touch as a model for self-absenting: "[t]he subject's self-touching is always discontinuous – absent to itself, as it were – as if it were the touching of any other" (23). Interruption, in the Nancy interpretation, can be re-imagined in this way as a fold in continuity, like the parasite who is inside, outside, and beside the self. And, if the subject's "self-touching is always discontinuous," the idea of self-same self undergoes a radical change by the "intrusion of alterity," as Johnston and Malabou put it (23–24). Like Cole and Hage, Abbasi draws on kinetic and spatial metaphors to describe the analytic process. Journeying through these cases over time and cultural intertexts, she refutes C. P. Oberndorf's prevailing theory that transference, in its most positive form, "is most likely to be easily established and examined (analysed) between patient and hospital and patient and physician if their psychological biases do not differ too widely" (cited in Abbasi 133). Between Oberndorf's 1954 paper on the fear of strangers and the late 1990s, there had been only a few papers on the impact of ethnic and other differences on the psychoanalytic dyad, Abbasi observes – a curious phenomenon, given that many early analysts in the US were immigrants. It is only now, in the twenty-first century, that the sporadic research on interracial and cross-cultural psychoanalysis is beginning to gather critical mass. "With my patients as well, the obvious difference between us presented a visible structure onto which they could project their feelings of exclusion and devaluation," Abbasi states (134). The ability to see (through) the patient's co-optation of cultural stereotypes, both negative and positive, could help the analyst to better confront their own prejudices and inner conflicts: "this constitutes important work in one's own personal/training analysis" (135). In closing the case report, Abbasi writes with this altered self-awareness that she understood, with Mr. Gupta, "that his sadistic fantasy of my bodily orifices being viciously searched and attacked had to do not only with his rage at feeling excluded from my life and my body, but also his wish to find a way into me and within me" (133). Interruption is the affected subject's desire for touch, but it does not transform the non-parallel lives of the analyst and analyzand into homegenistic community. Keeping this model of therapeutic contact as parting and partitioning, we turn to the final chapter of the book. Here we ask what the affordances of psychoanalysis or psychotherapy might be for the unhomed in New York City, the torture survivors at Bellevue, the undocumented homeless in Harlem, or the "pathological parents" of a therapeutic nursery.

CHAPTER 6

Psychoanalysis of the Unhomed: Free Clinics, New York

The arduous and often thankless work of free clinics originates with and is sustained by guerrilla activists, one of whom is Jimmie Holland, fondly known as Jimmie. The founder and "mother" of psycho-oncology, Holland worked tirelessly to bring together the fields of psychiatry and oncology, from her appointment in 1977 as the inaugural Chief of the Psychiatry Service at the Memorial Sloan Kettering hospital until her death in December 2017 as Chair of MSK's Department of Psychiatry and Behavioral Sciences. She was instrumental in the founding of the Psycho-Oncology Society in 1984 and co-founded its journal, *Psycho-Oncology*, in 1992. She launched the American Psychosocial Oncology Society in 1986. In the influential article "History of Psycho-Oncology: Overcoming Attitudinal and Conceptual Barriers,"[1] Holland ponders the impact of two histories of prejudice impinging on the emergent field of scholarship on the psychological dimensions of cancer: the culture of silence around cancer, and the stigma attached to mental illness. Given the undeniability of the psychological impact of cancer, she examines the social factors that contributed to the integrative, behavioral, and psychosomatic branch of medicine that is psycho-oncology emerging as late as the last quarter of the twentieth century. It is a heterogeneous and interdisciplinary field, Holland points out – one which has benefited from the research and clinical experience of psychiatrists, behavioral psychologists, social work-ers, oncologists, nurses, and the patients themselves. To this list of con-tributors Holland adds clergy and pastoral counselors.[2] Citing *King Lear*'s "We are not ourselves when nature, being oppressed, commands the mind to suffer with the body," she adds that the core of psycho-oncology addresses "this suffering of the mind that occurs with cancer" (215).

Holland challenges the prejudice in "mainstream medicine" against behavioral interventions, which, despite being backed by strong empirical data, are seen as "alternative therapies" comparable to praying or making dietary changes: every intervention in cancer is deemed complementary "if it is not surgery, radiation, or chemotherapy" (218). What this also fails to recognize is that patients turning to so-called alternative or complementary therapies are demonstrating distress that has gone unseen or untreated by their oncologists. Citing a study by H. J. Burstein and collaborators on the use of alternative therapies by women diagnosed with early-stage breast cancer, Holland observes that these patients had demonstrated more distress, more severe depression and decreased sexual function, and a poorer quality of life than counterparts who had not turned to such therapies. The rise of psycho-oncology de-stigmatizes the range of interventions in cancer treatment and aftercare that focus on mental health: group therapies and group sessions; the screening of distress; the initiation of dialogue on the experience of pain. Holland herself was instrumental in campaigning for patient distress to be recognized as the sixth vital sign in medicine (after temperature, pulse, blood, respiration, and pain). Holland raged against the "tyranny of positive thinking"[3] cancer patients and survivors suffered. Pep talks were not enough, she insisted, and competent medical care would have to be put in place to address the suffering of cancer patients negotiating the cultural "burden to be positive."[4]

Jimmie Holland, whom I interviewed at Sloan Kettering Hospital in October 2017 (we had been in sporadic email correspondence since 2014), provided me with a detailed list of mental health resources which accepted Medicare, the federal health insurance program: low-cost psychotherapy clinics in Manhattan, psychiatrists, psychologists, social workers, therapists. Jimmie worked full days at the hospital and had time only for working lunches (of fresh, hot soup, brought in by her assistant), of which my visit was one – when she died two months later on December 24, more than one obituary called the octogenarian's death (at 89) "sudden," such was the unrelenting force of her medical progressivism and fight for raising awareness about the human vulnerabilities inflicted by cancer. Meaning-centered Psychotherapy (MCP) – a short, structured intervention which helps patients to cope with the loss of meaning in life brought on by the onset of severe illness – is an integral part of the psycho-oncology training and education program at the Memorial Sloan Kettering Cancer Center, and it draws on the neurologist, psychiatrist, and Holocaust survivor Viktor Frankl's theory of logotherapy.[5] Holland herself has championed talk therapy throughout her career, using its efficacy in anxiety reduction as an evidence base to justify psycho-oncology. As she said to her students, "you have to treat the whole person, not just the tumor."[6] Recognizing the deficit of psychotherapy for mental health problems of the urban poor, Holland has treated the problems as culturally endemic and not simply restricted to the travails of one's racial or social embodiment. However, psychoanalysis in its conventional form was not a solution, Holland maintained. She cited, instead, translations and variations of psychoanalysis, including the existential psychotherapy inaugurated by Irvin Yalom's *Staring at the Sun*. She then recommended – picking up the phone then and there for introductions – three key psychotherapeutic interventions in urban poverty in New York that I would proceed to study and collaborate with: the Program for Survivors of Torture at Bellevue; the United Transitional Living Community in Harlem; the community outreach of analysts at the William Alanson White Institute.

In *The Architectural Uncanny*, Anthony Vidler proposes the uncanny – discussed in detail in Chapter 3 of this book – as a response to "the real shock of the modern": "a homelessness generated sometimes by war, sometimes by the unequal distribution of wealth" (9). This chapter presents three case studies, adding the legacies of chattel slavery to the causative factors listed by Vidler for the physical and psychic unhomeliness – and the phobic inhospitality – of the Western nation to the asylum seeker and refugee, as well as the internal immigrant, the noncitizen. The first of the three sections is an account of psychotherapy as it is used to treat torture survivors in New York, a major entry point for immigrants to the United States. The second section is about a different category of homesickness, and provides an account of the mental health needs of New York's homeless poor. The third looks at the home as a Gothic carceral, where the natural guardians and protectors of children have turned predators, linking the therapy of traumatized survivors of childhood sexual abuse to interventions in the legacy of slavery in the US.

On Transience

Sigmund Freud's "On Transience," written in 1915 at the invitation of the Berlin Goethe Society, has an early articulation of the profoundly impactful theory of mourning which would be elaborated in "Mourning and Melancholia" (1917). It begins cheerfully, with Freud taking a summer walk through the "smiling countryside" with a "taciturn" friend and a young but already famous poet (305). His travel companions seem overburdened with "aching despondency" because the ambient beauty of the scene is ephemeral, already fading into nothing (305). Does transience of beauty lead to a loss or increase in the value of the (beautiful) object, Freud speculates: why should the beauty or perfection of a work of art or of an intellectual achievement "lose its worth because of its temporal limitation" (306)? Failing to convince the present company, Freud considers the possibility of "a revolt in their minds against mourning" (306). In the essay, the melancholic summer of his companions is the one immediately preceding the outbreak of the Great War, a cataclysmic event that, Freud writes, robbed the world of the "beauty of its countrysides," "the achievements of our civilisation," "the lofty impartiality of our science," the hopes of a triumph over "the differences between nations and races" (307). Waking up from a nation's dogmatic slumber – "our country [was] small again and . . . the rest of the world far remote" – Freud wonders if the lost certainties and cultural possessions are now valueless (because proven impermanent). What is preferable, mourning occasioned by loss or a "permanent renunciation" of the precious but passing loves? The former, Freud indicates, because mourning, "however painful it may be, comes to a spontaneous end":

> When it has renounced everything that has been lost, then it has consumed itself, and our libido is once more free . . . to replace the lost objects by fresh ones equally or more precious. It is to be hoped that the same will be true of the losses caused by this war. (307)

This essay, Anthony Vidler remarks, is among those works by Freud which not only grapple with the traumas of war but "anticipate in many respects the extension of psychoanalysis to social concerns" (7). The war had "robbed us of very much that we had loved" but "we shall build up again . . . and perhaps on firmer ground and more lastingly than before," Freud cautiously hopes in "On Transience" (307).

As we have seen with the PCPCS horticultural initiative, and in the fictional representation of displacement in the last chapter, for the poorest migrants, refugees, and asylum seekers in the colonial metropolis, unhomeliness is the loss of territorial security in the natal home resulting from global or internecine war, the unsettledness of exile, and the receding horizon of hopes of rehabilitation (or acculturation in the adoptive home). The task of the analyst is to turn the permanent mournfulness of these denied citizens into mourning, which, as Freud stated, has a "spontaneous end." For it is possible, Freud had concluded, that "if the objects are destroyed or if they are lost to us, our capacity for love (our libido) is once more liberated" (306).

"To help meet the needs of the estimated 400,000 torture survivors living in the United States today, the U.S. Office of Refugee Resettlement (ORR) will distribute $7.3 million in grants to 10 to 15 of the nation's most comprehensive torture treatment centers," writes Leslie

Knowlton in an article in *Psychiatric Times*. The funding is a result of the Torture Victims Relief Act (TVRA), legislation passed by the US Congress in 1998. The population of survivors of torture in New York City is high, and the PSOT center at Bellevue, the epicenter of public health in the country, has provided multidisciplinary care to this category of immigrant patients since March 1995. Bellevue integrates medical and psychiatric care: medically ill patients get psychiatric care, in other words. While the NYU School of Medicine, with which it is affiliated, is more focused on surgical specialities, Bellevue strives to make mental health a priority. The Torture Survivors center is based in the primary care medical clinic and run by primary care doctors, psychiatrists, psychologists, gynaecologists, rehabilitative teams (ranging from physicians to art therapists), and social workers. "The center was founded with hospital funds and donations from various private foundations and government agencies," Knowlton notes. With a budget of $1–7 million, the program raises donations from federal authorities, private individuals and foundations, and the UN Voluntary Fund for Victims of Torture. All physicians and psychologists in the program have faculty appointments at NYU School of Medicine, and the program is supported by other medical center resources, including the Rusk Institute of Rehabilitative Medicine. Though the Bellevue/NYU PSOT is not a mental health program, it functions as a free clinic: fees are waived for patients who cannot afford treatment, others are seen on a sliding fee scale.

Speaking to Knowlton in the year 2000, Edna Impalli, clinical psychologist and educational and cultural coordinator of the Survivors of Torture program, estimated that there were 75,000 to 90,000 torture victims in New York City alone, with up to 35 percent of refugees coming to the US from countries where torture is systematically practiced. Patients are referred to the SOT program by legal agencies, community organizations, and current and former participants. All patients have either experienced traumatic events consistent with the United Nation's definition of torture (UN Convention Against Torture, 1984/1987)[7] or have experienced states of exception, including genocide, war, political violence. The program offers ethnoculturally specific supportive group therapy for torture survivors, therapy oriented toward "adaptation" – restoration of capability and psychological functioning – rather than "emotional exploration." The program currently has six groups: two Francophone and one Anglophone African, an international English-speaking group, a Tibetan group, and an LGBT one.

"Clients" come in presenting non-psychiatric medical problems, Impalli states, "physical sequelae" such as broken bones, muscle pain, headaches, dizziness, burns, hearing loss and loss of sensation, or tuberculosis, and "emotional sequelae" including memory loss, sexual dysfunction, social withdrawal, insomnia, flashbacks, and nightmares. The program offers individual and group therapy (to homogeneous and mixed groups): "Psychological treatments include cognitive-behavioral therapies, psycho-dynamic therapies, family therapy, narrative/solution-focused therapy, group therapy, testimony therapy, hypnosis and EMDR (eye movement desensitization and reprocessing), activity therapies, and expressive art therapies." The program researches the types of torture and trauma relevant for each demographic, their symptoms, and expedient diagnoses. Each patient has a database form with standardized measures of PTSD and psychological symptoms, and this data is scrutinized for information on the specific effects of torture and trauma on refugees, their adaptive and survivalist capabilities, and the efficacy of various treatment approaches.

Urged and introduced by Jimmy Holland, I met Dr. Asher Aladjem at Bellevue. Despite his international renown, the unassuming Aladjem did not seem put out when he had to use an empty room in the hospital as his makeshift office for our interview. As I introduced my topic to him, Aladjem said he regretted the decline in in-patient services for the chronically and persistently mentally ill. Hospital stays of 45 to 60 days were now down to 16: "not cost saving but cost shifting," he remarked, with prisons and shelters bearing the brunt of housing the de-institutionalized and homeless afflicted. A pathbreaking study co-authored by Aladjem uses a convenience sample to examine the psychological consequences of torture and refugee trauma.[8] As the specialists point out, while most studies of this type focus on homogeneous samples drawn from a single region, this research drew on the refugees seeking medical assistance in an urban torture treatment center. Using psychological distress instruments – the Harvard Trauma Questionnaire (HTQ) and the Hopkins Symptom Checklist (HSCL-25)[9] – this study looked at a sample which included 199 men and 126 women from 54 countries (with Tibet, Sierra Leone, and Guinea among the most heavily represented). The most common reason for persecution cited was political activism (65.8%), followed by other factors such as religion, ethnicity, family relation to other victims, gender and sexual identity.

Most of the participants reported having been beaten; 18% of the sample reported rape and 11% sexual assault. Psychological torture, reported by 90% of the participants, involved the individual concerned or their family members. The responses to HSCL-25 and HTQ showed extremely high levels of psychological distress across the sample, with 80% of the patients above the threshold on measures of depression and anxiety. The standardized symptom rating scales also revealed nearly half of all the patients (46%) to be above the cut-off for identifying "clinically significant PTSD" (192). The study offered unique insights into factors generating psychological distress – survivors of rape, for instance, demonstrated more symptoms on the anxiety, depression, and PTSD scales – as well as the singular cultural manifestations of such distress. The rate of PTSD symptoms among Buddhist refugees (most of whom were Tibetan) was significantly lower. While this finding, the authors point out, was consistent with existing research that Buddhist monks are less prone to PTSD than other torture survivors (despite experiencing comparable traumatic experiences), they emphasize the validity of medical constructs such as PTSD despite cultural differences: "the high level of internal consistency found for the Tibetan translation of the Harvard Trauma Questionnaire suggests that the phenomenon of PTSD may be equally valid in Tibetan Buddhist survivors of torture, even if considerably less common" (193).

Aladjem started his medical practice at the height of the AIDS epidemic in the 1980s, with dire survival rates. He was with an uptown program that provided care to refugees with AIDS from all over the world. "Even within a [cohesive] community you have no support if you are gay and have AIDS," Aladjem stated in his interview with me. After the AIDS epidemic, the program focused on expanding psychiatric service to patients with cancer or in primary care. "You do population management," the hospital administrators at Bellevue say admiringly to Aladjem, the hospital's only psychiatrist in ambulatory care.[10] The survivors (not victims) of torture Aladjem has treated constitute a heterogeneous trauma population: the young Rohingya from Bangladesh with sarcoma of the bone, his arm excised below the elbow; the Tibetan monk fleeing the Chinese government who "hears voices telling him to go to Bellevue"; West African Muslims whose limb amputations were categorized into "short sleeve" (up to elbow) and "long sleeve" (entire arm); Bosnian women raped by Serbian soldiers in detention camps; slaves from Mauritania; LGBT populations from Chechnya, Azerbaijan, Ukraine, Iraq.

In a *Lancet* article, Sharmila Devi points out the pivotal role played by stories in this mode of treatment:

> In a modern room at New York's Bellevue Hospital, Marie's story of rape and torture by African soldiers sounded like a medieval chronicle, but it was an all-too-familiar tale for Adam Keller, the doctor who examined her.

> Although Keller has heard countless similar stories in his 15 years of heading the Programme for Survivors of Torture (PSOT), he listened to Marie's story with such empathy and understanding that it was as though he was hearing everything for the first time. (1527)

In the conversation with Keller, Marie talks about her kidnapping and solitary confinement in a dirty cell in May 2006. She talks about her broken nose and the gash on her leg made with a knife. "[W]ere you raped, sexually assaulted?" Keller asks Marie (1527). She nods. Though she does not volunteer the information at first, we learn that she was raped and sodomized in captivity. Marie had come to the NYU School of Medicine from a homeless shelter in New York with suspected malaria, where she was referred to the PSOT. After a diagnosis of severe PTSD, she was prescribed sleeping pills there and started therapy. In these cases, the medical treatment of physical and mental illness doubles as the documentation the patient will use for her application for asylum, a process assisted by PSOT's legal services manager, who is an experienced paralegal and a Board of Immigration Appeals accredited representative.

Aladjem peppers his conversation with me with stories of his own life. "I grew up in Israel, in the biggest refugee camp in the world, with neighbors from India, Warsaw, Yemen." "I always saw myself as a citizen of the world," he says. He wanted to be a diplomat but knew he wouldn't get security clearance from Israel because of his sexual orientation. Aladjem decided to become a hands-on doctor, not an Israeli bureaucrat – "I needed to find the humanity in medicine." Aladjem says that treating patients who have endured chronic, long-lasting catastrophes – twenty years of war, for instance – has made him realize that "a lot of bad things happen to people, but life doesn't end there." As had Jimmy Holland, he cites the Austrian psychiatrist and Holocaust survivor Viktor E. Frankl's concept of resilience: resilience, Aladjem states, is not an emotion but a cognitive state of mind. His use of psychotherapy is along psychodynamic principles: where he sees depression, he sees also resilience, the wish to move on and be better. Aladjem mentions a 70-year-old woman patient from the Dominican Republic. Her daughter died of AIDS, and of grandchildren she left behind, one has cerebral palsy, the other a hyperactive disorder. The patient came to Aladjem from a shelter, soon after her own breast cancer diagnosis. In the course of her treatment, she developed the capability to contact a journalist and arrange a scholarship for the granddaughter with cerebral palsy to attend medical school. "Everything is a long process, but everything I do has good outcomes," Aladjem says simply. He encourages patients to make decisions for themselves: "they come in chains of old cultures; I help them out of these chains." A Tibetan priest, who had arrived traumatized and tortured, his hand covered with burns, said he needed Aladjem's permission to become a sushi chef in Michigan. Aladjem says he is happy to be instrumentalized in this way, as the patient returns to his own self the confidence and agency he had lost.

Aladjem talks about traumatic and narrative memory and the particular difficulty posed by the forced cultural forgetting of "disappeared" political activists. In this instance, he is referring to the Mothers of the Plaza de Mayo, the Argentine mothers whose children were abducted during the military dictatorship and who mobilized a movement between 1973 and 2006. He is referring also to Chinese patients whose fathers "disappeared" during the cultural revolution. Can you rebuild memory when it is devastated by personal loss which doubles as a symptom of the breakdown of civil order? What do you say to a mother from Bosnia who receives a letter from the son conceived of rape? In answer to the latter, Aladjem advises the mother to "meet him." The outcomes he works toward are the following: developing trust in humanity; enabling the patient to become a productive member of society; enabling the patient to create a community, starting with a family. "I am not the anonymous analyst," Aladjem states, joking that this may be a non-traditional use of psychodynamic psychotherapy. He is convinced that "you can't do good psychopharmacology without psychotherapy": "pills don't solve problems."

Sharmila Devi recounts a case study with Aladjem as the psychiatrist in charge. Agnes had been visiting the Armenian parliament building in Yerevan when a group of armed men attacked, shooting dead the prime minister and seven high-ranking officials in 1999. Security forces, believing she was involved with the perpetrators of the attack, harassed her. She fled to the USA, her three children separated from each other and relocated to France, Germany, and Russia. Aladjem informs us that when Agnes first arrived at the PSOT in 2006, she was mute and unable to communicate. When she was able to speak eventually, she complained of chest pains. These symptoms, Aladjem states, were not dismissed by her PSOT assessors as psychosomatic and further medical examination revealed that Agnes had a heart defect, for which she was able to get surgery.

"Aladjem speaks six languages, but Armenian is not one of them, while Agnes still has a poor grasp of English," writes Devi. The two of them met in person, communicating through an interpreter on a telephone. "After men followed me in Armenia I ran away and stayed far away and that's why I'm scared," Agnes said between tears, via the interpreter. "Until now, [the

US] didn't deport me because what I'm saying is the truth" (1528). Aladjem notes significant improvement in Agnes's confidence from the time she first came to Bellevue. She is noticeably more assertive, but continues to suffer from extreme anxiety and fear, which impede her learning abilities and language skills. "She has average intelligence but seems impaired cognitively and people don't take her seriously," Aladjem observes. "She's trapped between lawyers and lives hand-to-mouth with friends, and is one step away from being homeless. Her children might be in a similar situation. It's an all too familiar story to us" (1528).

Aladjem, a psychiatrist by training, argues that his discipline has a vital role in the "identification, evaluation, and treatment of torture and refugee trauma" (217). At Bellevue, however, psychiatry is practiced in conjunction with primary care medicine and behavioral health psychology. Clients are not always directly referred to the psychiatrist after their intake interview. The primary care physicians in the program, trained in "psychopharmacological interventions" (258), can prescribe medication. The psychiatrist is consulted only when there is insufficient clinical progress or when the need for a psychiatric follow-up is felt after the initial prescription. As Aladjem observes of this challenging biopsychosocial model:

> This integration has increased the range of available interventions, and enabled the program to offer a wide range of multi-disciplinary treatment options. This is a collaborative model in which mental health, medical and social services combine forces to construct a new arena in which to provide care. (220)

Aladjem does not view PTSD and the traumatic symptoms of survivors of torture as identical. It is a diverse group of neuropsychiatric symptoms which generate diverse diagnoses because of comorbidity – psychiatric and medical – premorbid psychopathology, and ongoing stressors.[11] Therefore, it is crucial to consider a client's current presentation of symptoms in the context of the client's individual life. Citing the research of Yehuda and Macfarlane, Aladjem notes that the prevalence of PTSD among those exposed to traumatizing stressors can range from 3% to 58%, the low prevalence rates pertaining to those exposed to natural disasters, while the high (47% to 50%) to victims of man-made traumas, such as prisoners of war, and torture and concentration camp survivors. Even then, Aladjem argues, PTSD cannot be understood solely in terms of the traumatic experience: there is "a significant percentage of people exposed to these stressors who do not develop the clinically significant threshold of symptoms for a diagnosis of PTSD" (223).

Similar to the bipolar dancer from the old Soviet Union, a lot of premorbid victims of torture present co-morbid conditions. Aladjem outlines a case study in which depression and substance abuse were the co-morbid symptoms accompanying PTSD, and which showcases the dialogue between psychiatry, psychotherapy, and social services that the PSOT initiative stands for. A 35-year-old Tibetan activist was tortured and forced to flee, leaving his wife and two small children behind. He found work at a construction site in NYC and lived in cramped conditions with several others. He had severe symptoms of depression and anxiety and was self-medicating: "drinking myself to sleep" (226). Recurrent flashbacks of his torture, homesickness, and sleep disturbances became so debilitating that he could no longer imagine a future for himself. His hopelessness and helplessness impeded even his work with the immigration attorney preparing his asylum application. Aladjem records that the patient was started on psychotropic medication instantly – Benzodiazepine, Clonazepam 0.5 mg PO at bedtime, and Mirtazapine 15 mg PO at bedtime – and he simultaneously participated in psychotherapy, primarily to address the concurrent alcohol abuse. This "psychopharmacological" (228) intervention, he argues, was the most expedient one, given the intensity of the patient's symptoms, his alcohol addiction, and his potentially dangerous day job in construction. Not psychiatric hospitalization, but outpatient therapeutic treatment, can work favorably in this way for a psyche battered by forced imprisonment and torture. If the dosage of Mirtazapine had to be increased, the Benzodiazepine was slowly tapered off. After about ten weeks of treatment, the patient, who once felt incapacitated by guilt and self-loathing ("the notion of feeling well was contrary to his experience," 227), stopped drinking and started being able to fall asleep.

Citing Scott and Briere, Aladjem states that "no one model will suffice to describe the entire pathophysiology involved in the manifestation of post-traumatic stress" (241). Individuals differ in their neuro-anatomical make-up, and this influences their singular responses to the traumatic event. The event itself causes neuro-anatomical changes: the brain responds to acute stress by releasing neurotransmitters that help the body to behave adaptively, but these reactions too vary from person to person. Aladjem argues that a firm grasp of biological systems is imperative for gaining insight on how the brain is reacting to repetitive traumas. The classes of medication used in psychopharmacological treatment are as follows: anxiolytics; antidepressants; antipsychotics; mood stabilizers; pain medications; psychostimulants; cognition-improving medication; adrenergic blocking agents. Pain is one of the most common symptoms, often presented without a recognizable aetiology.

Aladjem cites the example of a patient who discontinued her treatment with psychotropic medications because they threatened her suffering subjectivity with erasure: "When I feel sad at least I know the pain is mine" (258). Ms Q, the patient in question, is a professional woman from a nation in northwest Africa. Her traumatic suffering dates back twenty years prior to her arrival, in her thirties, at the Bellevue/NYU PSOT. She and a sibling were arrested with their father, a human rights advocate, and subsequently separated. He was executed and the children imprisoned. Ms Q was beaten, berated, and sexually abused: the sibling died in prison. Ms Q, who was referred to the program by an international human rights group, had symptoms of Major Depression and was prescribed medication immediately. Within a few days, she complained that she was feeling benumbed, not quite herself. (Aladjem notes that her medication would not reach the therapeutic level for another couple of weeks at least.) Reflecting a pattern we have encountered before, in other clinical scenarios, the idea of being relieved of her symptoms triggered guilt, loss, emptiness, and was unbearable to her. She was allowed to discontinue her medication but continued with (psycho)therapy. The symptoms of depression remitted gradually.

"Psychotherapy and psychopharmacology should not be viewed as disjunctive, but rather as points along a continuum of care," argues Aladjem (256–257). Psychopharmacology of the kind practiced by Aladjem concerns itself with psychodynamics and an in-depth comprehension of the patient's experience. Medication alone is not enough, although it offers symptom relief, Aladjem insists. A careful monitoring of outcome measures with psychotropic medications can enable patients to engage in therapy, "which then facilitates the painful process of addressing profound changes in one's self" (256). Ms Q, whose alleviated depression symptoms are periodically triggered by the human rights advocacy works she has immersed herself in, uses supportive therapy to achieve a viable balance between "her needs to heal and to advocate for change" (258). The Program for Survivors of Torture, thus, functions as a twenty-first-century free clinic where one could be freed from destructive neuroses and prepare to work and love again. Helen Schur, the wife of Freud's physician Max Schur, had said of the postwar psychoanalysts trying to democratize the discipline that they truly believed "this would be the liberation of the people" (Danto 10).

Transients

In an ethnographic study of the homeless poor of New York City conducted between 1979 and 1982, Kim Hopper addresses the undeniable rise in psychiatric disorder in the shelter population. However, she critiques the "impaired capacity" model of homelessness – which sees mental disorder as instrumental in displacement, not the other way around – to argue that interlinked socioeconomic factors (such as housing, employment, household composition, and government assistance), which have caused "disorders in the system of care" (159), should be held responsible for the individual's inability to secure stable habitation. She discusses, for instance, as some of the causative factors, the scrapping of federal housing-assistance programs for poor households, gentrification, and the decline of single-room occupancy (SRO) hotels. Disaffiliated, disaffected, troubled, and troublesome, "homelessness remains locked with the conceptual brace of 'deviancy,'" Hopper states (164). There are three devious consequences of this public perception: it turns the homeless poor into victims and casualties; tackling this "problem population" takes the form of control and containment, not repair and rehabilitation; larger developments in the economy and policy pertaining to the disabled and dependent are not scrutinized unless they are egregious failures, such as deinstitutionalization.[12] This "reclassification" of the dependent poor from vagrants to patients, Hopper argues, avoids an uncomfortable question: "how much money, under what auspices and in accord with what terms and conditions, will be devoted to the effort to resettle these aliens amongst us?" (164).

The psychiatric model of homelessness has severe shortcomings, Hopper warned in 1988. The data was not collected systematically and comprehensively, with appropriate diagnostic instruments. It is not easy, she argues, to distinguish mental illness symptoms from behavioral patterns developed from a homeless way of life, whose baseline levels of functioning are poorly defined. The specific contribution of homelessness to a given dysfunction could not be established without doubt: the cross-sectional nature of the studies (by Bachrach, Koegel, Burnam, and others) would make it impossible to establish a time sequence. The time lag between deinstitutionalization and ex-patient showing up in shelters showed also that it was not just "personal impairment" but "social handicap" and the ecology of an unequal, divided city which were to blame (160).

The Central Harlem Housing Guide, created by the Manhattan Community Board 10, lists the United Transitional Living Community as a homeless shelter. New York is one of the five states that accounts for nearly half of the nation's homeless population: 98 percent of the state's homeless population is in New York City. It has a homeless population of

75,323 people, most of whom are sheltered because of the Callahan Decree, a legal mandate that the city council provide safe temporary housing for this vulnerable sub-population (Otokiti et al.). Located in the northwest corner of 133rd street and 7th, TLC, as it is called, defines itself as not just a shelter but a source of "strength-based empowerment," as Athea Thomas, a licensed clinical social worker, puts it. Funded primarily (70 percent) by the city while the occupants pay the remaining amount, the program is guided by principles of "harm reduction" and "trauma-informed care": "we create and reinforce stabilization." TLC is an apartment-style shelter for single adults, unique in the way it lets residents shop; cook; participate in choice-oriented discussions about their past, present, and future; and, most importantly, complete the housing pack for city-funded housing. What makes TLC unique is that it is a mental health shelter for homeless populations, including undocumented persons, and addresses psychosocial issues arising from being homeless. Residents arrive here from assessment sites including the 30th Street Central Shelter (for men), and the Franklin Center in the Bronx and HELP Women's Center in Brooklyn (for women).

The psychiatric evaluation TLC offers mainly reveals diagnoses of schizoaffective disorder, depression, paranoia, bipolar disorder, PTSD, and major depression with psychotic features, among others. When I ask about common symptoms ("common" both in the sense of prevalent as well as that of characterizing the homeless as a collectivity), the attending psychiatrist, Tony Stern, mentions mood dysregulation and psychotic difficulties with "reality testing." Self-isolating paranoia and misplaced grandiosity intensify the solipsism of the displaced, becoming more impenetrable with time. This in turn leads to hopelessness. Speaking of the "unholy trio" of paranoia, narcissism, and hopelessness, Stern says his aim "is to see it in action and to begin to defuse it as best I can – and to help the TLC person to begin to notice its undermining dynamic in their own lives." "Do most residents present similar or related symptoms?" I persist. He answers in the affirmative, repeating that the core trio of paranoia, grandiosity, and hopelessness can be seen as a single common problem. "All three symptoms result from and result in a tendency toward self-isolating," he states.

Most of the residents have had more than one cycle of homelessness: many, if not most, of the residents have substance abuse problems. "We do our best to go beyond the assembly line approach to helping people," Stern says. He discusses the drawbacks of managed healthcare: the time limitation of ten sessions only; the inability of the psychiatrist to give a prescription for more than thirty days; the impossibility of the time-strapped public-sector psychiatrist properly evaluating a patient before renewing prescription. "These days many outpatient clinics are more like outpatient factories, unfortunately," Athea adds. TLC, on the other hand, aims at building a community that offers a more holistic physical and mental space. Most clients live here for more than a year (and usually a minimum of six months), and "we often see actual change," she states. They change behaviors that made them struggle. Mental illness does not go away magically – episodes of depression, for instance, can occur with stressors – but residents learn to cope with these episodes.

Formal therapy is not suitable for everyone, Stern points out, but some form of counseling or pre-therapy is an option for most TLC residents. What the TLC team provide is not formal "therapy" as these residents either already have or are about to have their own psychiatrist and therapist, either at a clinic, an ACT (Assertive Community Treatment) team, or another setting.[13] "We see ourselves as the eyes and ears of those providers who then back them up and coordinate our more holistic care with them in a variety of ways," Stern says. By "holistic," Stern implies inner and outer changes, getting the residents' attitudes more in line with the world and trying, at the same time, to ease that interaction by securing them housing. The discussions and daily interactions with residents are focused on the vicissitudes of their worldly encounters. How, for instance, did she or he fare on an interview for permanent housing? The interactions between the team and residents are daily, no topic considered inconsequential if it is deemed relevant by the resident.

I ask whether the residents were receiving therapy or on any psycho-tropic drugs already when they arrived at TLC. That is the case "about 60% of the time," Stern states, adding that residents are encouraged to seek medical help when they are not receiving any. "The bigger problem," he observes, "is often that a resident is on meds but in no real therapy." The mistaken priorities and misplaced resources of the mental health system are to blame for this, Stern says. Stern and Thomas talk about a patient with schizoaffective disorder. He had come to TLC after being denied housing repeatedly, and nineteen different hospitalizations. He displayed symptoms of severe PTSD and was on medication when he arrived, which he started taking regularly after joining the TLC community. His social skills were so poor that he could not articulate his own history. The support of staff and peers, as well as the stability of a roof over his head, helped him to re-engage in outpatient treatment. "You have to convince them that they are capable," Athea Thomas states, and this is a confidence boost they are less likely to find within themselves in the confines of an outpatient clinic alone. TLC, Thomas and Stern insist, is a living community between peers and staff. They practice an informal type of "milieu therapy," addressing poor communication, anger management, time management, and social skills. TLC focuses on harm reduction through controlled substance use: if substance use supersedes mental health issues, clients are sent to detox. The more serious cases involve a treatment of heavy substance abuse and co-occurring depression: "when we've exhausted all the options, we suggest they go to detox," Stern states.

I pointedly ask Stern and Thomas about technique. Stern is an experienced psychiatrist and Thomas is a clinical social worker. It is a holistic, needs-based approach, they state, designed to reinforce the more formal psychiatric treatment of their residents. Stern had mentioned "milieu therapy" in our initial conversations, a structured therapy approach used in inpatient psychiatric units and group living situations, its central emphasis on community building based on mutual respect and communication. As the name indicates, the "milieu" itself is seen as an environment of healing. "We don't offer *formal* milieu therapy here at TLC," Stern clarifies, "but we strive to create a supportive setting in which people can learn about themselves and prepare to live in the wider community." This is reflected in the way the program is structured as a therapeutic community: weekly community meetings, several weekly groups[14] conducted by staff to teach coping skills, frequent mediation between residents when conflicts inevitably arise. "We attempt to frame these conflicts as good opportunities to learn communication skills," Stern informs me. The mediation sessions involve individual and paired counseling sessions. The psychotherapy background of Athea Thomas, her successor Raquel Barrett, and Tony Stern informs these linked initiatives, as do their concerted efforts to provide a place for inner learning.

The case manager for each resident looks after not only mental health needs but the client's savings plan, documentation for their care package, and progress with the housing pack (for city-funded housing). TLC aims at an individualized approach for each person, non-judgmental yet motivational. "How are you doing today?" often reinforces the non-rigid structure of meetings. The team draws on therapy models such as Behavioral Activation, centered around positive reinforcement, Problem Solving Therapy, Acceptance and Commitment Therapy, and Dialectical Behavior Therapy, among others. "All good help involves a dialectic between accepting someone and helping them change," Stern states. TLC encourages non-confrontational methods such as Motivational

Interviewing to clarify strengths and aspirations in clients and deploy their own motivations for affecting change. "We are not a jail," Thomas states with a smile, and success is mostly measured by the resident's consistency in returning to the shelter in a non-coercive framework (as well as slowly taking the steps to secure more permanent housing). "At our best, we steer our residents to a balanced focus between their inner and outer lives," Stern states. "Naturally most of them want more stable housing. Our team often helps them get there. When we have also encouraged them to find new levels of emotional stability and self-reflection, we have truly done our job."

I will now present two case studies provided by Stern which shed light on the unconventional yet effective therapeutic scene at TLC. Joe is a 63-year-old African-American man, never married. He has carried the diagnosis of schizophrenia most of his life, and he presents with the flat affect and a preoccupation with internal stimuli that goes with it. He talks in a disjointed fashion, skipping topics randomly.

PSYCHIATRIST: It's our job to help you feel comfortable here. Also to help you get what you want.
He nods.
PSYCHIATRIST: What do you want?
JOE: Money.
PSYCHIATRIST: What will the money buy you?
JOE: Housing.
PSYCHIATRIST: It's our other priority to find you housing.
JOE: Mom and dad, living down in Florida, they paid.
PSYCHIATRIST: You'd like to pay for your own place, like them?
JOE: Like a normal life. Like anyone.

In the conversation that ensues, Stern observes how Joe's self-assessment is abnormal and inadequate, tinged with palpable sadness about his life's outcomes. He became more animated as he shared these real feelings. The thought process became harder to follow at times, but the patient spoke with a new "aliveness," Stern records, as they explored his wish to pay his way from practical as well as emotional vantage points. Joe had worked for a time as a part-time barber. Could he conceive of taking this up again? If not, would he be willing to accept the housing TLC were able to obtain for him?

In the next session, conducted five days later, Joe starts with "It helped" – talking to Stern, that is. Stern's focus in the first two or three sessions was to establish rapport, without which he wouldn't be able to elicit the history he needed to profile Joe's housing package. For someone like Joe, unaccustomed to connecting with another, this situation is unprecedented, and Stern finds that he wants to see the psychiatrist more frequently than his schedule would allow. The hunger for further contact, however, is better from the grinding self-isolation, Stern states. In future sessions, Joe expresses more and more signs of accepting his situation, including the fact that he cannot pay for housing at this stage in his life. "This is not formal psychotherapy," Stern reminds me. He has also been mindful of the fact that Joe is a habitual marijuana user. It's "supportive counseling," embedded in the process of Stern's preparing his psychiatric evaluation, required for Joe to secure housing. The medicalization implied by "schizophrenia" is hardly the whole story, Stern emphasizes.

Stern mentions a rule he applies to the residents: "the good, the bad, and the wild card." This has an old rabbinical basis, going back to Reb Nachman of Bratslav, who founded a branch of Hasidic Judaism, in its focus on the positive. In the current parlance of CBT, it would be the equivalent of putting aside ANTs (automatic negative thoughts) to focus on happy counter-thoughts. He mentions a resident, Luke, diagnosed with schizophrenia. He has never held down a job because he is terrified of the aggression of others. He feels continually judged and ostracized, stemming from his father's harsh treatment of him, and cannot cope with most work situations. He is also terrified of his own aggression, these inner and outer threats debilitating him. Stern wonders if it is possible to look at this another way: Is Luke a truly peaceful person, too in love with peace, perhaps, for this world? He dwells on the goodwill Luke enjoys in the community, and how the deli counter guy at the corner bodega just up the 7th Avenue, where Luke does odd jobs, makes it a point to say to him every time that "Luke's SUCH a nice man." This Stern calls the wild card, revelations about a patient that go beyond the protocols of positive thinking on the part of the psychiatrist. Looking for these unexpected dimensions in a resident, he says, "is a fairly important part of how we aim to be helpful to these residents, though its informality makes it easy to overlook."

John has had ten years of treatment as bipolar. When asked if he likes poetry, John says, "I'm a poet myself. In fact, I've done 'improv' poetry to audiences over the years." Stern responds to him with lines from Blake – a gesture, he points out, that is "a good step in rapport-building": "He who binds to himself a joy / Does the wingèd life destroy. / He who kisses the joy as it flies, / Lives in Eternity's sunrise."[15] This has a positive effect on John, as does a comment Stern made a few minutes later: "It's often struck me that improv poets can be misinterpreted as bipolar by muggle doctors with no wizardly blood." He laughed a knowing laugh, Stern notes. Does he believe his "psych" evaluation, the psychiatrist inquires? Not really, John answers, paving the way for a conversation. Is John "a fast-talking charmer and schemer prone to mood swings" (the bad) or "a quick-witted poet and true people person with keen wit and wisdom" (the good), Stern speculates. Perhaps he is both, Stern thinks as he records the conversation. After two rapport-building sessions, John is ready to confess that he has an "ugly temper." Secure in the non-judgmental technique deployed by Stern, John begins to let down his guard. There are also reports that he has embarked on a romantic relationship with a woman in the shelter. Stern mentions two incidents that bear testimony to the "shadow side"[16] even before John has confessed to the same: an altercation with another resident in the community room near his office, and a fight in the TV room where John is calling one of the residents a b**** because she is watching her own program, not letting him watch *Jeopardy* at 7 p.m.

Stern talks to the woman involved in the fracas. She identifies as Christian proudly and persistently, a characteristic he has drawn on before to resolve a physical altercation between her and another female resident. She reminds him that they have discussed Jesus' "Love thine enemies" before: "Yes, I guess you are right. But it's hard!" Stern's case notes show that he has also invited John to talk more about this "current conflagration," but that he was too angry to engage at the moment.

> I'll look for the right moment in the next few days to invite him again to reflect on what happened. He had calmed down somewhat by the time I left for the evening a half hour later, and I made it a point to say a "hi, are you okay?" on my way out the door. He nodded a yes.

The Unhomed

Athea Thomas did not elaborate on the relationship between mental illness, race, and homelessness. "It [race] is not a major issue," she said, while also acknowledging the stigma around mental health in African and Hispanic cultures. Carol Valentin, on the other hand, starts the conversation with racism and the psychopathologies it generates. Dr. Valentin is a clinical psychologist and graduate of the William Alanson White training program in psychoanalysis. She has been in private practice in New York and New Jersey since 1985, and is also the Clinical Director and supervisor of the Episcopal Social Services Therapeutic Nursery in Harlem and the

Lower East Side, where I interviewed her. Valentin's work focuses on biracial and multicultural identity formation, as well as the impact of racism on mental health.

Every day, she sees households scarred by the legacy of slavery and segregation. "The parents are very fragile themselves," the demands on their time to survive such that they can't give children "the means to attachment." In a formidable work of scholarship Valentin cites as an influence, Selma Fraiberg and others had elaborated on unwelcome intruders in the nursery: "How is it that ghosts of the parental past can invade the nursery with such insistence and ownership, claiming their rights above the baby's own rights?" ("Ghosts in the Nursery" 390). Valentin's interventions in infant mental health enjoin the treatment of imperiled children with preternatural attention to the repetition of the past in the present. Morbidity in parental history is not, in itself, a predictor of the repetition of the past: the presence of pathological figures in parental history, in other words, does not mean the parents would go on to replicate these figures and transmit the pathological experience to their children. Ghosts haunt the nursery, Fraiberg et al. conclude on the basis of clinical studies, when parents, in the extremity of childhood terror, go on to form "a pathological identification with the dangerous and assaultive enemies of the ego" (419). The so-called "pathological parents," in other words, were those who formed identifications with their aggressors, turning into aggressors themselves. The Fraiberg study identifies this as an act of desperate survivalism, with the parents revealing memories of childhood abuse, tyranny, and desertion in explicit detail when interviewed: "What was not remembered was the associated affective experience" (419).

Sheltering Arms offers treatment to preschool children who have suffered trauma. It functions more as an educational institute – and as a community – and less as a mental hospital, seeking to address what each child needs.[17] Children who have suffered abuse spend half-an-hour every week with a therapist. They qualify for the special needs program through a psychological evaluation carried out by a school psychologist, a clinical social worker, or psychometric testing. The evaluations, Valentin points out, are not dynamic emotional assessments but about behavior, language, speech, and development instead. Once the children are admitted, their parents are called in by the therapist or team of therapists to talk about their wards, inaugurating a dynamic relationship: "we want to make parents feel this is a safe space," Valentin states. "We can't [explicitly] say we are doing therapy here," she states cautiously: "we say we are helping parents." Counseling takes the form of a play therapy, instrumentalized to help a child to do better in the classroom environment.

The children at Sheltering Arms have been abused physically or sexually or both. Common symptoms include speech and language delays, behavior problems, hyperactivity, tantrums, and showdowns. The parents themselves often manifest borderline and impulse control disorders, hostility, aggression, and what Valentin calls "dysregulated emotion." Parents are not always the perpetrators, Valentin states, adding that her psychodynamic training has helped her to use non-judgmental techniques. Parents from the African-American communities are visibly afraid of psychologists and clinical social workers, and the damning diagnoses they are associated with. Valentin takes me through a few case studies. The first involves a 3-year-old boy, mean, aggressive, and angry, whose teachers bring him to Valentin for evaluation. She begins with trying to pacify the violently agitated boy:

> It can take up to an hour to calm down a child. He fought and fought and fought. "I know you are angry," I said. "I know you are afraid." "I'll help you." With some kids restraining is necessary. And you can't get angry as you try to calm the child. You hold him, not restrain.

After three days of consultations, the only chilling certainty Valentin has is that the child was being abused: the boy was even experiencing her reassuring embrace as an attack. She remembers the teachers telling her that he did not want to pull his pants down in the toilet and, when he did, they saw welts on his body.

This case is reported to the police immediately, the mother summoned by ACS (Administration for Children's Services). They remove the child from the home he shares with his mother and stepfather, who were both mercilessly beating the boy. Months later, the stepfather is arrested for domestic violence and the child returned to the mother. He now feels reassured, protected, and his aggression toward other children has lessened. Valentin's notes show that the child, who had grown up manipulative and angry, his sense of reality distorted, had reacted favorably to his teacher's "I love you." "He saw a hope," Valentin explains. The mother, who was advised by Valentin to receive therapy, did not eventually go to a counselor. The boy, however, responded favorably to play therapy and is gradually transformed from an aggressor to someone who feels love and attachment. In the psychodynamic practice of play therapy, which uses play to comprehend and address the child's psychosocial problems, the boy would always want to be the baby. He was never aggressive in the therapy

room with Valentin and the clinical social worker, where he struggled to
move out of the paranoid-schizoid position instead. "He needed to be
rocked."

Valentin takes me through another case where the mother behaved liked
an adolescent, harboring hostile feelings toward her child. It is yet another
instance when the psychotherapy of the child – "Where are they?" "Where
did they (or their development) get stuck?" – traces the mother's history of
attachment. "You have to be able to tolerate her, not judge her," Valentin
observes. "If the mother is to become a good enough mother, you, the
therapist must lead by example." Valentin is referring to Winnicott's idea
of the "holding environment" necessary to allow the good enough – not
perfect or ever-present – mother to carry out the daily care of her baby
(Winnicott, *Maturational Processes* 145). These processes take place in
a complex psychological field, Winnicott observes, and should not be
dismissed as instinctual and physiological activities. The mother is "good
enough" when she is "held" in networks of support: when this sustenance is
not forthcoming from the family, the infant's personality "becomes built
on the basis of reactions to environmental impingements" (54). This is an
elaboration of Winnicott's environmental thought, mentioned in
Chapter 4, which engages with interferences with the mother's ability to
hold. The psychotherapist at Sheltering Arms provides the mother with the
pastoral care and environmental modifications – the maternal means of
holding, containing, mirroring – that will allow her to provide a similar
facilitating environment for her infant.

Valentin talks about her own travails as a light-skinned African-
American – in the world of interpersonal psychoanalysis in particular,
and public mental health in general. Most psychoanalysts "don't have
a life like mine," she states, referring to her nine siblings, the children of
different fathers. She observes how, until recently, psychoanalytic society
wasn't actively seeking to train people of color: those who were trained did
not always return to the community to work. She was an exception, but her
volunteering at the nursery entails "getting paid as much as I was in 1985."
The free clinic structure, she says without bitterness, necessitates personal
sacrifice on behalf of practitioners. She draws no salary or pension benefits
for her consultancy work at Sheltering Arms and sustains herself through
private practice in New York and New Jersey. "I use what I know of
psychoanalysis," she says, downplaying her extensive training in Freudian
and Winnicottian methodologies, to help out the children, whom she
describes as "locked in the trunk [of a car], with no one to get them out
of it."

The Analyst in the Unhomely City

"[E]conomic factors do not fully explain the traditional exclusion of the lower-class patient," writes the psychoanalyst Neil Altman, explaining that, even in low-fee training clinics attached to universities or hospitals, poor patients have been selectively offered treatment ("Psychoanalysis," 29). In recent years (Altman is writing in 1993), with dwindling numbers of middle- to upper-class patients, training clinics have had to accept patients from lower socioeconomic strata "out of necessity" (30). In this article, Altman is describing the clinical work carried out in a community mental health center associated with a large inner-city hospital in New York City. The community around the hospital was traditionally populated by working- and middle-class Jewish, Irish, and Italian residents, with a new influx of immigrants from the Dominican Republic and the war-torn countries of Central America. As such it presents a complex ethnic mix and "various levels of acculturation to North American industrial and postindustrial society" (32). The people of the area are in the lowest social classes, with livelihoods ranging from blue-collar to clerical jobs. There are a large number of families subsisting on public assistance, high school-dropout rates, and drug and AIDs crises.

As I briefly mentioned in the introduction, Altman addresses the question of analyzability that inevitably comes up in relation to the treatment of lower-class or culturally different, non-English-speaking patients. Traditional psychoanalysis, whether it is the classic Freudian model of creating a "blank screen" for analytical work or the ego psychological approach, which defines pathology in terms of defect or deficit, both fall short of the needs of the public clinic. The first does not take into account the multiple roles the analyst is called upon to fill, as we have seen with Stern's or Valentin's engagement with social welfare agencies: it also requires that the "analyzable" patient tolerates the analyst's strategic withholding during the session. The second approach, predicated on "ego strength," is marred by its constitutive prejudices around race, ethnicity, and class. "In a society in which everyone is presumed to have equal opportunity to advance socially, one's lower-class standing is easily seen as evidence of personal failure," Altman observes (33). He offers an object relational approach instead, drawing on the work of W. R. D. Fairburn, a contemporary of the British psychoanalysts Melanie Klein and D. W. Winnicott, and the American ego psychologist Fred Pine. Altman offers two case studies in the article, both of which involve scenarios where the patient is testing the "abstinence" – the neutrality of stance and non-involvement – of the psychoanalyst by directly beseeching them to help.[18] In the second, which I shall discuss here, Nancy, a teenager from a low-income family now in its third generation on welfare, is in the second year of her once-a-week treatment. For the first time, the therapist asks her about her dreams and Nancy narrates one where she had sneakily put her hand in his (Altman's) pocket and found a $100 bill. While Nancy had associated this with instinctive thinking that she was about to come into some money, she had no idea what the therapist was doing in her dream. She proceeded to talk about her resentment at the lack of child support from the father of her baby and wondered if she could locate her father, who was supportive when she was young, and who had just been released from prison.

Usually, at the end of the session, the therapist would write a slip for the clinic receptionist to allow Nancy to receive bus fare, as was the reimbursement scheme of Medicaid, which Nancy was on. On being handed the slip, Nancy asked the therapist if he would write two slips for her younger brothers, who had escorted her to the clinic and were now in the waiting room. The therapist had written a slip for one of the brothers before, on the grounds that Nancy had never ventured out alone in the troubled neighborhood. He hesitated to extend the generosity to another brother, possibly a drug user, and offered bus fare for one brother alone. The dream begins to make sense to the therapist now: had the patient seen him as someone who could be duped for money? A drive-based interpretation, Altman notes, would prioritize the sexual element in the intimate touch of the dream, while an ego psychological perspective would call attention to the patient's frustration with the therapeutic situation, leading to an attempt to get him to gratify her in a concrete way (sexually or financially). An object relations reading, Altman states, would force us to contemplate that the analyst is a sexually exciting object as well as a denying, rejecting object (requiring the act of stealth). By denying her request, instead of examining further the nature of the dream, the analyst has also lapsed into an old object, the improvident men in Nancy's life who continue to refuse the patient support.

In the public clinic, the therapist has to perform bureaucratic as well as advocacy functions for the patient, not just intensive therapeutic treatment. The work of Fred Pine challenges the artificial antagonism between insight-oriented therapy and supportive therapy, while that of Fairburn urges the therapist to treat transference in relation to the patient's internalized objects. "Who am I in this patient's object world?" (39) could be, Altman argues, the start of a new relational configuration between the analyst and the analyzand in inner-city therapy. The therapist can take practical measures to "shift one's position away from enacting the internal drama with the patient," such as letting a clerk or administrative staff deal with reimbursement (45). In that way, the therapist, who is both old object (withholding) and new object (dispensing) for the patient at the start of the dream analysis, can strike the proper balance with someone from a very different socioeconomic background. Altman scrutinizes the question of (financial) speculation and transaction in the therapeutic relationship further. How might the public/free clinic function properly, he goes on to ask, given that, with Medicaid, the egalitarian gesture of the patient paying the therapist for their treatment does not shape transferential ideation? "While transference tends to put the therapist into a parental role, the economic arrangements provide some degree of counterpoint," he states (46–47). For the therapist to assume new object status, should public clinics require at least token payments?

In his influential 1995 work, *The Analyst in the Inner City*, the second edition of which was published in 2009, Altman adds a key phrase to the damning indictment of "nonanalyzable" meted out to the disenfranchised and dispossessed of society examined in the 1993 essay: "the psychically disowned" (xix). He begins the work by describing the difference between his private practice and his work in inner-city public clinics – separated by twenty minutes on the subway – as a "culture shock" (xi). Psychoanalysis, historically, has shown little affinity for inner-city public clinic work, he declares at the outset. The book, he states, not only aims to offer guidance to the clinician working in the inner city, but is also an experiment in what "we can learn about psychoanalysis and its theory by taking analytic work into the inner city" (xx). With this insight derived from Altman, the work of *Unseen City* comes full circle: it is about not only an applied psychoanalysis, but a traveling psychoanalysis. As the subtitle of chapter 9 of *The Analyst in the Inner City*, "Bringing Psychoanalysis to Community-Based Clinical Work," suggests, psychoanalysis will have to unhouse itself from a dyadic, office-based practice.

Altman describes how concepts of transference and countertransference change as the clinician walks up to a client's home for an in-house session, parking her car a couple of spots away from the building to make her arrival less intrusive (215). Like the analyst of this example, coming to terms with having a session in a living room filled with children, music, barking dogs, a hissing cat, and the smell of fried chicken,[19] traveling psychoanalysis will have to rethink and redraw its spatial boundaries. Altman narrates another anecdote to illustrate the challenges and salutary self-estrangement that community-based work can bring home to the analyst on the move. Here, he is on a consultation visit at the Westcoast Children's Clinic in Oakland, California. In the short time left after a nearly two-hour meeting with the clinical staff, a clinician volunteers a brief case study. She had been sent to interview a boy in a group home over an hour away from Oakland. The adolescent was a Native American boy, removed from his home in an impoverished neighborhood in Richmond, California. He was now in the wine country, with its predominantly white community, in a group home with mostly white kids. The clinician said she felt an "unaccountable sadness" when the boy said with some hesitation – not wanting to give offense to a woman he had assumed was white (she was mixed race) – that his fellow companions were "nerds" (217). Altman writes about how this vignette, heard in a jet-lagged state, made him visualize the wine country, with its spiffy spas, inns, and restaurants built on purloined Native American land. With tears in his eyes (which he seems to partly blame on exhaustion), Altman tells the clinician that her sadness stemmed from the cultural guilt around the fact that the land this adolescent felt so alienated in was once his and should have been his rightful home. Another clinician "opened up her unconscious," and volunteered that wine was an agent of the destruction of Native Americans (218). Albeit momentarily, the boy's unspoken history of deterritorialization is acknowledged in the emotional experience of "pain and loss" of his therapist, and translated from "unaccountable" to thinkable in the therapeutic consultation that followed (217).

Afterword: Second Sight

In *The Souls of Black Folk*, W. E. B. Du Bois memorably posits the "Negro" as "born with a veil, and gifted with second-sight in this American world, – a world which yields him no true self-consciousness, but only lets him see himself through the revelation of the other world" (8). The Du Boisian enigma of double-consciousness – "this sense of always looking at one's self through the eyes of others" (8) – continues to generate voluble discussion and debate, including questions of the elite or esoteric positioning of the cultivated author and his problematic universalizing of the black condition. Du Bois's "two warring ideals in one dark body, whose dogged strength alone keeps it from being torn asunder" (8) poses a causal circularity: is the "dogged strength" pre-existing or did it materialize from the clash of ideals and imperatives it is mobilized against? Is the black subject born with a veil and also preternaturally gifted with second sight? Is second sight a form of awakening or a de-programming of awake selves? Such is the visceral immediacy of Du Bois's words that we even wonder if the veil is to be negotiated vertically (rising above) or laterally (stepping past). The current context does not allow a tracing of the play of the signifier in Du Bois's meditations on the epidermalized soul, but I cite the words for their relevance to the binaries I have traced throughout this work: the individual vs. the group, the impoverished and raced subject vs. the citizen, human vs. animal, the dialectic of multiple identifications and affiliations vs. the malady of multiple identifications and affiliations. The "peculiar sensation" (8) of what Du Bois calls double-consciousness defines the sensorium of *Unseen City*. Here, double threatens division, not multiplication; "second sight" is a countervailing practice that seeks to correct historically inflicted blindness; and consciousness itself is aversively wrested from the very social and psychic regimens which had sought to deny it.

Unseen City argues that a humanistic understanding of both psychoanalysis and the psychic lives of the poor is urgent, revealing in the course of the book the importance of adapted psychoanalysis for sustained efficacy and wider dissemination and application. The status of psychoanalysis in this project is worth revisiting briefly. While my inaugural gesture is a critique of normative and classical psychoanalysis, I argue for its continued relevance as the argument unfolds, albeit in the different morphologies examined in three of the chapters. Is it psychoanalysis or is it psychotherapy, the reader may ask? I start with psychoanalysis and end in the fringes of global cities with practices which are psychoanalytically oriented psychotherapies at best (and ad hoc, short-term counseling with no resemblance to classical psychoanalysis in some instances). Psychoanalysis – its history and theory, particularly the free clinic movement – provides a logical copula for disparate and diachronic practices which draw on its fundamental components but may not themselves be identified as psychoanalysis. The components include the idea of the unconscious; talk therapy; addressing the unspeakable, the ineffable, the ambiguous; a non-pharmaceutical engagement with and healing of trauma, individual and collective; the cultivation of a rich and complex inner life (over time) in the modern psychoanalytic subject. The deployment of the framework of Freud's free clinics serves to make psychoanalysis responsive to the plight of the poor: it ushers in an overhaul of the time, duration, and cost of the analytic session and the training of lay counselors, who will make possible an ambulatory and more flexible and accessible psychoanalysis. The free clinic model connects psychoanalysis to its translated forms, its black-letter epistemology to the ontology of being poor in the city and poor in the world.

"He is Tiresias and Oedipus and Sophocles rolled into one," Jonathan Lear says of Sigmund Freud (31). What the quote suggests is that the founder of psychoanalysis is both a historic figure and a self-fabricated one, who posed as author, actor, and bystander in the theoretical (and theatrical) account he gave of the modern human, bracketed by atavistic infantilism on one side and teleology on the other. "Freudian" is the privileged term in this work, its starting point a democratic experiment that tested the perceptual limits, boundaries, and the very praxis of the discipline Freud had founded. The mainstays of psychoanalytic theory of the twentieth and twenty-first centuries that I have engaged with in *Unseen City* have a Freudian provenance: fort-da, the passivity of the experience sublated in the activity of the game; the more retrograde form of fort-da, which is repetition compulsion; the uncanny; Tancred and Clorinda's erotic wounding; the death drive as interior to life, the desire for death definitive of the very interiority posited by psychoanalysis; the "beyond" which is not spatial but temporal, "an earlier state of things" (*Beyond the*

Pleasure Principle 38), to name a few. Psychoanalysis also refers to a wide range of concepts and movements that Freudian metapsychology has influenced, even those which have crystallized in reactive modes to its specific or wider culture: trauma studies, with its focus on the unbinding of the death drive; the Klein-influenced British School; Winnicott's revisionist work on infant development and relationship; Kristeva's use of *unheimlich* to articulate the foreigner's melancholy; neurobiological approaches to psychoanalysis; ego psychology. I was also concerned throughout with discovering and charting different forms of psychoanalytically oriented psychotherapy that addressed the needs of the resource-poor, noting at the same time that, efficacious though these were, they did not offer opportunities for mid- to long-term therapy.

While it may seem naïve and futile to agitate for a more equitable geopolitical distribution of psychoanalysis when the theory and techniques themselves seem to have fallen into disuse in countries such as the UK and India, it is neither naïve nor futile to challenge the damning prejudice that the poor may not have cognitive resources to sustain deep analytic work, or the stratificatory prejudice – a caste system in itself – which dictates that the chronic poor need immediate relief and contributions, not psychotherapeutic assistance. As Honey Oberoi Vahali, who runs a free clinic at Delhi's Ambedkar University, says, unlike psychiatry, where the illness metaphor reigns, psychoanalysis can enable us to *work with* the patients, not just *work on* them.[1] Psychoanalysis has not just a curative function but an epistemological one, and interpretation involves the cultivation of complex temporalities and psychic depths. Girindrasekhar Bose's indigenized term for it was "introspective meditation" (Nandy, *Savage Freud* 143). One of the reasons why psychoanalysis and literature have had such brisk commerce with each other is their mutual reliance on imaginative powers to bring cursory description to life, build atmosphere, and create plausible characters, with convincing backstories.[2]

A defining characteristic of free market economics is the ability of individual actors to take decisions to optimize and improve their wellbeing. What I have documented in *Unseen City* are the complex challenges that adverse social conditions impose on self-actualization. Without interventions that improve the mental health of the urban poor, the rhetoric of social mobility toward a dynamic and vibrant society is rigged from the start. I am not arguing that we bestow soulmaking and self-fashioning instruments on the primitive or prehistoric other of psychoanalysis. As Anna Kornbluh points out, "as subjects under capitalism, our identities, our feelings, and our urges are profoundly embedded in the structures of private ownership of means of production, exploitation of labour, and abjection of a permanent underclass" (139). I am arguing instead that psychoanalysis, which has long attacked the false autonomy of identification, be repurposed to help to expose this "integrality . . . of intimacy and economy" (Kornbluh 140) so that the myth of the auto-constitutive psyche and its autobiography gives way to the heterography of socially constituted selves. The future of mental health lies in community healthcare, says Ratnaboli Ray, founder of Anjali and the Janamanas initiative (discussed in Chapter 4). Ray, who has spent most of her adult life rehabilitating people forcefully treated in public-sector psychiatric institutions that were predatory, not protective, of these lives, insists that building "resistant, empowered communities goes a long way in reducing stigma associated with mental health and preventing institutionalisation, abandonment and erosion of citizenship."[3]

Cities such as Mumbai, London, and New York present an interesting duality in that, while these are sites of the contingent local which allow a study of poverty in specific contexts, they also baffle self-contained, nation-based accounts. The global city can therefore help us to imagine a new universalism of the oppressed as capitalism rationalizes the use of free human labor and surplus populations for the "self-determination of capital" (Spivak, "Speculation on Reading Marx" 53). The cities represent speed and change as well as ossified hierarchies and segregationist politics: the three chapters on contemporary fiction (and creative non-fiction) portray otherwise dynamic narrators/protagonists stopped in their tracks by stultifying norms. The disjointedness of the global city is temporal as well as spatial, forcing the reader to confront historic legacies of caste, colonialism, slavery, neoliberal *governmentality* (a term I borrow from Povinelli), social death. The modernity of Mumbai and Kolkata needs to be reviewed in the light of their treatment of the slum poor as a biohazardous and pollutable entity, while the modernity of New York must be rethought "via the history of the black Atlantic and the African diaspora into the western hemisphere" as Paul Gilroy argues in *Black Atlantic* (17). Similarly, the toxic xenophobia directed at settlers (from erstwhile colonies) in the ghettoes of London, the intricate relation between raciological thinking and the rise of ethnic nationalism, or the pernicious characterization of immigration as infestation, occupation, and war, can only be understood in relation to Britain's inability to mourn or expiate for its violent occupation of the colonies for centuries.

Jacqueline Rose's reflection on her literary psychoanalytic criticism defines my approach too: "literature is not being offered as a complement to psychoanalysis, more as a supplement, as in Freud's own suggestion that we should look to the poets when he stalls" (9). The supplement completes the deficit of micro- and macro- structural explanations of poverty, tidy but ultimately doxic accounts if they do not take into consideration cultural difference, human diversity, and the contentious mess of lives and stories. The "literary" in these chapters could be attributed to representational techniques such as negative capability; the hard-won autonomy of art from normativity and discursivity; the novel form's inherent suspicion of nation and nationalism; immanent analysis and critique. More crucially, however, the "literary" in *Unseen City* stands for the second sight Du Bois talks about: the ability of the dispossessed to see through murky cultural screens; the ability to take a second look – powered by a double-consciousness that was once split, and is now multiplied – at deadening constructs as well as potential new selves.

The "literary" is not restricted to chapters which read novels. In the clinical chapters, I treat case studies as multiple shattered narratives which supplement sociographic, ethnographic, quantitative, and medical research on mental illness at the intersection of race and class. These chapters end with hopes of social transformation either partly actualized or in the horizon, another function of the second sight acquired in the throes of what Fred Moten calls "the scene of objection" (*In the Break* 1).[4] Literary humanism says this imaginary, unborn, and alternative life is real. In a scene from Arundhati Roy's *The Ministry of Utmost Happiness*, two hippie filmmakers are shooting a documentary on "Protest and Resistance," and they ask passers-by to recite "Another World Is Possible" as if they were protesters and to say it in their mother tongue. If your language was Hindi or Urdu, your line could be "doosri duniya mumkin hai." Not quite understanding the brief, Anjum, the penniless *hijra* (intersex) woman who has taken up residence in the Muslim cemetery and redefined kinship and community outside the codes of social production and reproduction, earnestly says "Hum doosri Duniya se aaye hain" (We *are* the denizens of that Other World) (110).

The interdisciplinarity of *Unseen City* has taken risks with the geopolitical scope of the investigation and in the juxtaposition of literature and (critical and philosophical) theorizing with empirical work with the free clinics of today. In the introduction, I describe this optimistically as breaking new ground in comparative studies. While I remain a researcher and teacher of the humanities, I have used my scholarly collaborations to build this account of the relationship between cities, poverty, and psychoanalysis, with medical research and quantitative as well as qualitative evidence. The manuscript was read by literary critics as well as psychoanalysts, and I have revised the material in response to the technical questions and suggestions that arose. The (medically) trained health workers at the sites where I have conducted research – Janamanas, NALAM, PCPCS, and Transitional Living Community, in particular – have participated in the making of the case studies, and my reconstruction of their psychoanalysis of the future for the poor. I evoked the idea of *jugaad* or intrepidness – playfully suggested by Leela Gandhi – in the introduction to speak of a dispossessive psychoanalytic commons. I think of the integrated critical approach of this book as a hack too: not a shortcut or a deceptive ruse but thrifty resourcefulness at a time of crisis. As Inspector Hathi Ram Chaudhary of the critically acclaimed serial *Paatal Lok* tells his junior, Imran Ansari, "bahaane mat mar, jugaad kar": "stop making excuses, figure something out!" Let us stop making excuses; let us figure something out. Vikram Patel et al. preface *Global Mental Health* with the hope that scientific developments in the field will "renew the passion and commitment of the armies of advocates, from academics and practitioners to those who live with mental illness and their loved ones" (20). Alongside advancements in pharmacotherapy, biomedical research, and psychological or psychosocial interventions, this mass mobilization of passion and commitment is crucial.

    Paatal Lok[5] begins with Hathiram explaining the lie of the land to his sidekick in terms of the cosmological divisions of *swarg* (heaven), *dharti* (earth), and *paatal* (hell). "It's in the scriptures," he grins, "but I read it on WhatsApp." Unlike the vertical stratification of the realms in (Hindu) mythology, the three worlds are laterally distributed and synchronous in contemporary Delhi. Gods and rich folk live in heaven, ordinary humans on earth, and hell crawls with vermin: Hathiram's precinct in East Delhi, Outer Jamuna Paar, is *paatal lok*, a netherworld of petty crime, lowly officials, the assorted wretched of the earth. It takes a spectacular event (Hathiram uses the Hindi word *kaand*, or "scandal"), such as the parasites of *paatal lok* attacking respectable homes in the middle-class *dharti lok*, for everyone to realize that the classifications are contiguous, egregious though the inequality between classes may be. The outbreak of a global pandemic in 2020 was one such event for unequal cities, mobilizing a global fight and solidarity response as it did, and simultaneously exposing extreme health and other inequalities. The more deprived the area, the higher the risk of fatal Covid-19. In the UK, for instance, the health impact of belonging to some minority ethnic groups is equivalent to being twenty years older than your actual age.[6] In the meantime, the world's ten richest people have amassed wealth (£200 bn) which could apparently vaccinate every adult on earth and pay back the income lost in 2020 to the world's poorest people.

On January 1, 2021, the *Guardian* newspaper reported that pharmaco-therapy of mental illness in England had soared in 2020: "Calls to mental health helplines and prescriptions for antidepressants have reached an all-time high, while access to potentially life-saving talking therapies has plunged during the coronavirus pandemic."[7] The article cited Esther Cohen-Tovée, chair of the British Psychological Society's division of clinical psychology, expressing her serious concern at the drastic reduction she saw in referrals for psychological help, a development made particularly problematic by the concomitant rise in prescribed antidepressants. The ostensible explanation for the latter is that, when patients present with severe symptoms in the middle of a pandemic, the risk factors for self-harm are higher, a consideration GPs take very seriously.

The drop in attendance for extant hospital appointments for acute cases (in the psychological and psychiatric categories) that the article mentions in passing points to larger infrastructural failures: service interruptions, such as the inevitable cancellation of group therapies; fears of infection in a hospital environment; and, finally, a worsening of the mental health vulnerabilities and inequalities which existed before the pandemic. In a searing article in the research journal *Nature*, Rochelle Burgess, a community psychologist who has worked on mental healthcare in South Africa, Colombia, and the United Kingdom, speaks of a "familiar disappointment" with Covid management, despite public health guide-lines advocating an intensification of mental health support during the coronavirus crisis: "Once again, recommendations forget half of the equa-tion: our need to address the social and economic conditions that contrib-ute to poor mental health."[8] She mentions the 1 billion living in slums, the more than 700 million living in poverty, millions of people of color in Western societies whose environments are fetid and livelihoods precarious, to point out the everyday challenges to mental health that have been exacerbated by the pandemic. Instead of taking into account the systemic oppression of these lives, those who craft mental health plans focus exclusively on the individual, Burgess argues. This is a crucial layering of the relationship between the individual and the group in therapeutic approaches I have discussed from the start: my invocation of Karl Marx's *Poverty of Philosophy* and Irigaray's reading of Marx on Proudhon proposed a historically contingent mode of psychoanalysis that pushes against uni-versalizing ideas of the human condition. To be truly patient-centered, we need to take into account the deprived life circumstances of poor and marginalized groups, the mind *and* the world, Burgess insists. The activists, analysts, authors, and humanitarians I have written about in this book are the amanuenses and translators of the psychic lives of the urban poor twisting between the mind and the world.

I emailed Tim Kent and Ahmet Caglar in January 2021 to ask how the new class of their green-fingered charges was faring in the midst of the nation's draconian third lockdown. The gardening group has been indefinitely suspended during the pandemic. The City and Hackney PCPCS team moved it to Zoom and it is now an online program of twenty weeks. "We are planning to add some gardening-related activities to the group," Caglar writes. The first round of virtual group therapy sessions has now ended: Caglar reports that the initiative was well received. He saw enthusiastic engagement and contributions despite the majority of participants never having used the internet before. "We have lost the richness of nature with all its metaphors, but the virtual world also provided us a fertile ground for symbolism," Caglar says before signing off. Kent writes that interest in the Hackney horticultural therapy program has inspired the team to try to start a new trauma-related gardening project at the Tavistock.

Notes

Introduction: "The Poverty of Philosophy" – A Critique of Psychoanalytic Knowledge and Power

1. Some of the classics of feminist theory analyze Irigaray's critique of psychoanalysis in further detail. See Teresa Brennan, *Between Feminism and Psychoanalysis* (Routledge, 2002); Jane Gallop, *Reading Lacan* (Cornell University Press, 1985); and *Feminine Sexuality: Jacques Lacan and the école freudienne*, ed. Juliet Mitchell and Jacqueline Rose (Norton, 1982) – texts which also serve as introductions to the vexed relationship between feminism and psychoanalysis.

2. In her essay "Freud in the Tropics," Jacqueline Rose suggests that it is not clear if the ambivalence "Freud characterises as typical of primitive emotion" is something to be suppressed or overcome (134).

3. See also Jacques Derrida's "Geopsychoanalysis" in this collection, his excoriating critique of the geopolitically restricted imaginary of the International Psychoanalytic Association.

4. In the introduction to *The Crowd*, Le Bon states that the "claims of the masses ... amount to nothing less than a determination to utterly destroy society as it now exists, with a view to making it hark back to that primitive communism which was the normal condition of all human groups before the dawn of civilization" (cited in Brickman, 104). Gustave Le Bon was a French social psychologist, sociologist, and anthropologist. His 1895 work *La Psychologie des foules* (translated in 1896 as *The Crowd: A Study of the Popular Mind*) brought crowd theory to the public sphere, imbuing it with ideas of the psychopathology of race. For an excellent interpretation of the concept of the crowd in relation to racial/racist ideas, see "Hatred and the Crowd," in Gilman and Thomas 75–122.

5. Freud, *The Ego and the Id*, SE 19: 29.

6. "Psychoanalysis makes use of the particular relation of the transference in order to reveal, on the outer confines of representation, Desire, Law, Death, which outline, at the extremity of analytic language and practice, the concrete figures

of finitude" (*The Order of Things 388*). Not everyone agrees on the perceived difference between psychoanalysis and ethnography, however. Mary Ann Doane, for example, sees psychoanalysis as an elaborate form of ethnography, a writing of the ethnicity of the white Western psyche: "repression becomes the prerequisite for the construction of a white culture which stipulates that female sexuality act as the trace within of what has been excluded" (209). For Freud's "anthropological archive," see Khanna ch. 2.

7. www.sciencedirect.com/science/article/pii/S0165032717320232?via%3Dihub</int_i>.

8. In her speech on behalf of all three winners of the prize that year – Abhijit Banerjee and Michael Kremer included – Duflo talks about the movement toward poverty alleviation of which she was a part: "We believed that like the war on cancer, the war on poverty was not going to be won in one major battle, but in a series of small triumphs, with no doubt many setbacks along the way" (www.nobelprize.org/prizes/economic-sciences/2019/duflo/speech).

9. Apter is talking about world literature here and offering alternatives to the putative "possessive collectivism" (a phrase used by Rebecca Walkowitz in *Born Translated*) of the field, accused often of "homogenizing difference, flattening forms, and minimizing cultural untranslatablity" (*Against World Literature* 328).

10. I am using "dissimilation" in the sense in which Natalie Melas deploys the word to describe a singularity that sets apart the individual from their public or social group, which divides them from their similar, or exposes them "as similar to them but definitely not the 'same'" (82). Melas draws on Althusser and Nancy to articulate a "differential effect" (93) which is both separateness, the absence of common ground, *and* a kind of estranged attachment.

11. I elaborate on the workings of this unit of the Tavistock, titled The City and Hackney Primary Care Psychotherapy Consultation Service (PCPCS), in Chapter 2. PCPCS is a free mental health service provided by the Tavistock and Portman NHS Foundation Trust and the team, based in St. Leonard's Hospital in Hackney, runs a horticultural therapy program which I describe and analyze in Chapter 2.

12. Report on horticultural project prepared by Ahmet Caglar and others, quoted here with his permission.

13. Caglar is making a reference to the theories of E. Goffman here. See *Stigma: Notes on the Management of Spoiled Identity* (Penguin Books, 1990).

14. Butler points out that "subject" is not a term interchangeable with "individual," and is deployed here as a linguistic, not human, category, "a structure in formation" (10).

15. Butler is talking about love in a Kleinian psychoanalytic frame here, wherein its aggressivity toward love objects is mitigated through the operations of

guilt. Butler's somewhat convoluted logic is that with demographics who are dead or dying – and she thinks here of the minority populations of a largely heteronormative libidinal economy – the victim becomes the persecutor in not allowing themselves to be saved, or to be loved. If, as potential objects of love, "they assume a mark of destruction," it is possible to believe "they may threaten one's own destruction as well" (27).

16. I discuss MUS further in Chapter 4.

17. In Rushdie's novel *Shame*, the narrator says "I, too, am a translated man. I have been borne across" (29). This is one of his many expressive statements on the lost authenticity of postcolonial identity and the mixed-up and hybrid cosmopolitanism that can attach to it.

18. The British-Bangladeshi residents of Brick Lane, protesting against the Booker-nominated Monica Ali novel of that title published in 2003, compared its "despicable" representation to that of *Satanic Verses*. The Greater Sylhet Welfare and Development Council (GSWDC), representing about 500,000 Bangladeshis living in Britain, claimed that *Brick Lane* was "a completely stereotypical view of Bangladeshis living in Brick Lane and one we simply do not recognise. The book says we got here by jumping ships and it says we have lice and live like rats in holes." While Ali has every right to claim her Bangladeshi heritage imaginatively, these perspectives cannot be ignored and point to the quandaries of visibility and invisibility Rushdie himself addresses in delineating what Chamcha can or cannot see in the migrant ghetto, and what he will learn to see therein: www.standard.co.uk/home/bri ck-lane-novel-is-an-insult-7437170.html.

19. See James Clifford's critique of the salvage mode of anthropology in "Of Other Peoples: Beyond the Salvage Paradigm," *Discussions in Contemporary Culture*, ed. Hal Foster (Bay Press, 1987). He identifies the salvage mode as a historical practice that has characterized Western practices of art, culture, and "collecting." Speaking specifically about the recidivist colonial attitudes informing early twentieth-century anthropology, Clifford states that this historical and geopolitical paradigm reflects "a desire to rescue something 'authentic' out of destructive historical changes" (121).

20. www.youtube.com/watch?v=p-ClpJxVYYY<int_sup>.

21. Judith Butler uses this term with reference to Giorgio Agamben's observation in *Homo Sacer: Sovereign Power and Bare Life* that we live in a time when populations without full citizenship exist within states, "their ontological status as legal subjects . . . suspended" (*Antigone's Claim* 149).

22. Cited in Derrida's "Geopsychoanalysis," which takes to task the European and North American bias of the psychoanalytic world, as seen in the wording of the 1977 Constitution of the International Psycho-Analytic Association.

1 Eco-cosmopolitanism as Trauma Cure

1. Mannoni analyzes several dreams of the Malagasy, interpreting the images therein in terms of the Oedipal conflict that he subsequently claimed was structuring Malagasy servitude. Whereas Mannoni saw the rifle in the dream as the symbol of a penis, Fanon refuted the psychoanalytic and intrapsychic reading by stating the rifle was nothing more than rifle, the phobogenic "model Lebel 1916" (*Black Skin* 79). During his Madagascar years, Mannoni also recorded his own dreams in a journal, published posthumously in 1990. See Christopher Lane, "Psychoanalysis and Colonialism Redux: Why Mannoni's 'Prospero Complex' Still Haunts Us," *Journal of Modern Literature* 25.3/4 (Summer 2002), pp. 127–50.

2. Fanon here cites testimonies given at a trial in Tananarive.

3. http://windhamcampbell.org/2014/winner/aminatta-forna.

4. Ruth Leys, *Trauma: A Genealogy* (University of Chicago Press, 2000), p. 3.

5. See George A. Bonanno, "Loss, Trauma, and Human Resilience: Have We Underestimated the Human Capacity to Thrive after Extremely Aversive Events?" *American Psychologist* 59.1 (January 2004), pp. 20–28, and A. S. Masten, "Ordinary Magic: Resilience Processes in Development," *American Psychology* 56 (2001), pp. 227–238. See also Bonanno, Maren Westphal, and Anthony D. Mancini, "Resilience to Loss and Potential Trauma," *Annual Review of Clinical Psychology* (2011): www .annualreviews.org/doi/10.1146/annurev-clinpsy–032210–104526.

6. David Scott, *Conscripts of Modernity: The Tragedy of Colonial Enlightenment* (Duke University Press, 2004).

7. Later in the novel, we learn that there is no sanctuary for Agnes in postwar Sierra Leone, for she is living under the same roof as the man she witnessed murdering her husband. This man has now married her daughter, so Agnes gags herself to protect her daughter from the devastating knowledge.

8. See Carolyn Pedwell, *Affective Relations: The Transnational Politics of Empathy* (2014).

9. I use this term to mean "in the wake," living in the aftermaths of atrocity and mass death, well as the more colloquial sense of being ideologically demystified and critically aware of cultural structures. I discuss Christina Sharpe's "orthography of the wake" in detail in Chapter 5.

10. Ian Baucom, "Frantz Fanon's Radio: Solidarity, Diaspora, and the Tactics of Listening," *Contemporary Literature* 42.1 (Spring 2001), pp. 15–49.

11. Frantz Fanon and Raymond Lacaton, "Conducts of Confession in North Africa," a hitherto unpublished manuscript, now anthologized in Khalfa and Young 412–416.

12. The Arabic term "djounn" or "djinn" refers to supernatural creatures – genies – who can exercise psychic control over humans. In "Maghrebi

Muslims and their Attitude to Madness," Fanon and his co-author François Sanchez explain that in Maghrebi belief, the mentally ill patient is "absolutely alienated, he is not responsible for his disorder; the genies alone bear full responsibility for it" (Khalfa and Young 422). The mentally ill person, in this culture, commands respect and is never to be held culpable for abnormal behavior, which is the work of "morbid genies" (423). This "madness" is deemed temporary and is treated through local psychotherapeutic practices, such as visits to a healer. Someone who is considered mentally ill is not confined in an asylum but "protected, fed, maintained, looked after by his own within the realm of possibility" (424).

2 The Analyst as Muse of History in Disaster Zones: Free Clinics, London

1. Wajahat Habibullah, cited Hogan 140.
2. The term "imperial democracies" was coined by Arundhati Roy and Zillah Eisenstein. Roy has long courted controversy with the Indian government with her campaigning for Kashmir's independence. *The Ministry of Utmost Happiness*, her much-awaited second novel published in 2017, narrates the benighted history of Kashmir in multiple voices. See Zilla Eisenstein, *Sexual Decoys, Gender, Race and War in Imperial Democracy* (Zed Books, 2007).
3. In the sample studied, 68.15 percent of patients had immediate onset of PTSD, while 31.34 percent had delayed onset; 85.07 percent of patients had chronic PTSD, leading the investigators to conclude that they had sought treatment after 40 months. The authors observe that only a small proportion of the general population was seeking treatment for PTSD despite the prevalence of trauma exposure.
4. www.nytimes.com/2014/10/28/arts/international/in-haider-vishal-bhardwaj-draws-from-hamlet.html.
5. www.cnbc.com/2019/08/05/article-370-what-is-happening-in-kashmir-india-revokes-special-status.html. This Tariq Ali article, "Kashmir on the Edge of the Abyss," reads the 2019 move in the context of India's engagement with Kashmir in the fifty years preceding it. For a legal interpretation of the constitutional validity of the abrogation of Article 370, see Balu G. Nair, "Abrogation of Article 370: Can the President Act without the Recommendation of the Constituent Assembly?" *Indian Law Review* 3.3 (2019).
6. www.nytimes.com/2019/08/15/opinion/sunday/kashmir-siege-modi.html.
7. Basharat Peer's *Curfewed Night: A Frontline Memoir of Life, Love and War in Kashmir* (Random House India, 2011) was a key inspiration for the movie, Vishal Bhardwaj has said, and provides an incisive as well as affective critique of Kashmir at war. Sumantra Bose's *Kashmir: Roots of Conflict, Paths of Peace*

(Harvard University Press, 2005) is a powerful study of the complex problem of Kashmir which also suggests possible pathways of resolving it, based on the author's comparative study of ethnic, religious, regional, and sectarian conflicts across the globe.

8. The in-joke for Bhardwaj's cultured cinegoers is that this Kashmiri everyman is none other than Basharat Peer himself.

9. https://indianexpress.com/article/entertainment/bollywood/kashmir-is-the-hamlet-of-my-film.

10. For a detailed history of the "Ceasefire Line" – later known as the Line of Control or LOC – designated by the United Nations in 1949, see Ravina Aggarwal, *Beyond Lines of Control: Performance and Politics on the Disputed Borders of Ladakh, India* (Duke University Press, 2004). Article 2 of the Geneva Convention mandates that the conventions, vital for ensuring the basic rights of wartime prisoners, apply to all cases of international conflict. For more details, see International Committee of the Red Cross (ICRC) website: https://ihl-databases.icrc.org/applic/ihl/ihl.nsf/Comment.xsp?actio n=openDocument&documentId=BE2D518CF5DE54EAC1257F7D0036 B518. The work of the ICRC is based on the Geneva Conventions of 1949. Finally, Article 370 of the Indian Constitution grants autonomous status to the state of Jammu and Kashmir. A. J. Noorani's *Article 370: A Constitutional History of Jammu and Kashmir* (Oxford University Press, 2011) provides the political contexts in which the Article was formulated and enacted in 1949 and traces, through this optic, the vicissitudes of Jammu and Kashmir's relationship with the Union of India in the troubled decades following.

11. The answer to Haider's existential questioning in the public sphere depicted in this scene is a resounding "Azadi" or '"freedom." In Bhardwaj's account of the experience of filming this part, he recalls that members of the crowd, all of them local Kashmiris, were immediately responsive: "we didn't need to prompt them" (in conversation with Preti Taneja, Pre-Screening Q&A).

12. His argument in this essay is that both the deconstructibility of law and the indeconstructibility of justice make deconstruction possible. Deconstruction takes place in the aporetic gap between law and justice: "It is possible as an experience of the impossible, there where, even if it does not exist (or does not yet exist, or never does exist), *there is* justice. Wherever one can replace, translate, determine the x of justice, one should say: deconstruction is possible, as impossible" (15). Deconstruction is that which reveals the self-authorization of the law: it is also the unrepresentable which exceeds (the law of) the determinable.

13. According to Rose, "A psy-ontology has come to inhabit us, an inescapable interiority that hollows us out, in the depths of the human, a psychic universe with a topography that has its own characteristics" (*Inventing our Selves*, 190).

14. Herman notes how academic interventions in the field of trauma studies unwittingly mimic the symptomatology we have come to associate with the pathology of trauma: it has a history of "episodic amnesia," she argues, with "active investigation" alternating with "periods of oblivion" (7), the cycles corresponding to fleeting affiliations with political movements that help trauma scholars to "counteract the ordinary social processes of silencing and denial" (9). Similarly, in *Trauma: A Genealogy*, Ruth Leys points out that the generational history of trauma is marked by "an alteration between episodes of forgetting and remembering" (15).

15. The first Janet quote is from *Psychological Healing* (Macmillan, 1925); the second from *The Major Symptoms of Hysteria* (Macmillan, 1907). Cited in van der Kolk 180.

16. Ruth Leys uses this term to describe the concepts initiated by Janet which not only were very influential for Freud and Breuer, but have proved to be foundational for recent theorists of trauma such as Judith Herman, Bessel van der Kolk, and Onno van der Hart. See Leys's influential article "Traumatic Cures," 647.

17. Complex PTSD or C-PTSD was first proposed by Judith Herman in *Trauma and Recovery* (1992). Psychologists Gillian Eagle and Debra Kaminer's work on traumatic stress in South Africa highlights the prevalence of continuous, chronic stress in populations which suffer endemic violence and poverty. See *Traumatic Stress in South Africa* (Wits University Press, 2010).

18. Transcript of talk reproduced with author's permission.

19. "Lines of Advance in Psychoanalytic Therapy," SE 17: 168. Elizabeth Danto cites this too, though she gets the date wrong (1918, instead of 1919), to make the point that experiments with the variable length of the session or duration of analysis were controversial topics in the free clinic movement. The analysts of the Berlin Poliklinik "found no suitable substitute for the analytic method and condemned as metaphorically useless 'the copper of direct suggestion,'" Danto states (179).

20. Brenman's report, prepared with the Nafsiyat research team, can be found here: www.nafsiyat.org.uk/index.php/2019/01/14/our-research.

21. M. Murray, "Levels of Narrative Analysis in Health Psychology," *Journal of Health Psychology* 5.3 (2000), pp. 337–347.

22. For detailed information, see: www.centreformentalhealth.org.uk. The case studies listed here are drawn from a report titled "Managing Patients with Complex Needs," available on the website above, and interviews with Ahmet Caglar and Tim Kent, the Primary Care Service Lead at PCPCS Hackney. The report, co-authored by Michael Parsonage, Emily Hard, and Brian Rock, uses a sample of 282 patients treated by the PCPCS. The cost of one session of treatment, which is free, is £109 (including therapist salary, overheads,

management, and supervision costs). See also Stern et al. for the history of this public-sector service.

23. For more on the migration patterns and mental health needs of the Turkish-speaking immigrants in London, see www.ncbi.nlm.nih.gov/pmc/articles/PMC3275503.

24. http://sprc.info/wp-content/uploads/2013/07/DayMer-Final-Report-final.pdf.

25. www.npi.org.uk/files/5714/4533/2889/LPP_2015_report.pdf.

26. Cited in Jordan and Hinds 63. Martin Jordan's "Ecotherapy as Psychotherapy – Towards an Ecopsychotherapy" provides useful distinctions between ecotherapy and ecopsychology, and contextual information on the emotional turn in geography influencing movements such as horticultural psychotherapy. For a short introduction to Winnicott's object-relations theory, see Phillips. Chapter 5, "Real-Making," touches on Winnicott's views of the self as a plant which requires a nurturing environment.

27. Winnicott 230. It is important to remember that Winnicott envisioned this space as the infant's transition from absolute dependence on the mother to becoming separate from her, and finding objects belonging to an external reality, "beyond omnipotent control," as Adam Phillips puts it (114).

28. Cited in PCPCS report co-authored by Ahmet Caglar, used here with his permission.

29. They are drawing on Porges's theories of the power of feeling safe.

30. Data provided by PCPCS. Feedback from Horticultural Therapy Group, Spitalfields Farm (July 2016–July 2017). Caglar and Kent also shared a video recording of the group providing these responses in Turkish. The questionnaire had six talking points and answers had been translated by Caglar:
Did the group help you change in the way that you hoped?
Did your group experience meet your expectations? In what way?
What aspects of your group experience were different from your expectations, and how?
What did you find most useful about taking part in this group?
What did you find least useful about taking part in this group?
Other comments?

31. This is a reference to attachment theory, a developmental theory of personality outlined by John Bowlby, which has been influential in psychotherapy. This interpersonal approach sees bonding with others as an essential survival strategy for human beings, whether it is in the relational domain of the infant–parent or adult–adult. See *Attachment Theory and Research in Clinical Work with Adults*, ed. Joseph H. Obegi et al. (The Guilford Press, 2009).

32. Cathy Caruth discusses this at length in *Unclaimed Experience* 135.

33. This critical stance supplements the "wound-and-the-voice" theoretical model elaborated in great depth by academic trauma theorists such as Cathy Caruth, who, in *Unclaimed Experience,* describes trauma as a wound of the mind. In Caruth's Freudian interpretation, the text and rhetorical potential of trauma, even when it is a beguiling itinerary of recurrences and repetitions, is where historical testimony can be located by the reader/listener/analyst.

3 Slums and the Postcolonial Uncanny

1. The Sanskrit term literally means "original occupants" and is used to describe indigenous tribal populations who lived in India before the arrival of the Aryans in the second millennium BC, and their descendants. Oraon are also an aboriginal people who speak a Dravidian language.

2. Haraway is, of course, writing about the late twentieth century, not newly minted postcolonial India, and she sees in this fusing of machine and human – part social reality, part myth – an emancipatory promise for gender politics.

3. In *State of Exception,* where Agamben develops the theory of the sovereignty he had extrapolated from Carl Schmitt in *Homo Sacer* even further, he defines the phrase as a situation where a rare and extreme mode of governance "tends increasingly to appear as the dominant paradigm of government in modern politics" (2).

4. www.sinema.sg/2010/12/01/nair-i-would-not-refer-them-as-dogs.

5. In one of the ironies of late liberalism, Nair's *Queen of Katwe,* on a chess prodigy who emerged from a Kampala ghetto, has been praised as the "new *Slumdog Millionaire."* Nair's comments on *Slumdog Millionaire* can be found here: www.sinema.sg/2010/12/01/nair-i-would-not-refer-them-as-dogs.

6. The phrase occurs in *Three Guineas.* "The Lives of the Obscure" is the title of an essay in Virginia Woolf's *The Common Reader.*

7. http://jhbwtc.blogspot.com/2009/10/unthinkable-nigeriana-social-imaginary.html.

8. www.urbz.net/about.

9. www.nytimes.com/2009/02/21/opinion/21srivastava.html.

10. www.nytimes.com/2012/02/09/books/katherine-boo-on-her-book-behind-the-beautiful-forevers.html.

11. www.newyorker.com/magazine/2009/02/23/opening-night-3.

12. Anna is the Tamil word for "brother": in multilingual communities, it serves also as a generic marker of the man's Tamil origin.

13. Freud concluded *Studies on Hysteria*, co-authored with Joseph Breuer, with the hope that "much will be gained if we succeed in transforming hysterical misery . . . into common unhappiness" (393).

14. She calls them Santas presumably because of the "gunny sacks of garbage on their backs" (xii).

15. I am referring here to Judith Butler's argument in *Frames of War*, where she examines the political epistemologies that determine the "ontologies of the subject" (3). Livability is dependent on the intelligibility conferred on lives by this frame.

16. www.bookbrowse.com/author_interviews/full/index.cfm/author_number/21 29/katherine-boo.

17. www.thehindu.com/features/metroplus/None-so-blind%E2%80%A6/art icle15714567.ece.

18. Woman-oriented Hindi movies, where the golden-hearted prostitute has been rehabilitated to the heteronormative family and bourgeois respectability, include *Pyaasa*, *Mausam*, *Amar Prem*, *Sadak*, *Chameli*, and *Laga Chunari Main Daag*.

19. www.nytimes.com/2012/11/25/books/review/up-front.html.

20. www.bookbrowse.com/author_interviews/full/index.cfm/author_number/21 29/katherine-boo.

21. https://timesofindia.indiatimes.com/life-style/spotlight/Leela-was-a-beauti ful-thing-Sonia-Faleiro/articleshow/8269573.cms.

4 Psychoanalysis of the Oppressed, a Practice of Freedom: Free Clinics in Urban India

1. Freire further elaborates on this idea in works such as *Cultural Action for Freedom* and *Cultural Freedom in Latin America*.

2. Christine Hartnack's "Vishnu on Freud's Desk: Psychoanalysis in Colonial India" and "British Psychoanalysts in Colonial India" provide a detailed and nuanced account of the politics behind the establishment of the psychoanalytical society. Hartnack sheds light not only on the cross-cultural dialogue between Bose and Freud – which she interprets as a failure of cross-cultural dialogue – but also the friendship between Owen Berkeley-Hill, the medical superintendent of the European Mental Hospital in Ranchi (Bihar), and Ernest Jones. In "The Primitive as Analyst," Kalpana Seshadri-Crooks challenges Hartnack's reading of the power relations between Bose and Freud and between Berkeley-Hill and his Indian subjects. The danger, she states convincingly, is that of "forcing a familiar (master/slave) narrative and perhaps obfuscating deeper problems": "For instance, Freud's attitude does not seem as simply condescending as Hartnack makes it out to be. In fact, her reading of

Freud as a generic European with clichéd colonialist attitudes is induced by her rather cursory glance at histories of colonial India, and it ignores her own struggles to come to terms with the difference of his Jewish background in a culturally homogenous country" (186).

3. See Shruti Kapila's "The 'Godless' Freud and his Indian Friend," which traces the genealogy of the Indian psychoanalytic movement, bringing classic psychoanalytical literature and Indian writings on Freud "within a single field of interpretation" while focusing on the question of religion (125).

4. Alf Hiltebeitel's *Freud's India: Sigmund Freud and India's First Psychoanalyst Girindrasekhar Bose* (2018) is a recent and substantial contribution to extant scholarship on the Freud–Bose correspondence. Hiltebeitel focuses on the implications of cultural and religious difference for psychological thought.

5. *Lumbini Park Silver Jubilee Souvenir* (1966), Indian Psychoanalytical Society archive.

6. In *Psychology in a Third World Country*, Durganand Sinha names four successive phases of psychological research in India: imitation, expansion, problem-oriented research, and indigenization (38). Cited in Seshadri-Crooks, "The Primitive as Analyst."

7. Seshadri-Crooks's "The Primitive as Analyst" builds on this insight to chart restitutive postcolonial feminist approaches to psychoanalysis.

8. Text of the lecture provided by author and reproduced with her permission.

9. See https://economictimes.indiatimes.com/magazines/panache/mental-health-in-india-7-5-of-country-affected-less-than-4000-experts-available/articleshow/71500130.cms.

10. http://infochangeindia.org/agenda-issues/access-to-healthcare/399-less-than-1-of-our-health-budget-is-spent-on-mental-health. According to a national epidemiological survey of 2016, the treatment gap is 73.6 percent for severe mental illnesses, and 85 percent for common mental illnesses: G. Gururaj et al., *National Mental Health Survey of India, 2015–16: Mental Health Systems* (National Institute of Mental Health and Neuro Sciences, Bengaluru). See also Giriswar Misra, ed. *Psychology in India: Clinical and Health Psychology* (Pearson, 2010).

11. For a detailed analysis of the different parts of the Mental Healthcare Act, see www.india-seminar.com/2019/714/714_arjun_soumitra.htm.

12. http://pukar.org.in/about-us.

13. www.sciencedirect.com/science/article/pii/S0277953614005383?via%3Dihub.

14. Povinelli cites this term with an endnote reference to Foucault's *Security, Population, Territory*. It was coined by Guy Davidson in an article titled "Sexuality and the Statistical Imaginary in Samuel R. Delany's *Trouble on Triton*" (2008).

15. https://economictimes.indiatimes.com/news/politics-and-nation/dr-cr-chan drashekar-peoples-psychiatrist-gives-free-treatment/articleshow/54778520.c ms?from=mdr.

16. https://economictimes.indiatimes.com/news/politics-and-nation/dr-cr-chan drashekar-peoples-psychiatrist-gives-free-treatment/articleshow/54778520. cms.

17. The phrase is taken from the Anjali website, where detailed information of this human rights organization may be found: www.anjalimentalhealth.org.

18. *Mental Health Care Services in Community Settings: Discussions on NGO Approaches in India*, p. 41. This work provides a detailed description of the work undertaken by Janamanas in Rajarhat-Gopalpur as well as other sites, and in the context of other NGO interventions in the community after the Mental Healthcare Act of 2017.

19. The Pali word "Bahujan," the literal meaning of which is "the many," is used as an umbrella term for Scheduled Caste (Dalit), Scheduled Tribe (Adivasi), Other Backward Classes, Shudra, and Denotified, Nomadic, and Semi-Nomadic tribes (who are not classified in caste categories).

20. The phrase is taken from the Banyan website, where detailed information of the organization's history, scope, chapters, and initiatives can also be found: https://thebanyan.org/history.

21. www.thehindu.com/features/downtown/the-banyan-providing-hope-not-ju st-shelter/article3421284.ece. See also https://frontline.thehindu.com/cover-story/the-banyan-model/article9049917.ece on the "Banyan model."

22. Data cited from: https://thebanyan.org/mentalhealth.

23. The reference here is to the Mahatma Gandhi National Rural Employment Guarantee Act (MGNREGA), passed in 2005, which guarantees 100 days of employment in a financial year to any rural household whose adult members are willing to do unskilled manual labor: https://tnrd.gov.in/schemes/nrega .html.

24. See www.thelancet.com/journals/lancet/article/PIIS0140-6736(11)61093-3/ful ltext, cited in Pathare et al. 1.

25. M. Slade, M. Omering, and L. Oades, "Recovery: An International Perspective," *Epidemiology and Psychiatric Sciences* 17 (2008), pp. 128–137.

26. Pathare is also on the team of a unique peer-support intervention in rural Maharashtra. Titled "Atmiyata," a word which means "filiation" in Sanskrit and other regional languages, it is a community-based intervention model which taps into extant community resources which are democratically run and have elected leaders. The Atmiyata "Champions," as they are called, aim to build informal community care for people with CMDs and mental distress. See Joag et al., "Feasibility and Acceptability of a Novel Community-Based Mental Health Intervention Delivered by Community Volunteers in

Maharashtra, India: The Atmiyata Programme," *BMC Psychiatry* 20.48 (2020).

27. The translator's note states that "conscientização" refers to "learning to perceive social, political, and economic contradictions, and to take action against the oppressive elements of reality" (17). The term was invented by a team from the Instituto Superior de Estudos Brasileiros, founded in 1955 in Rio de Janeiro and attached to the Ministry of Education and Culture as an independent research group. The ISEB was dissolved by the military leaders of the 1964 coup, and many of its members were exiled from Brazil. See Torres.

28. https://frontline.thehindu.com/cover-story/the-banyan-model/art icle9049917.ece.

5 Open, Closed, and Interrupted City

1. This evocative phrase is attributed to the Surrealist poet André Breton and was an avowed goal of the Bureau of Surrealist Research established in 1924. It has been used without quotation marks by thinkers such as Stefania Pandolfo and Judith Butler.

2. De Certeau makes a distinction between the voyeur, "seeing Manhattan from the 110th floor of the World Trade Center," for example, and the *flâneur*, a "practitioner" of the city whose (re-)organizing of a bustling city through restive walking is unintentional and "blind" (91, 93).

3. Gilbert translated the line simply as "Mother died today." Two more translations of *L'Étranger* appeared in 1982, by Joseph Laredo and Kate Griffith, respectively, but the rendering of the first line remained the same. In his 1988 translation, the American poet Matthew Ward changed the word back to Maman but did not echo the ordering of the words in the Camus original (a translation of which would be "Today, Maman died").

4. The Dutch appropriated Manhatta island from the Lenape tribe in 1626, forcing their eventual mass migration from their homeland. The wall that started appearing on maps in the 1660s, built to keep away Native Americans, became Wall Street.

5. www.nytimes.com/2011/05/19/books/open-city-by-teju-cole-book-review.html.

6. Inspired by the 1902 novel, Freud wrote "Delusion and Dream in Jensen's *Gradiva*" in 1907.

7. The term "necropolitics" is from Achille Mbembe's 2003 article of the same name. The *Public Culture* essay led to the book, *Necropolitics*.

8. See also Mikko Tuhkanen's interpretation of Bigger Thomas's awakening in "*Native Son* and Diasporic Modernity." Citing Wai Chee Dimock and others,

Tuhkanen suggests that American literature – in particular, African-American literature – be read as a diasporic formation and as signaling a diasporic modernity.

9. In *Elements of the Philosophy of Right*, Hegel wrote of the perfectibility of human substance, related to our infinite capacity to labor on and transform original natures to second, spiritual natures, a spirituality that becomes habitual.

10. See also Hartman, *Scenes of Subjection*, for a critical appraisal of the ways in which the spectacle of blackness, from the antebellum era to the end of the nineteenth century, was co-opted as a source of terror to refigure relations of mastery and servitude.

11. A report titled "The Educational and Mental Health Needs of Syrian Refugee Children" gives an excellent account of the psychic aftermaths of the Syrian conflict, which began in March 2011 with the military crackdown on antigovernment protesters and resulted eventually in the displacement of nearly 12 million people: http://old.worldomep.org/wp-content/uploads/201 6/02/FCD-Sirin-Rogers-FINAL-4.pdf.

12. www.unhcr.org/uk/news/stories/2015/12/56ec1ebde/2015-year-europes-refu gee-crisis.html.

13. www.bbc.co.uk/news/uk-politics-33716501. The article reports that the UN Special Representative for International Migration had criticized British politicians for their "xenophobic responses" to the migrant crisis and their manipulative use of "grossly excessive language." Human Rights groups such as the Refugee Council condemned the Prime Minister's description as "irresponsible, dehumanising language to describe the desperate men, women, and children." See www.theguardian.com/uk-news/2016/jan/27/davi d-camerons-bunch-of-migrants-quip-is-latest-of-several-such-comments. The dehumanizing rhetoric around migrants (and internal migrants) is a distinctive feature of right-wing majoritarian regimes. In May 2018, President Trump called some deported immigrants "animals" during a roundtable discussion on immigration policy: "These aren't people. They are animals and we are taking them out of the country at a level and at a rate that hasn't happened before, and because of the weak laws they come in fast . . . it's crazy." See www.huffington post.co.uk/entry/trump-calls-some-undocumented-immigrants-animals_u s_5afcae35e4b0a8ec921b85e4?ri18n=true. Amit Shah, head of the Bharatiya Janata Party, the ruling (nationalist) party in India, called Muslim refugees "termites" at a rally in West Bengal during the election campaign of 2019. Referring to illegal immigrants from Bangladesh, he stated: "Infiltrators are like termites in the soil of Bengal. A Bharatiya Janata Party government will pick up infiltrators one by one and throw them into the Bay of Bengal" (www

.reuters.com/article/india-election-speech/amit-shah-vows-to-throw-illegal-im
migrants-into-bay-of-bengal-idUSKCN1RO1YD).

14. A 328-page Human Rights Commission (of Quebec) report, documenting
cases of minorities – particularly blacks, Muslims, and Arabs – being attacked
between 2007 and 2017, urges the province to formulate substantive anti-
racism policy. According to the report, 72 percent of the interviewees
identified as Black and/or Arab, with 51 percent identifying themselves as
Muslim. Each person in this group said they had faced verbal and physical
assaults or had had their property vandalized: on average, each was the victim
of three hate crimes in the ten-year period (www.nationalobserver.com/2019/
09/25/news/quebec-human-rights-commission-asks-government-take-hate-r
acism-seriously).

15. This collection of essays examines varieties of identity formations and their
literary expression as a largely monolingual, white-settler colonial province
becomes culturally plural. See also *Managing Immigration and Diversity in
Canada: A Transatlantic Dialogue in the New Age of Migration*, ed.
Dan Rodríguez García (McGill-Queen's University Press, 2012) for wide-
ranging perspectives on different facets of the Canadian immigration
experience, including multiculturalism and multinationalism, examined in
the frame of comparative migration studies.

16. *The Colonizer and the Colonized* 85.

17. www.theguardian.com/books/2009/may/23/cockroach-rawl-hage-review.

18. See Brian Massumi's profound examination of nomad thought in *A User's
Guide to Capitalism and Schizophrenia: Deviations from Deleuze and Guattari*
(Cambridge, MA: MIT Press, 1992).

19. The anthropologist art historian Anny Milovanoff's short article on
nomadism, titled "La seconde peau du nomade," which appeared in the
journal *Les Nouvelles Littéraires* in 1978, is seen as a source for Deleuze and
Guattari's nomadology in *A Thousand Plateaus*.

20. Cited in Elizabeth Wright, *Psychoanalytic Criticism* (London and New York:
Routledge, 2002), p. 172.

21. *Placeless People* traces selected mass displacements of the mid twentieth
century and is about statelessness and the concomitant rightlessness.

22. Bong Joon-ho's critically acclaimed (and popular) movie *Parasite* plays on the
coeval existence and mutual mistrust of the vertical and the subterranean
(semi-basement) lives of the rich and poor, respectively. Capital vampirically
sucks the blood of workers; the poor infiltrate and occupy the host to take
back what they can.

23. Christopher Norris accurately describes the work's countervailing stress
on the "foreign," the "strange," and the "uncanny" as phenomena
which prevent Enlightenment reason from becoming a monological

discourse: "Kristeva moves on from acknowledging the worst possibilities (difference as a cause of hatred, paranoia, ethnic persecution) to the prospect of a better, more enlightened alternative where the difference *within* each and every subject is envisaged as providing the common ground, the measure of shared humanity, whereby to transcend such differences *between* ethnic and national ties" (*Truth and the Ethics of Criticism* 94).

6　Psychoanalysis of the Unhomed: Free Clinics, New York

1. Medicare covers people who are 65 and older; certain younger people with disabilities; people with end-stage renal disease. The different parts of Medicare cover medical insurance, hospital insurance, prescription drug cover. For detailed information, see the US Government site www.medicare.gov.

2. Psycho-oncology is a speciality of cancer treatment that has two dimensions: the psychological impact of cancer on patients and their families across all stages of the disease, and the psychological, social, and behavioral factors that contribute to cancer cause and survival. For a comprehensive introduction to the field, see Jimmie Holland et al. See also Jimmie C. Holland and Sheldon Lewis, *The Human Side of Cancer: Living with Hope, Coping with Uncertainty* (New York: Harper Collins, 2000).

3. The phrase from Holland's *The Human Side of Cancer*, also the title of one of the book chapters, is cited in the *New York Times* obituary for her (January 4, 2018), a powerful snapshot of this extraordinary life: www.nytimes.com/2018/01/04/obituaries/jimmie-holland-who-cared-for-the-cancer-patients-mind-dies-at-89.html?auth=login-email&login=email.

4. See Jimmie Holland's interview with Winfield Boerckel, Lung Cancer Program Director at CancerCare, a not-for-profit organization that offers support to cancer patients and their carers: www.medscape.com/viewarticle/842747#vp_2.

5. The primary force animating human life, Frankl stated, was the quest for meaning (not the Freudian will to pleasure or the Nietzschean will to power). This, he argued in *Man's Search for Meaning* and other works, was based on his experience of suffering and concomitant efforts to find meaning through the suffering. Logotherapy, or meaning therapy, is recognized as the third school of Viennese psychotherapy (after Freud's psychoanalysis and Alfred Adler's individual psychology). The American Medical Society,

American Psychiatric Association, and the American Psychological Association treat it as a scientifically based school of psychotherapy.

6. See www.curetoday.com/articles/jimmie-holland-never-stopped-working-in-the-field-she-founded-psychosocial-oncology.

7. UN Convention Against Torture (1984/1987), *The Convention Against Torture and Other Cruel, Inhuman or Degrading Treatment or Punishment*, Article 14(1).

8. http://citeseerx.ist.psu.edu/viewdoc/download?doi=10.1.1.548.5326&rep=rep1&type=pdf.

9. See Raghavan, who argues that the Harvard Trauma Questionnaire, a 16-item rating scale with items corresponding to DSM-IV symptoms of PTSD, is the only empirically validated tool for use with traumatized refugees. HTQ, Raghavan states, has "extensive normative data on community, clinical and culturally diverse samples. These data display considerable variation across cultural groups, confirming the importance of culture specific norms" (590). A mean score of 2.5 on HTQ represents clinically significant PTSD symptoms, and research shows that 93 percent of PTSD patients and 84 percent of non-PTSD patients classified thus have coincided with expert clinicians' diagnoses. Raghavan rates the Hopkins Symptom Checklist highly but finds it inadequate for treating refugees on the grounds of its lack of population-specific assessment instruments.

10. The information on Asher Aladjem's work in the PSOT, unless cited otherwise, is based on an interview conducted in October 2017 and subsequent correspondence.

11. The term "premorbid" refers to the underlying emotional susceptibility to the development of a pathological response to traumatic events. Aladjem cites the example of a "flamboyant" male dancer from the former Soviet Union who was arrested and beaten by the police in his former country for what was considered socially unacceptable behavior. He presented several PTSD symptoms upon arrival at Bellevue, including flashbacks, insomnia, hypervigilance. A careful evaluation led to a diagnosis of bipolar disorder in the patient. The symptoms of bipolar disorder, in other words, were premorbid and were seen to coexist with the "co-morbid" symptoms of PTSD. "This better understanding of the patient's psychopathology allowed [a] more focused remedy with Mood Stabilizer medication (Depakote) resulting in [a] better outcome of treatment of the target symptoms and improved longitudinal adherence to therapy," Aladjem concludes (224).

12. Hopper points out that it is common practice to attribute the rise of homelessness to the demise of the asylum. The logic was compelling: in the 1980s, "Hospital censuses were at their lowest point in decades and examples

of florid psychopathology were common on city streets" (159). This logic, Hopper argues in the rest of the essay, is just as flawed as calls for the reinstatement of the asylum.

13. Courtenay Harding's famous 32-year longitudinal study shows that a third of the cohort of the 269 patients from Vermont State Hospital had not improved despite participating in a comprehensive rehabilitation program. It sheds light on the varying times of recovery and heterogeneity of outcomes in patients with severe mental illnesses and, more positively, emphasizes that "contrary to the expected downward and deteriorating course for schizophrenia or for other severe and chronic psychiatric disorders, symptoms can be ameliorated over time and functioning can be restored" (724). See Courtenay Harding et al., "The Vermont Longitudinal Study of Persons with Severe Mental Illness I: Methodology, Study Sample, and Overall Status 32 Years Later," *American Journal of Psychiatry* 44.6 (June 1987), pp. 718–726. The TLC team concurs. Residents are encouraged to be on treatment courses, but the encouragement itself needs to be balanced between aggressive imposition and passive nonintervention.

14. Topics include independent living skills, behavioral health, and housing information and there is a men's group, a women's group, an art group, etc.

15. William Blake, notebook poem "Eternity." See Leopold Damrosch, *Eternity's Sunrise: The Imaginative World of William Blake* (Yale University Press, 2015), p. 3.

16. Stern is making a reference to Carl Jung's idea of the shadow self, which is a multivalent concept meaning the unconscious, the hidden or the repressed, negative feelings, etc. This occurs across Jung's oeuvre.

17. Valentin mentions that the Psychiatry Department at Columbia University has used this outreach program to train their analysts. The working-class daycare workers resented professionals descending on them from the hospital, which led to the creation of the in-house team in 1985, headed by Valentin. Carol Valentin has been the Clinical Director at Sheltering Arms since, training psychologists and clinical social workers in psychoanalytic approaches to the treatment of trauma in children.

18. In Altman's therapeutic parlance, terms such as "anxiety" and "frustration" imply the (psychoanalyst's) anxiety regarding the patient's emerging awareness of repressed drives and (the patient's) frustration at the abstinence of the psychoanalyst, respectively.

19. Altman is citing A. Fernando here from "Examples from the Road: Mindlessness In-Home," *Journal of Infant, Child and Adolescent Psychotherapy* 7 (2008), pp. 88–99.

Afterword: Second Sight

1. Personal interview, Ambedkar University, July 20, 2016.
2. In *The Doctor and Mrs A.*, Sarah Pinto writes about the limits of a strictly historical method for the ethnographer in a medical archive. "I found that it is *exceedingly* difficult, almost impossible, to treat medical archives as my discipline seemed to want me to do, to enflesh them into stories and description". Referring to details which came not from human interactions but clinical files, Pinto writes that to record these "without filling voids with imagined back-stories" felt like "a feat of anti-imagination" (35).
3. Personal correspondence, February 1, 2021.
4. Moten is writing about the resistance of the object and the objectified here. Objection, therefore, is used in the sense of objectification or dehumanization. Moten relates it to Butler's definition of "psychic life" as the scene of subjectivity, which can also imply subjection and subjugation.
5. The nine episodes of *Pataal Lok* were streamed on Amazon Prime video in 2020. For an excellent review see: www.ndtv.com/opinion/the-patal-lok-world-and-its-big-truths-by-mukul-kesavan-2245733.
6. www.theguardian.com/uk-news/2021/jan/28/study-reveals-depth-of-bame-health-inequality-in-england.
7. www.theguardian.com/society/2021/jan/01/covid-antidepressant-use-at-all-time-high-as-access-to-counselling-in-england-plunges?CMP=Share_iOSApp_Other.
8. www.nature.com/articles/d41586-020-01313-9.

Works Cited

Abbasi, Aisha. *The Rupture of Serenity: External Intrusions and Psychoanalytic Technique*. Karnac Books, 2014.

Acharyya, Sourangshu, et al., "Nafsiyat: A Psychotherapy Centre for Ethnic Minorities." *Psychiatric Bulletin* 13 (1989), pp. 358–360.

Adorno, Theodor. *Negative Dialectics*. Trans. E. B. Ashton. Routledge, 1990.

Agamben, Giorgio. *Homo Sacer: Sovereign Power and Bare Life*. Trans. Daniel Heller-Roazen. Stanford University Press, 1998.

The Open: Man and Animal. Trans. Kevin Attell. Stanford University Press, 2002.

Remnants of Auschwitz: The Witness and the Archive. Trans. Daniel Heller-Roazen. MIT Press, 2000.

State of Exception. Trans. Kevin Attell. University of Chicago Press, 2005.

Akhtar, Salman, ed. *Freud Along the Ganges: Psychoanalytic Reflections on the People and Culture of India*. Other Press, 2005.

Aladjem, Asher. "The Psychiatric Care of Survivors of Torture, Refugee Trauma, and Other Human Rights Abuses." *Like a Refugee Camp on First Avenue: Insights and Experiences from the Bellevue/NYU Program for Survivors of Torture*. Ed. Hawthorne E. Smith. Bellevue, 2007.

Alter, Robert. *Pen of Iron: American Prose and the King James Bible*. Princeton University Press, 2010.

Altman, Neil. *The Analyst in the Inner City: Race, Class, and Culture Through a Psychoanalytic Lens*. Routledge, 2009.

"Psychoanalysis and the Urban Poor." *Psychoanalytic Dialogues: The International Journal of Relational Perspectives* 3.1 (1993), pp. 29–49.

Psychoanalysis in an Age of Accelerating Cultural Change: Spiritual Globalization. Routledge, 2015.

American Psychiatric Association. *Diagnostic and Statistical Manual of Mental Disorders, Fourth Edition, Text Revision (DSM-IV-TR)*. American Psychiatric Association, 2000.

Diagnostic and Statistical Manual of Mental Disorders, Third Edition (DSM-III). American Psychiatric Association, 1980.

Diagnostic and Statistical Manual of Mental Disorders, Third Edition, Revised (DSM-III-R). American Psychiatric Association, 1987.

Anderson, Warwick, et al. *Unconscious Dominions: Psychoanalysis, Colonial Trauma, and Global Sovereignties.* Duke University Press, 2011.

Apter, Emily. *Against World Literature: On the Politics of Untranslatability.* Verso, 2013.

——. *Continental Drift: From National Characters to Virtual Subjects.* University of Chicago Press, 1999.

Austin, J. L. *How to Do Things with Words. The William James Lectures delivered at Harvard University in 1955.* Ed. J. O. Urmson and Marina Sbisà. Oxford University Press, 1975.

Balagopal, Gayathri, and Aruna Rose Mary Kapanee. *Mental Health Care Services in Community Settings: Discussions on NGO Approaches in India.* Springer, 2019.

Ball, John Clement. "An Interview with Salman Rushdie." *Conversations with Salman Rushdie.* Ed. Michael Reder. University Press of Mississippi, 2000, pp. 101–109.

Barad, Karen. *Meeting the Universe Halfway: Quantum Physics and the Entanglement of Matter and Meaning.* Duke University Press, 2007.

——. "Posthumanist Performativity: Toward an Understanding of How Matter Comes to Matter." *Signs* 28.3 (Spring 2003), pp. 801–831.

——. "Quantum Entanglements and Hauntological Relations of Inheritance: Dis/continuities, SpaceTime Enfoldings, and Justice-to-Come." *Derrida Today* 3.2 (2010), pp. 240–268.

Benjamin, Walter. *Understanding Brecht.* Verso, 2003.

Benslama, Fethi. *Psychoanalysis and the Challenge of Islam.* University of Minnesota Press, 2009.

Bhabha, Homi K. "How Newness Enters the World: Postmodern Space, Postcolonial Times, and the Trials of Cultural Translation." *Writing Black Britain: 1948–1998.* Ed. James Procter. Manchester University Press, 2000, pp. 300–306.

Blackwell, Dick, and Farideh Dizadji. "Demonised, Blamed, Negated, and Disappeared: The Victimisation of the Poor in the Globalised Economy." *Psychotherapy and Politics International* 14.1 (2016), pp. 5–16.

Boo, Katherine. *Behind the Beautiful Forevers.* Portobello Books, 2012.

——. "Opening Night: The Scene from the Airport Slums." *The New Yorker* (Feb. 16, 2009): www.newyorker.com/magazine/2009/02/23/opening-night-3.

——. "Q&A with Katherine." www.behindthebeautifulforevers.com/qa-with-katherine.

Bowlby, Rachel. *Still Crazy After All These Years: Women, Writing and Psychoanalysis.* Routledge, 1992.

Boyarin, Daniel. "What Does a Jew Want? Or, the Political Meaning of the Phallus." *The Psychoanalysis of Race.* Ed. Christopher Lane. Columbia University Press, 1998, pp. 211–40.

Brenmann, Natassia. "Stories from Nafsiyat": www.nafsiyat.org.uk/index.php/2019/01/14/our-research.

Brickman, Celia. *Race in Psychoanalysis: Aboriginal Populations in the Mind.* Routledge, 2018.

Butler, Judith. *Antigone's Claim: Kinship Between Life and Death.* Columbia University Press, 2000.

Frames of War: When Is Life Grievable? Verso, 2016.

The Psychic Life of Power: Theories in Subjection. Stanford University Press, 1997.

Callard, Felicity, and Constantina Papoulias. "Affect and Embodiment." *Memory: Histories, Theories, Debates.* Ed. Bill Schwarz et al. Fordham University Press, 2010, pp. 246–262.

Camus, Albert. *L'Étranger. The Outsider.* Trans. Stuart Gilbert. Penguin Books, 1961.

The Stranger. Trans. Matthew Ward. Vintage, 1989.

Caruth, Cathy. "After the End: Psychoanalysis in the Ashes of History." *Trauma in Contemporary Literature: Narrative and Representation.* Ed. Marita Nadal et al. Routledge, 2014, pp. 17–34.

Unclaimed Experience: Trauma, Narrative, and History. Johns Hopkins University Press, 1996.

Cefalu, Paul A. "'Damnéd Custom . . . Habits Devil': Shakespeare's Hamlet, Anti-Dualism, and the Early Modern Philosophy of the Mind." *ELH* 67.2 (Summer 2000), pp. 399–431.

Chakrabarty, Dipesh. "The Time of History and the Times of Gods." *The Politics of Culture in the Shadow of Capital.* Ed. Lisa Lowe and David Lloyd. Duke University Press, 1997.

Chandrashekar, C. R. *You Too Can Learn the Art of Counselling.* Navakarnataka Publications, 2013.

Chattopadhyay, Swati. *Representing Calcutta: Modernity, Nationalism, and the Colonial Uncanny.* Routledge, 2006.

Unlearning the City: Infrastructure in a New Optical Field. University of Minnesota Press, 2012.

Cherki, Alice. *Frantz Fanon: A Portrait.* Trans. Nadia Benabid. Cornell University Press, 2006.

Chow, Rey. "Where Have All the Natives Gone?" *Feminist Postcolonial Theory: A Reader.* Ed. Reina Lewis and Sara Mills. Edinburgh University Press, 2003, pp. 324–350.

Christinidis, Georgia. "Slumdog Millionaire and the Knowledge-based Economy: Poverty as Ontology." *Cultural Critique* 89 (Winter 2015), pp. 38–60.

Cixous, Hélène. "Fiction and Its Phantoms: A Reading of Freud's Das Unheimliche (the 'Uncanny')." *Volleys of Humanity: Essays 1972–2009.* Ed. Eric Prenowitz. Edinburgh University Press, 2011, pp. 15–40.

Volleys of Humanity: Essays (1972–2009). Edinburgh University Press, 2011.

Cole, Teju. *Every Day Is for the Thief.* Faber and Faber, 2014.

Open City. Faber and Faber, 2011.

Craps, Stef. "Beyond Eurocentrism: Trauma Theory in the Global Age." *The Future of Trauma Theory: Contemporary Literary and Cultural Criticism.* Ed. Gert Buelens et al. Routledge, 2014, pp. 417–442.

Cyrulnik, Boris. *Resilience: How Your Inner Strength Can Set You Free from the Past*. Trans. David Macey. Penguin Books, 2009.

D'Angelo, Alessio, et al. "Welfare Needs of Turkish and Kurdish Communities in London: A Community-based Research Project": http://sprc.info/wp-content/uploads/2013/07/DayMer-Final-Report-final.pdf.

Danto, Elizabeth Ann. *Freud's Free Clinics: Psychoanalysis and Social Justice, 1918–1938*. Columbia University Press, 2007.

Das, Veena. *Affliction: Health, Disease, Poverty*. Fordham University Press, 2015.

Davis, Mike. *Planet of Slums*. Verso, 2007.

Deb, Siddhartha. *The Beautiful and the Damned*. Viking, 2011.

De Certeau, Michel. *The Practice of Everyday Life*. Trans. Steven F. Rendall. University of California Press, 1984.

Deleuze, Gilles, and Félix Guattari. *A Thousand Plateaus: Capitalism and Schizophrenia*. Trans. Brian Massumi. Continuum, 2004.

Derrida, Jacques. *Archive Fever: A Freudian Impression*. Trans. Eric Prenowitz. University of Chicago Press, 1996.

"Force of Law: The 'Mystical Foundation of Authority.'" *Deconstruction and the Possibility of Justice*. Ed. Druscilla Cornell et al. Routledge, 1992.

"Geopsychoanalysis ' . . . and the rest of the world.'" *The Psychoanalysis of Race*. Ed. Christopher Lane. Columbia University Press, 1998, pp. 65–90.

Limited Inc. Trans. Jeffrey Mehlman and Samuel Weber. Northwestern University Press, 1988.

The Post Card: From Socrates to Freud and Beyond. University of Chigago Press, 1987.

Specters of Marx: The State of the Debt, the Work of Mourning, and the New International. Routledge, 2012.

Devi, Sharmila. "Healing the Scars of Torture." *The Lancet* 376.9752 (2010), pp. 1527–1528.

Dey, Ishita, et al. *Beyond Kolkata: Rajarhat and the Dystopia of Urban Imagination*. Routledge, 2013.

Rajarhat and the Dystopia of Urban Imagination. Routledge, 2013.

Dickens, Charles. *Bleak House*. Ed. Nicola Bradbury. Penguin Books, 1996.

Oliver Twist. Ed. Peter Fairclough. Penguin Books, 1986.

Our Mutual Friend. Ed. Adrian Poole. Penguin Classics, 1997.

Doane, Mary Ann. "Dark Continents: Epistemologies of Racial and Sexual Difference in Psychoanalysis and the Cinema." *Femme Fatales: Feminism, Film Theory, Psychoanalysis*. Routledge, 1991, pp. 209–249.

Du Bois, W. E. B. *The Souls of Black Folk*. Ed. Brent Hayes Edwards. Oxford University Press, 2007.

Duflo, Esther. "Poor but Rational?" *Understanding Poverty*. Ed. Abhijit Vinayak Banerjee et al. Oxford University Press, 2006, pp. 367–378.

Eagle G., and D. Kaminer. "Continuous Traumatic Stress: Expanding the Lexicon of Traumatic Stress." *Peace and Conflict: Journal of Peace Psychology* 19.2 (2013), pp. 85–99.

Echanove, Matias, and Rahul Srivastava. "Taking the Slum out of 'Slumdog'": www.nytimes.com/2009/02/21/opinion/21srivastava.html.

Ecker, Bruce, et al. *Unlocking the Emotional Brain: Eliminating Symptoms at Their Roots Using Memory Reconsolidation*. Routledge, 2012.

Ellmann, Maud. "The Ghosts of *Ulysses*." *James Joyce's Ulysses: A Casebook*. Ed. Derek Attridge. Oxford University Press, 2004, pp. 83–101.

El Shakry, Omnia. *The Arabic Freud: Psychoanalysis and Islam in Modern Egypt*. Princeton University Press, 2017.

Erdelyi, Matthew Hugh. "Dissociation, Defense, and the Unconscious." *Dissociation: Culture, Mind, and Body*. Ed. David Spiegel. American Psychiatric Press, 1994, pp. 3–20.

Fabian, Johannes. *Time and the Other: How Anthropology Makes Its Object*. Columbia University Press, 1983.

Faleiro, Sonia. *Beautiful Thing*. Canongate, 2011.

Fanon, Frantz. *Black Skin, White Masks*. Trans. Charles Lam Markmann. Grove Press, 1967.

Toward the African Revolution: Political Essays. Trans. Haakon Chevalier. Grove Press, 1988.

The Wretched of the Earth. Trans. Richard Philcox. Grove Press, 2004.

Fassin, Didier, and Richard Rechtman. *The Empire of Trauma: An Inquiry into the Condition of Victimhood*. Princeton University Press, 2009.

Forna, Aminatta. *Ancestor Stones*. Bloomsbury, 2006.

"Don't Judge a Book by Its Author": www.theguardian.com/books/2015/feb/13/aminatta-forna-dont-judge-book-by-cover.

Happiness. Bloomsbury, 2018.

The Hired Man. Bloomsbury, 2013.

The Memory of Love. Bloomsbury, 2010.

Foucault, Michel. *Abnormal: Lectures at the Collège de France, 1974–75*. Picador, 2007.

The Order of Things: An Archaeology of the Human Sciences. Routledge, 2002.

Fraiberg, Selma, Edna Adelson, and Vivian Shapiro. "Ghosts in the Nursery: A Psychoanalytic Approach to the Problems of Impaired Infant–Mother Relationships." *Journal of the American Academy of Child Psychiatry* 14 (1975), pp. 387–421.

Freire, Paulo. *Pedagogy of the Oppressed*. Penguin Books, 2017.

Freud, Sigmund. *The Standard Edition of the Complete Psychological Works of Sigmund Freud* (hereafter SE). 24 vols. Trans. James Strachey. The Hogarth Press, 1961.

Beyond the Pleasure Principle (1920). SE 18 (1920–1922), pp. 1–64.

Civilization and Its Discontents (1930). SE 21 (1927–1931), pp. 58–146.

"Delusions and Dreams in Jensen's Gradiva" (1907). SE 9 (1906–1908), pp. 1–96.

"Further Recommendations on the Technique of Psycho-analysis" (1913). SE 12 (1911–1913), pp. 121–174.

Group Psychology and the Analysis of the Ego (1921). SE 18 (1920–1922), pp. 69–143.

"Lines of Advance in Psycho-analytic Therapy" (1918–19). SE 17 (1917–1919), pp. 157–168.

"On Transience" (1915). SE 14 (1914–1916), pp. 305–307.

"Postscript to an Autobiographical Study" (1927). SE 20 (1925–1926), pp. 71–76.

"The Taboo of Virginity" (1918). SE 11 (1910), pp. 191–208.

"Thoughts for the Times on War and Death" (1915). *SE* 14 ((1914–1916), pp. 273–300.

Totem and Taboo (1913). SE 13 (1913–14), pp. 1–100.

"The 'Uncanny'" (1919). SE 17 (1917–1919), pp. 217–256.

"The Unconscious" (1915). SE 14 (1914–1916), pp. 159–214.

Beyond the Pleasure Principle. Ed. and Trans. James Strachey. W. W. Norton and Company, 1961.

Gallo, Rubén. *Freud's Mexico: Into the Wilds of Psychoanalysis*. MIT Press, 2010.

Gandhi, Leela. *Postcolonial Theory: A Critical Edition (Second Edition)*. Columbia University Press, 2019.

Ganguly, Debjani. *This Thing Called the World: The Contemporary Novel as Global Form*. Duke University Press, 2016.

Gates Jr., Henry Louis. "Critical Fanonism." *Critical Inquiry* 17.3 (1991), pp. 457–470.

Gilman, Sander L., and James M. Thomas. *Are Racists Crazy? How Prejudice, Racism, and Antisemitism Became Markers of Insanity*. NYU Press, 2016.

Gilroy, Paul. *Against Race: Imagining Political Culture beyond the Color Line*. Harvard University Press, 2002.

The Black Atlantic: Modernity and Double-Consciousness. Harvard University Press, 1995.

Güneli, Gün. "Review." *World Literature Today* 67.4 (1993), pp. 886–887.

Hacking, Ian. *Mad Travelers: Reflections on the Reality of Transient Mental Illnesses*. Harvard University Press, 2002.

Hage, Rawi. *Cockroach*. Penguin Books, 2010.

Hall, Stuart. "The After-Life of Frantz Fanon: Why Fanon? Why Now? Why Black Skin, White Masks?" *Fact of Blackness: Frantz Fanon and Visual Representation*. Ed. Alan Read. Bay Press, 1996, pp. 12–31.

Haraway, Donna. "A Cyborg Manifesto: Science, Technology, and Socialist-Feminism in the Late Twentieth Century." *Simians, Cyborgs, and Women: The Reinvention of Nature*. Routledge, 1991, pp. 149–181.

Hartman, Saidiya. "Fugitive Dreams of Diaspora: Conversations with Saidiya Hartman." Interview with Patricia J. Saunders. *Anthurium: A Caribbean Studies Journal* 6.1 (Spring 2008), pp. 1–16.

Lose Your Mother: A Journey Across the Slave Route. Farrar Straus Giroux, 2008.

Scenes of Subjection: Terror, Slavery, and Self-Making in Nineteenth-Century America. Oxford University Press, 1997.

Hartnack, Christine. "British Psychoanalysis in Colonial India." *Psychology in Twentieth-Century Thought and Society*. Ed. Mitchell G. Ash and William Woodward. Cambridge University Press, 1987, pp. 233–257.

"Vishnu on Freud's Desk." *Social Research* 57 (1990), pp. 921–949.

Harvey, David. "Globalization and the Spatial Fix." *Geographische Revue* 2 (2001), pp. 23–30.

Rebel Cities: From the Right to the City to the Urban Revolution. Verso, 2012.

Social Justice and the City. University of Georgia Press, 2009.

Hayles, N. Katherine. *The Cosmic Web: Scientific Field Models and Literary Strategies in the Twentieth Century.* Cornell University Press, 1984.

Hegel, G. W. F. *Elements of the Philosophy of Right.* Ed. Alan W. Wood. Trans. H. B. Nisbet. Cambridge University Press, 1991.

Heise, Ursula K. *Sense of Place and Sense of Planet: The Environmental Imagination of the Global.* Oxford University Press, 2008.

Herman, Judith. "The Politics of Trauma: A Conversation with Judith Herman." *Listening to Trauma: Conversations with Leaders in the Theory and Treatment of Catastrophic Experience.* Ed. Cathy Caruth. Johns Hopkins University Press, 2014.

Trauma and Recovery: The Aftermath of Violence – From Domestic Abuse to Political Terror. Basic Books, 1992.

Hertz, Neil. "Freud and the Sandman." *Deconstruction: Critical Concepts in Literary and Critical Studies,* vol. III. Ed. Jonathan Culler. Routledge, 2003.

Hiltebeitel, Alf. *Freud's India: Sigmund Freud and India's First Psychoanalyst Girindrasekhar Bose.* Oxford University Press, 2018.

Hogan, Patrick Colm. *Imagining Kashmir: Emplotment and Colonialism.* University of Nebraska Press, 2016.

Holland, Jimmie C. "History of Psycho-Oncology: Overcoming Attitudinal and Conceptual Barriers." *Psychosomatic Medicine* 64.2 (March–April 2002), pp. 206–221.

Holland, Jimmie, et al., eds. *Psycho-Oncology.* Oxford University Press, 1998.

Hopper, Kim. "More than Passing Strange: Homelessness and Mental Illness in New York City." *American Ethnologist: Journal of the American Ethnological Society* 15.1 (1988), pp. 155–167.

Ireland, Susan, and Patrice J. Proulx, eds. *Textualizing the Immigrant Experience in Contemporary Quebec,* vol. IV. Westport, CT: Greenwood Publishing Group, 2004.

Irigaray, Luce. "The Poverty of Psychoanalysis." *The Irigaray Reader.* Ed. Margaret Whitford. Blackwell, 1991, pp. 79–104.

Jameson, Fredric. *The Antinomies of Realism.* Verso, 2013.

Jay, Martin. "The Uncanny Nineties." *Salmagundi* 108.20 (1995).

Johnston, Adrian, and Catherine Malabou, *Self and Emotional Life: Philosophy, Psychoanalysis, and Neuroscience.* Columbia University Press, 2013.

Jones, Gavin. *American Hungers: The Problem of Poverty in US Literature, 1840–1945.* Princeton University Press, 2007.

Jordan, Martin, and Joe Hinds, eds. *Ecotherapy: Theory, Research and Practice.* Palgrave Macmillan, 2016.

Kakar, Sudhir. *The Colors of Violence: Cultural Identities, Region, and Conflict.* University of Chicago Press, 1996.

Culture and Psyche: Selected Essays. Oxford University Press, 1997.

Kapila, Shruti. "The 'Godless' Freud and His Indian Friends: An Indian Agenda for Psychoanalysis." *Psychiatry and Empire*. Ed. Megan Vaughan et al. Palgrave Macmillan, pp. 124–152.

Kareem, Jafar, and Roland Littlewood. *Intercultural Therapy: Themes, Interpretation, and Practice*. Blackwell Scientific Publications, 1992.

Kazi, Seema. *Between Democracy and Nation: Gender and Militarisation in Kashmir*. Oxford University Press, 2010.

Keller, Richard. "Madness and Colonization: Psychiatry in the British and French Empires." *Journal of Social History* 35.2 (2001), pp. 295–326.

Khalfa, Jean, and Robert J. C. Young, eds. *Frantz Fanon: Alienation and Freedom*. Trans. Steven Corcoran. Bloomsbury, 2018.

Khanna, Ranjana. *Dark Continents: Psychoanalysis and Colonialism*. Duke University Press, 2003.

Kirkmayer, Lawrence J., and Leslie Swartz. "Culture and Global Mental Health." *Global Mental Health: Principles and Practice*. Ed. Vikram Patel et al. Oxford University Press, 2014.

Knowlton, Leslie. "Bellevue's Torture Survivors Program Aids Victims." *Psychiatric Times* 17.12 (2000): www.psychiatrictimes.com/ptsd/bellevues-torture-survivors-program-aids-victims.

Koelen, Jurrijn A., et al. "Effectiveness of Psychotherapy for Severe Somatoform Disorder: Meta-analysis." *British Journal of Psychiatry* 204.1 (2014), pp. 12–19.

Kornbluh, Anna. "Romancing the Capital: Choice, Love, and Contradiction in *The Family Man* and *Memento*." *Lacan and Contemporary Film*. Ed. Todd McGowan and Shiela Kunkle. Other Press, 2004, pp. 111–144.

Kristeva, Julia. *Strangers to Ourselves*. Trans. Leon S. Roudiez. Columbia University Press, 1991.

Kumar, Manasi. "The Poverty in Psychoanalysis: 'Poverty' of Psychoanalysis?" *Psychology and Developing Societies* 24.1 (2012), pp. 1–34.

LaCapra, Dominic. "History and Psychoanalysis." *Critical Inquiry* 13.2 (Winter 1987), pp. 222–251.

Lear, Jonathan. *Open Minded: Working Out the Logic of the Soul*. Harvard University Press, 1998.

Leichsenring, Falk, and Susan Klein. "Evidence for Psychodynamic Psychotherapy in Specific Mental Disorders: A Systematic Review." *Psychoanalytic Psychotherapy* 28.1 (2014), pp. 4–32.

Leichsenring, Falk, and Sven Rabung. "Effectiveness of Long-term Psychodynamic Psychotherapy: A Meta-analysis." *JAMA* 300.13 (Oct. 1, 2008), pp. 1551–1565.

Leys, Ruth. *Trauma: A Genealogy*. University of Chicago Press, 2000.

"Traumatic Cures: Shell Shock, Janet, and the Question of Memory." *Critical Inquiry* 20.4 (Summer 1994), pp. 623–662.

Loury, Glenn. "Racial Stigma: Toward a New Paradigm for Discrimination Theory." *Understanding Poverty*. Ed. Abhijit Vinayak Banerjee et al. Oxford University Press, 2006, pp. 401–408.

Lund, Crick, and Annibale Cois. "Simultaneous Social Causation and Social Drift: Longitudinal Analysis of Depression and Poverty in South Africa." *Journal of Affective Disorders* 229 (2018), pp. 396–402.

Macey, David. *Frantz Fanon: A Biography*. Picador, 2000.

Makari, George. *Revolution in Mind: The Creation of Psychoanalysis*. Harper Perennial, 2008.

Makhdoomi, Rumani. *White Man in Dark*. PartridgeIndia, 2013.

Mannoni, Octave. *Prospero and Caliban: The Psychology of Colonization*. Trans. Pamela Powesland. University of Michigan Press, 1990.

Margoob, Mushtaq A., et al. "Treatment Seeking Posttraumatic Stress Disorder Patient Population Experience from Kashmir." *JK Practitioner: A Journal of Current Clinical Medicine and Surgery* 13 (January 2006), S57–S60.

Marx, Karl. *The Poverty of Philosophy*. Trans. H. Quelch. Martino Publishing, 2014.

Masschelein, A. *The Unconcept: The Freudian Uncanny in Late-Twentieth-Century Theory*. SUNY Press, 2011.

Massumi, Brian. *Parables for the Virtual: Movement, Affect, Sensation*. Duke University Press, 2002.

A User's Guide to Capitalism and Schizophrenia: Deviations from Deleuze and Guattari. MIT Press, 1992.

Mbembe, Achille. *Necropolitics*. Duke University Press, 2019.

McCulloch, Jock. *Black Soul White Artifact: Fanon's Clinical Psychology and Social Theory*. Cambridge University Press, 1983.

Mehta, Suketu. *Maximum City: Mumbai Lost and Found*. Viking, 2004.

Melas, Natalie. *All the Difference in the World: Postcoloniality and the Ends of Comparison*. Stanford University Press, 2007.

Memmi, Albert. *The Colonizer and the Colonized*. Trans. Howard Greenfield. Orion, 1965.

Mohamed, Saira. "Of Monsters and Men: Perpetrator Trauma and Mass Atrocity." *Columbia Law Review* (2015), pp. 1157–1216.

Mohanty, Chandra Talpade. "Imperial Democracies, Militarised Zones, Feminist Engagements." *Economic and Political Weekly* 46.13 (March 26–April 1, 2011), pp. 76–84.

Moretti, Franco. *Modern Epic: The World-System from Goethe to García Márquez*. Trans. Quintin Hoare. Verso, 1996.

Morrison, Toni. *Playing in the Dark: Whiteness and the Literary Imagination*. Harvard University Press, 1992.

Moten, Fred. *In the Break: The Aesthetics of the Black Radical Tradition*. University of Minnesota Press, 2003.

Mukherjee, Ankhi. "'This Traffic of Influence': Derrida and Spivak." *Parallax* 17.3 (2011), pp. 56–69.

Murthy, R. Srinivasa. "Hinduism and Mental Health." *Religion and Psychiatry: Beyond Boundaries*. Ed. Peter J. Verhagen et al. Wiley, 2010, pp. 159–180.

Nancy, Jean-Luc. *Corpus*. Trans. Richard Rand. Fordham University Press, 2008.

Nandy, Ashis. *The Intimate Enemy: Loss and Recovery of Self under Colonialism.* Oxford University Press, 1983.

Return from Exile. Oxford University Press, 1998.

The Savage Freud and Other Essays on Possible and Retrievable Selves. Oxford University Press, 1995.

Norris, Christopher. *Truth and the Ethics of Criticism.* Manchester University Press, 1995.

Nussbaum, Martha C. *Cultivating Humanity.* Harvard University Press, 1998.

Hiding from Humanity: Disgust, Shame, and the Law. Princeton University Press, 2015.

"Poverty and Human Functioning: Capabilities as Fundamental Entitlements." *Poverty and Inequality.* Ed. David B. Grusky and Ravi Kanbur. Stanford University Press, 2006, pp. 47–75.

Otokiti, Ahmed A. "Challenges Faced by the Homeless Population in New York City: An Analysis of Healthcare Delivery and Utilization of Care." *New York Medical Journal* (December 12, 2018): https://newyorkmedicaljournal.org/wp-content/uploads/2018/12/Otokiti-Challenges-Faced-by-homeless-12-12-2018.pdf.

Oxford English Dictionary Online: www.oed.com.

Pandolfo, Stefania. *Knot of the Soul: Madness, Psychoanalysis, Islam.* University of Chicago Press, 2018.

Patel, Vikram, et al., eds. *Global Mental Health: Principles and Practice.* Oxford University Press, 2014.

Patil-Deshmukh, Anita, et al. "The Psychological Toll of Slum Living in Mumbai, India: A Mixed Methods Study" (2014): www.sciencedirect.com/science/article/pii/S0277953614005383?via%3Dihub.

Pathare, Soumitra. "Less than 1% of Our Health Budget Is Spent on Mental Health": http://infochangeindia.org/agenda-issues/access-to-healthcare/399-less-than-1-ofour-health-budget-is-spent-on-mental-health.html.

Pathare, Soumitra, and Arjun Kapoor. "Section 377 and the Mental Healthcare Act: Breaking Barriers." *Indian Journal of Medical Ethics Online* (November 26, 2018): www.india-seminar.com/2019/714/714_arjun_soumitra.htm.

Pathare, Soumitra, et al. "Peer Support for Mental Illness in India: An Underutilised Resource." *Epidemiology and Psychiatric Sciences* 27.5 (2018), pp. 415–419.

Pedwell, Carolyn. *Affective Relations: The Transnational Politics of Empathy.* Palgrave Macmillan, 2014.

Peer, Basharat. *Curfewed Night: A Frontline Memoir of Life, Love and War in Kashmir.* Random House India, 2011.

Phillips, Adam. *Winnicott.* Penguin Books, 2007.

Pinto, Sarah. *The Doctor and Mrs A.* Women Unlimited, 2019.

"'The Tools of Your Chants and Spells': Stories of Madwomen and Indian Practical Healing." *Medical Anthropology: Cross Cultural Studies in Health and Illness* 35.3 (2016), pp. 263–277.

Plotkin, Mariano Ben. *Freud in the Pampas: The Emergence and Development of a Psychoanalytic Culture in Argentina.* Stanford University Press, 2001.

Povinelli, Elizabeth A. *Economies of Abandonment: Social Belonging and Endurance in Late Liberalism.* Duke University Press, 2011.

Quayson, Ato. "Unthinkable Nigeriana: The Social Imaginary of District 9" (October 16, 2009): http://jhbwtc.blogspot.com/2009/10/unthinkable-nigeriana-social-imaginary.html.

Raghavan, Sumitra. "Cultural Considerations in the Assessment of Survivors of Torture." *Journal of Immigrant and Minority Health* 21 (2019), pp. 586–595.

Rankine, Claudia. *Citizen: An American Lyric.* Graywolf Press, 2014.

Rose, Jacqueline. *On Not Being Able to Sleep: Psychoanalysis and the Modern World.* Chatto and Windus, 2003.

Rose, Nikolas. *Governing the Soul: Shaping of the Private Self.* Free Association Books, 1999.

  Inventing Our Selves: Psychology, Power, and Personhood. Cambridge University Press, 1998.

Roth, Anthony, and Peter Fonagy. *What Works for Whom? A Critical Review of Psychotherapy Research.* Guilford Press, 2005.

Roy, Arundhati. *The Ministry of Utmost Happiness.* Hamish Hamilton, 2017.

Roy, Nilanjana. "Happiness by Aminatta Forna – The London that Foxes Know." *Financial Times* (March 16, 2018): www.ft.com/content/47690282-2791-11e8-b27e-cc62a39d57a0.

Rushdie, Salman. *Satanic Verses.* Vintage Books, 1998.

  Shame. Vintage, 1995.

Schlicke, Paul. *The Oxford Companion to Charles Dickens.* Oxford University Press, 2011.

Scott, Catherine, Janelle Jones, and John N. Briere, "Psychobiology and Psychopharmacology of Trauma." *Principles of Trauma Therapy: A Guide to Symptoms, Evaluations, and Treatment.* Ed. John N. Briere and Catherine Scott. Thousand Oaks, 2006, pp. 259–331.

Scott, David. *Conscripts of Modernity: The Tragedy of Colonial Enlightenment.* Duke University Press, 2004.

Seshadri-Crooks, Kalpana. "The Primitive as Analyst: Postcolonial Feminism's Access to Psychoanalysis." *Cultural Critique* (Fall 1994), pp. 175–218.

Shakespeare, William. *Hamlet* (The Arden Shakespeare Third Series). Ed. Ann Thompson and Neil Taylor. Bloomsbury, 2016.

Sharma, Kalpana. *Rediscovering Dharavi: Stories from Asia's Largest Slum.* Penguin Books, 2000.

Sharpe, Christina. *In the Wake: On Blackness and Being.* Duke University Press, 2016.

Simmons Zuilkowski, Stephanie, et al. "Youth and Resilience in Postconflict Settings: An Intervention for War-Affected Youth in Sierra Leone." *Human Development* 59 (2016), pp. 64–80.

Singh, Harneet. "'Kashmir is the Hamlet of my film,' says Vishal Bhardwaj on Haider." https://indianexpress.com/article/entertainment/bollywood/kashmir-is-the-hamlet-of-my-film.

Sinha, Durganand. *Psychology in a Third World Country: The Indian Experience.* Sage, 1986.

Spivak, Gayatri Chakravorty. *An Aesthetic Education in the Era of Globalization.* Harvard University Press, 2012.

"Ghostwriting." *Diacritics* 25. 2 (Summer 1995), pp. 64–84.

"No Definitions for Activism." *Through the Roadblocks: Realities in Raw Motion.* Ed. Denise Robinson. NeMe, 2015, pp. 31–46.

"Speculation on Reading Marx: After Reading Derrida." *Post-structuralism and the Question of History.* Ed. Derek Attridge et al. Cambridge University Press, 1987, pp. 30–62.

Stern, Julian, et al. "Paradigms, Politics and Pragmatics: Psychotherapy in Primary Care in City and Hackney: A New Model for the NHS." *Psychoanalytic Psychotherapy* (online May 12, 2015): http://dx.doi.org/10.1080/02668734.2015.1033445.

Stonebridge, Lyndsey. *Placeless People: Writings, Rights, and Refugees.* Oxford University Press, 2018.

Tekin, Latife. *Berji Kristin: Tales from the Garbage Hills.* Trans. Ruth Christie and Saliha Paker. Marion Boyars, 1993.

Torres, Carlos Alberto. *The Wiley Handbook of Paolo Freire.* Wiley Blackwell, 2019.

Tschumi, Bernard. *Architecture and Disjunction.* MIT Press, 1994.

Tuhkanen, Mikko. "*Native Son* and Diasporic Modernity." *The Oxford History of the Novel in English*, vol. VI: *The American Novel 1879–1940.* Ed. Priscilla Wald and Michael A. Elliott. Oxford University Press, 2014, pp. 518–530.

Tyree, J. M. "Against the Clock: Slumdog Millionaire and The Curious Case of Benjamin Button." *Film Quarterly* 62.4 (Summer 2009), pp. 34–38.

Van der Kolk, Bessel. *The Body Keeps Score: Mind, Brain and Body in the Transformation of Trauma.* Penguin Books, 2014.

Van der Kolk, Bessel, et al. *Traumatic Stress: The Effects of Overwhelming Experience on Mind, Body, and Society.* Guilford Press, 1996.

Vidler, Anthony. *The Architectural Uncanny: Essays in the Modern Unhomely.* MIT Press, 1992.

Waheed, Mirza. *The Collaborator.* Penguin, 2011.

Walkowitz, Rebecca. *Born Translated: The Contemporary Novel in an Age of World Literature.* Columbia University Press, 2015.

Watters, Ethan. *Crazy Like Us: The Globalization of the Western Mind.* Hachette UK, 2011.

Weinstein, Liza. *The Durable Slum: Dharavi and the Right to Stay Put in Globalizing Mumbai.* University of Minnesota Press, 2014.

Winnicott, D. W. *Collected Papers: Through Paediatrics to Psycho-analysis.* Basic Books, 1958.

The Maturational Processes and the Facilitating Environment. The Hogarth Press and the Institute of Psycho-Analysis, 1965.

Winter, David, et al. *Trauma, Survival and Resilience in War Zones: The Psychological Impact of War in Sierra Leone and Beyond.* Routledge, 2015.

Wood, James. "The Arrival of Enigmas." *The New Yorker* (February 21, 2011): www.newyorker.com/magazine/2011/02/28/the-arrival-of-enigmas.

Woolf, Virginia. *Mrs Dalloway*. Ed. David Bradshaw. Oxford University Press, 2008.

　　A Room of One's Own and Three Guineas. Ed. Anna Snaith. Oxford University Press, 2015.

World Health Organization. *The World Health Report 2001. Mental Health: New Understanding, New Hope*. WHO, 2001.

Wright, Elizabeth. *Psychoanalytic Criticism*. Routledge, 2002.

Yehuda, R., and A. C. Macfarlane. "Conflict between Current Knowledge of Posttraumatic Stress Disorder and Its Original Conceptual Basis." *American Journal of Psychiatry* 152.12 (1995), pp. 1705–1713.

Young, Robert J. C. *Postcolonialism: An Historical Introduction*. Blackwell Publishers, 2001.

Zwarg, Christina. "Du Bois on Trauma: Psychoanalysis and the Would-Be Black Savant." *Cultural Critique* 51 (Spring 2002), pp. 1–39.

Index